Let Justice and Mercy Flow

Unraveling Cruel Cultures and Embracing Compassionate Ones

Ken Boutwell

Parson's Porch Books

Let Justice and Mercy Flow: Unraveling Cruel Cultures and Embracing Compassionate Ones
ISBN: Softcover 978-1-960326-40-9
Copyright © 2023 by Ken Boutwell

Parson's Porch Books is an imprint of Parson's Porch *&* Company (PP*&*C) in Cleveland, Tennessee. PP*&*C is a self-funded charity which earns money by publishing books of noted authors, representing all genres. Its face and voice is **David Russell Tullock** who you can contact at: dtullock@parsonsporch.com.

Parson's Porch *&* Company *turns books into bread & milk* by sharing its profits with the poor.

www.parsonsporch.com

Let Justice and Mercy Flow

Contents

Foreword

Ken Boutwell and I became fast friends soon after he sent me a manuscript to publish as his first book in 2016. He was referred to my publishing company by a mutual friend who was his pastor at First Baptist Church in Tallahassee, Florida..

He told me at that time that he was also working on a second book which would address racism and bigotry throughout history with an invitation to join him and others in changing these cruel cultures around the world

Knowing Ken's kind nature, I don't why I had this thought, but I did: "Another book by an angry and judgmental author who was trying to make a difference with the usual judgmental diatribe against other judgmental and angry bigots and racists.." That thought was totally wrong.

When I received the manuscript, I quickly realized that this book approached racism and bigotry with a different paradigm-kindness. Boutwell wrote about this malignancy with kindness and hope. And in doing so, he produced a book that every church should ask its members to read and discuss.

Let Justice and Mercy Flow is a primer for anyone who is seeking to live in the world as a non-racist and non-bigoted person.

Ken begins his book clearly aware that he, himself, was from a culture which was cruel and unyielding to anyone who was different than his white church, white family, and white friends. He knew there had to be a better way to live than where white people built and maintained an economy and society where non-white people were routinely oppressed and persecuted. As a result, Ken and his wife committed to live a a life and to teach their children to lead lives where they treated all people with the love, respect and equality that Christ worked so hard to teach us.

Boutwell ends his book with a call to a better way to live – a way of hope and love for all, especially for those who are non-white, non-Christian, and non-male.

The appeal of *Let Justice and Mercy Flow* is to join others of all faiths, genders, ethnicities who have committed to **L**oving **A**nd **S**erving **E**ach **O**ther (LASEO) Toward the end of the book, Boutwell invites his readers to sign a **L**oving **A**nd **S**erving **E**ach **O**ther Manifesto in order to change a cruel culture of bigotry and prejudice to a just and compassionate one.

As Bonhoeffer is quoted on the back cover, "Silence in the face of evil is itself evil. God will not hold us guiltless. Not to speak is to speak, Not to act is to act."

If you choose to join the LASEO movement, let us know by sending an email to join@laseonow,com. We'll add your name to our mailing list so you'll know what you and others are doing to unravel cruel cultures and embrace compassionate ones.

David Russell Tullock
Fall 2023

Preface

This book grew out of an exchange of letters that I had several years ago with one of the highly influential and well-respected leaders of the anti-gay movement in the United Methodist Church. I had written to the leader begging him to change sides on this issue to support the affirmation of LGBTQs by the United Methodist Church. He politely responded that he could not support the church's endorsement of gay lifestyles, observing that he was on the side of the great theologians.

As I wrote my initial letter (included in Appendix A) to the minister, I remembered my own history. Growing up in a white Mississippi family and church, we strongly supported the oppression and persecution of our black neighbors in a Jim Crow racially segregated society. So, I was no stranger to oppressing and persecuting people. Even as I now realized how cruel our oppression and persecution of our black brothers and sisters were back in those days, I also remembered how easy and comfortable it had been for us to do so. Something then made us think that this was simply the way it was supposed to be.

As I wrote my letter to the theologian, other memories came flooding back. I remembered my visits to the Holocaust Museum in Jerusalem and the Dachau holocaust concentration camp in Germany. I remembered going to the African American and Native American Smithsonian museums. I remembered my visit to the Black Hills of South Dakota and to the Crazy Horse Museum. I recalled the ministerial father of a girl that I dated being beaten unconscious because he was starting a racially integrated church near my hometown in Mississippi. I remembered my father telling me that my great uncle was a member of the KKK. I remembered a conversation that I had with a ministerial friend about the way his parents and church had damned his gay brother and the devastating effect that that cruel condemnation had on his brother. I remembered the first time that my young daughter asked me about what careers were open to her as a girl.

Because I was corresponding with a Methodist minister, my wondering included what role Christians and their institutions had played in all of these historical events. After the exchange of letters where the Methodist minister rejected my request, I couldn't stop wondering and began reading our Christian history about the witch trials, black slavery, Native Americans, anti-Semitism including the Holocaust, Jim Crow racial segregation, and the historic suppression of women and LGBTQs. The more I read, the more disturbed I became, and the big question of WHY? kept raising its head. Why did our Christian ancestors suppress and persecute others by keeping them in poverty, ostracizing them, enslaving them, lynching them, burning them at the stake, murdering them in gas chambers, and kicking them out of their churches? And why do we Christians continue to oppress and persecute people this very day? None of this is consistent with the values that we tell each other and the world we hold…values like "do unto others as we would have them do unto us, love our neighbors as we love ourselves and help the least of these."

This book reflects my own investigation of this critical question of WHY? and also an examination of my own personal history as I participated in some of these atrocities in my own life.

In some ways, the book was difficult to research and write because much of it concerns a history that few of us know or even want to know. It's vital though for us to face these things so that we will, hopefully, someday, stop treating other people with such cruelty.

The first chapter is comprised of fictional accounts based on historical testimonies of the victims, the observers, and my own experiences. The remaining chapters combine stories from my own history and that of friends along with extensive historical quotes from both the perpetrators of these atrocities as well as their victims.

As the evidence is presented, I draw conclusions with which you may disagree. I hope, however, that when you do disagree, you will search for your own conclusions and that those conclusions will lead you to oppose all Christian oppression and persecution of others. That will help us achieve that request in the Lord's prayer: "Thy will be done on earth as it is in heaven."

Author's Appreciation

Books like this one require a lot of research and even more advice from friends and family, both those who agreed with and those who disagreed with my findings and conclusions. I am deeply appreciative for their help and frequent frank discussions. Bill Carnes told me, in so many words, that my first attempt at my final chapter (Chapter 22) was a "wimp" and should be replaced with a much stronger vision for our future. He was right and I did. Regina E. Sofer and Barbara Goldstein supplied me with numerous reference materials. Charlie Dodson and Judi Fergus made suggestions that helped improve the thoughts and conclusions. My Sunday School class at Faith Presbyterian Church, Tallahassee, did the same. Nancy Stepina-Robison invited me to dinner after reading an early draft and spent the evening discussing and suggesting improvements. Jack Levine spent hours reviewing an early draft and suggested significant improvements in the structure. Linda Bianco had the patience and wisdom to help me when I faced dilemmas. Bill and Nancy Youngblood read early drafts and helped redirect some of my research and thoughts. My children, Jennifer, Jeff and Julie, provided much needed support and encouragement along the way. Lisa Blackwell took on the task of editing my rough writing and making it more understandable.

I am especially appreciative of help from Brian McLaren that I gleaned from his books and presentations at retreats that I attended. Both helped me to see the need for this book that strongly advocates treating all people with love, respect, dignity and equality.

And I will forever be grateful to my late wife, Jean. Over our 59 years of marriage, she helped redirect my values that provide the underlying theme for this book...a theme that every person, no matter race, ethnicity, gender, gender identification or religious beliefs, deserves to be treated with respect, dignity and equality.

Jean, I am who you helped me to be. I am so appreciative.

About The Author

I was born in 1939 and raised on a dairy farm in Newton, Mississippi. My entire youth was spent in a racially segregated society. I went to a white-only K-12 public school. I and my family were members of a small, rural, white-only Southern Baptist church. With our parents' encouragement , I and my two brothers were very active in the 4-H club, showing our cows at white-only local and state cattle contests. We attended white-only local, state and national 4-H meetings.

I obtained my undergraduate degree in Agricultural Economics from Mississippi State College (now University) when it was a white-only institution. I dated my absolutely wonderful high school sweetheart, Jean Youngblood, who attended the nearby white-only Mississippi State College for Women. After my graduation in 1961, Jean and I married and moved to Raleigh, North Carolina, where I entered graduate school at North Carolina State University and Jean continued her undergraduate studies at Meredith College. At the time, both were white-only institutions.

Upon earning my Ph.D. in economics and Jean earning her undergraduate degree in elementary education in 1965, I entered the U.S. Army to complete my two-year ROTC obligation and was assigned to the Office of the Secretary of Defense at the Pentagon. Our wonderful daughter, Jennifer, was born just a few months before we moved to Washington, D.C.

During all this time, the Civil Rights movement under the leadership of Martin Luther King, Jr. was picking up steam. Jean and I never participated in any of the protests. However, we did begin to see that the white supremacist culture in which we had been raised was unnaturally cruel to the black people who were being forced to live in an oppressive Jim Crow society and economy. But the pressure of the white culture in which we lived made us choose to remain silent as did most white people during those years.

We continued to be a member of an Arlington, Virginia, white-only Southern Baptist church. While Jean and I talked about the social, economic, education and justice inequities being forced on black people and pledged that we would raise our children to treat all people with respect, dignity, and equality, that is all that we did. We felt no obligation to help relieve the oppression and persecution of our black friends and neighbors, somehow concluding that it was their problem...not ours. As a side note, while living near D.C., our son, Jeff, was born and he was delivered by a very nice black physician. That posed no problem for us, but it would have been forbidden back in our Mississippi hometown, simply because we had different color skins. The fact that I even mention this shows how damaging the racial oppression was in those days.

Upon completing my military obligation, I took a job at the University of Florida teaching agricultural economics. However, after only one semester I was asked to take the job as Director of Budgeting at the university. Our third and last wonderful child, Julie, was born while we were in Gainesville. After only a year in that job, I was recruited by the State University System of Florida and became its Vice Chancellor for Administration. Our family moved to Tallahassee, Florida, in 1970 where we have lived for the past 53 years.

During my time at both the University of Florida and the State University System of Florida, students were protesting both against the Vietnam War and for racial rights. I found myself, along with other university administrators, in the middle of the dilemma of recognizing the legitimacy of the protests and maintaining "law and order." Our university system was also under federal court orders to desegregate, and we worked hard at finding ways to facilitate that integration. Fortunately, due to strong leadership from the Florida governor, Rueben Askew, State University System Chancellor Bob Mautz, and committed University presidents, we were able to complete the racial integration of all universities without any damaging incidents.

After five years with the State University System, I felt that I was at the point in my career that I could pursue a life time dream of starting my own private company. I left my job to found MGT of America, Inc., a consulting company that provided planning and management consulting services to universities, school districts, and local and state governments. It was a lot harder than I had envisioned, and our family lived for three years from the commissions that Jean earned as a real estate salesperson. Thank goodness she was a top-notch salesperson, always in the top ten percent of the real estate sales people in Tallahassee. Eventually, MGT grew to become a national firm with our home office in Tallahassee and other significant offices in the states of Washington, California, Texas and Michigan and smaller offices in other states.

When federal and state laws authorized state and local governments to establish programs to address the impacts of historical racial and gender discrimination, MGT became one of the nation's leading firms in conducting studies to assess the damages caused by decades of discriminatory hiring and purchasing policies and practices on both minorities and women and designing corrective programs. It was in conducting these studies that I came to more fully understand the extent of the damage caused by these discriminatory practices. I finally saw that the problems would never be solved until white people, who dominate and direct our nation's economy, society, and governmental laws, regulations, and policies, join with the victims to resolve those problems. It's only together that we can create a world where all people are treated with respect, dignity, and equality. The problems are simply too large and engrained to be solved by the victims alone.

All of this caused me to start re-examining my life and the roles that I and my white family and friends had played in keeping oppressive forces in place. That, in turn, caused me to start reading book after book after book about our world's extensive history of oppressing and persecuting people. What I found was devastating. For at least the past 2,000 years, dominant groups of people have joined together to oppress and persecute targeted victims. That oppression has included forcing them to live in ghettos, holding them in slavery, prohibiting them from learning to read and write, keeping them out of high-paying jobs, denying them justice, beating them, burning their homes, lynching them, burning them at the stake and many more atrocities. My greatest surprise was the role played by the world's religions (e.g., Christianity, Islam, Hinduism, et. al.) in oppressing and persecuting the victims. Naively, I had expected the exact opposite.

As I studied history, I began to look back at my own personal history and was shocked to realize that I, personally, have been a part of that oppression and persecution without fully realizing my role. That led to my beginning to speak out, such as I did with the letter mentioned in the preface. In turn, that led to my penning this book, which contains a combination of my own experiences in oppressing and persecuting victims as well as some (not all, by any means) of the world's crueler campaigns of oppression and persecution throughout history.

As I studied and remembered, my mind kept asking the question of *why?* Why, why, why have we treated each other so horribly? What makes us do it? I hope that as you read the pages that follow, you will ask yourself the same question: why, why why? And then I pray you will join with me in trying to make the world a better place for all of God's children.

Finally, as I neared the end of my writing, I unexpectedly lost my wife, Jean. She was my everything, and I could not write anything for almost a year after her passing. Just as I dedicated my life to her, I now dedicate this book to her.

Chapter 1

Victims Cry For Mercy
But Christians Give No Mercy

It was in the year of our Lord, 1633. Jerome cried out, "No, Mother! No, no, no! Stop them!" Then the hangman gave the signal, and the stool on which his Nanna was standing was kicked away by a nearby guard. Her body dropped, the noose around her neck jerked tight, and her eyes opened wide and then closed. Her neck snapped, and she gasped one last time as blood oozed out the corners of her mouth onto the floor. His Nanna was dead. Dead...gone forever!

She was more than his grandmother. She was his best friend. It was only six weeks ago that she and he were playing hide and seek in her garden. When she found him, they would both laugh, and she would give him a cookie that she "magically" made appear from under her apron. They would never play again—never!

The crowd cheered as the hangman, a local priest, proudly announced, "Satan and his cunning witch have been defeated. To God be the glory. Amen."

Jerome cried out again "No, no, no! No, Mother, *NOOO!*" but his cries were drowned out by the loud cheers of the celebrating Christians. His Nanna was gone...gone forever and the crowd cheered.

Although no definite records exist of the number of innocent people executed as witches during the years between 1200 and 1800, most historians agree that the number is in the thousands, maybe as many as 60,000 or even 100,000. Regardless of the total number, thousands of innocent people and their families suffered just like Jerome and his Nana suffered. And the Christian churches either participated in the executions or remained totally silent. Even great theologians like

Martin Luther and John Calvin gladly gave their support while preaching that "man is saved by faith, not what we do."

It was in the year of our Lord, 1838. An exhausted Dandalyn stumbled and caught herself just before she fell again into one of the mud holes lining the path. She had already fallen twice this day and had mud all over her arms, legs, and clothes. Even her hair was matted tightly with mud. The soldier closest to her called out, "Step it up, step it up! We ain't got all day." He could not see, or if he did, he did not care, that she was carrying burdens that no human should ever have to carry. His goal was to get this filthy, smelly, bedraggled group of heathen Indians to the new Indian territory as soon as possible. They were already behind today because they had had to dispose of the bodies of two old women and a small child who died last night.

Although there were other Indians walking nearby, Dandalyn walked alone in her own mind, never even looking up. It had not always been this way. Six months ago, she, her husband, Mikel, and their young daughter, Darla, sat happily in their north Georgia home, having supper with the new white Baptist missionary. He had explained how Jesus had given His life so that they too could join him in heaven someday. It was that very night that she and her husband, Mikel, who meant everything to her, gave their lives to Christ.

It was only two months later that God blessed them with a newborn son. That very evening, she, Mikel, and Darla knelt in prayer and thanked God for Billy, their new son. The following week, lots of friends came by to celebrate with them. She and her entire family could not have been happier.

Then three weeks ago, a troop of United States soldiers openly carrying guns arrived at their home and gave them a copy of a federal order. A treaty had been signed, and they were being moved immediately to a stockade about five miles away. They had to leave everything behind, carrying only a few clothes and blankets packed into some bags. With Mikel carrying the bags and Dandalyn carrying their newborn son wrapped in a shawl tied to her back, they began the five-mile walk, taking turns holding Darla's hand. The soldiers rode nearby on their horses and periodically prodded them with their bayonets to walk faster. As they were leaving, two wagons with white drivers passed them, stopping in front of their home to take whatever they wanted. Dandalyn ran to one the soldiers and told him what was happening. He just laughed and said, "You won't be needing all of that stuff."

At the stockade, they joined about three hundred other Cherokees and learned that the next morning all of them would begin the long march to the new Indian territory on the other side of the big river. With only blankets on the hard ground and Billy crying all night, they got very little sleep. But that didn't matter. The soldiers woke them before dawn to announce that everybody had to be ready to leave in one hour. Wagons would carry the supplies; the soldiers would ride horses, and everybody else would walk.

That was three weeks ago and everything since was now a blur. Four days into the march, one of the soldier's horses had knocked Mikel under a wagon wheel, breaking his leg. He couldn't walk, and Dandalyn had begged the soldiers to put him in one of the supply wagons. Instead, they left him on the side of the trail with only a few biscuits and a bowl of water. She begged to stay with him, but the soldiers said, "No." When she refused to move, the soldier laid his bayonet next to her throat and said that she had exactly one minute to start walking. Out of fear, Mikel begged her to go on, saying that he would catch up later. They held each other close for a moment, whispering "I love you," and parted when the soldier growled, "We ain't got all day." Every step for the rest of the day, Dandalyn prayed to God to protect Mikel and to bring their family back together. But that would never happen.

Three nights later, Darla, now exhausted, caught cholera and went into a coma. Dandalyn held her feverish body all night long, praying constantly and begging God to heal her small body. Just before dawn, Darla gasped twice and then stopped breathing. Her body went limp, and she died in her mother's arms. There was no time for a funeral. The soldiers simply placed her body between two logs and covered it with some brush—no service, no saying "goodbye," no nothing. They just tossed her tiny, precious body between two logs, threw a few tree branches over it, and ordered everyone to start walking. That was what they did every morning to those who had died during night.

Dandalyn struggled for the next two days to keep up with the march while carrying her son on her back. Billy was now running a fever and couldn't stop crying. Dandalyn was devastated. After losing Darla, she couldn't lose Billy. But the soldiers would not let her stop and comfort him. The march had to go on. Whenever she fell behind, she felt the sharp point of a bayonet in her back with an order to "step it up."

They came to a small town, and it must have been Sunday. Groups of white people were walking along the road toward a nice white church building with a tall steeple pointing to God in heaven while the bedraggled group of Indians marched down the other side of the road accompanied by the riding soldiers. Seeing a young white family walking towards them on their way to church, Dandalyn, out of sheer desperation, suddenly broke rank and rushed toward them. She knew that she was dirty. The only dress that she had worn for the past three weeks was covered with mud. Her face and her hair were matted with red dirt from the trail. But she was desperate.

She fell to her knees in front of the neatly dressed father and mother and burst into tears as she pleaded for their help. "I am a Christian. I've lost my husband, my daughter died two nights ago, and now my son is sick. Please help me, please, please," she sobbed. The couple looked at her a moment and then turned and walked away. They didn't want to be late for church.

Dandalyn slowly rose with a flood of tears running down her face, turning red as they gathered dirt and fell on her shoulders, walked back to join her kind. Inside the white church, nothing was said about the cruel persecution of Dandalyn and the other Native Americans who had just walked past their church. It was as if it had never happened. Instead, the title of the sermon was "Saved by Faith, Not What We Do."

As Billy's fever continued to rise, his crying became more desperate. His body was wracked with pain. Dandalyn held him close and prayed again to God, "God, I have already lost Darla. Please, please don't let Billy die. Please, God, please." But that was not to be. Somewhere around midnight, his crying slowed to a whimper and then he, like Darla, simply stopped breathing and died as she held him tightly against her chest. The pain was so great that she could not even cry.

She simply lowered his limp body to the ground beside her and prayed and prayed and prayed. She did not know what she was praying for, but she kept praying.

After Dandalyn could no longer pray, she made the decision that her son's body was not going to be tossed away and covered with a few limbs as the soldiers had done with Darla. So, while the others slept, she took out her knife and dug a small grave, laid him in it, kissed him one last time, and covered his tiny body with dirt and mud. She then tied two sticks together to form a small cross, laid it on his grave and prayed to God to take her precious Billy into His arms.

Now, Dandalyn walked alone with her kind, carrying burdens that no human should ever be made to carry. Over one hundred thousand more Native Americans would walk those trails of tears, throwing the dead bodies of thousands of their loved ones between two logs along the way. And the white Christian churches said nothing, choosing instead to preach that "man is saved by faith, not what he does."

It was in the year of Lord, 1845. Jimmy, his mother, and his two older sisters had just been auctioned off to a Methodist minister. They were loaded into a wagon being pulled by two spirited horses to an unknown place far, far away. Jimmy cried out, "Mommy, there's Daddy, there's Daddy! Daddy, stop them—stop them, Daddy, stop them!"

John ran toward the wagon that carried his family away and was able to briefly touch his son's hand and say, "I can't Jimmy, I can't" as his master yelled, "John, get back here, where' n the hell you think that you're going?". Two burley white men grabbed John by his shoulders, snarling, "Get back here, nigger." As they dragged him back to the auction block, John sobbed and quietly mouthed the words to his wife and three children, "I love you... I love you... I love you."

The wagon drove on down the street past Christ's Church where white members were gathering for the Saturday afternoon picnic after the monthly slave auctions. The picnicking Christians were having a great time, laughing and playing games as the wagon rode by, and Jimmy continued to cry out, "No, Daddy, no, no, no! Don't let them take us.

Daddy...Daddy...Daddy, help us, help us!" They would never see their daddy again and the church picnickers did not even notice. Tomorrow, their pastor would not even mention the wagon passing by or the monthly slave auctions. Instead, he would preach a rousing sermon on "we are saved by faith, alone, not by what we do."

It was in the year of our Lord, 1881. There was a loud knock on their front door, and Susie's mother shouted, "Susie, hide...in the closet! Quick... run....quick...in the closet! Run!" The lights from the burning torches made it look as if hell itself had descended on their home. The ten or so white-hooded men standing on their porch completed the picture. Hell had descended.

The knock came again, much louder this time, followed by, "Hey, nigger, we know you in there. You care anything at all bout yo family, you'll get yo black ass out here." Susie crouched under the quilts that her mother had hidden her under and watched through the crack in the closet door as her mother fell to her knees and prayed, "God, my God, please, please protect our family. Please, God, please." But there would be no protection.

The third knock shook the whole house. Her father said, "I have to go. If I don't, they'll kill all of us." Her mother begged, "No, Billy....no....you can't go. That man over there is holding a rope. They'll hang you. Susie and I can't live without you. You're our everything!"

Billy held his wife close for a moment and then responded, "I love you. Remember that forever," and opened the door. He had to protect his family.

Three hooded men grabbed him while the fourth slipped a noose over his head and snarled, "Joe Boss said that you been flirting with his wife this afternoon. Said that you looked her straight in the eyes and smiled at her." Billy responded, "All I said was "Good afternoon, Mrs. Boss."

"Ain't what he said. He said that you looked her straight in the eyes and smiled like you wanted her," the hooded man with a cross on his robe shouted so that his buddies could hear.

As they dragged Billy toward the nearby oak tree, another hooded man added, "If we hang nuff y'all niggers, y'all'a learn. Y'all ne'er gonna have our women." As the rope was thrown over a low hanging limb, Susie and her mother came running out of the house.

"No, no, no. Stop, stop, please! He's my daddy," Susie pleaded. The rope tightened, and just before the bones in his neck popped, Billy looked at his family and sobbed, "I love you." His body went limp. In an act of final cruelty, one of the executers gave the hanging body one last kick and exclaimed, "One less here and one more there."

As they mounted their horses to leave, the kicker asked his buddy, "Hey, you gonna be at church tomorrow? Hear we got a visit'n preacher from down south somewhere. Think they said he's gonna preach about our being 'saved by faith, not what we do' or something like that."

Susie and her mother ran to their father, wrapped their arms around his legs and held him tight as her mother sobbed "Why, God, why? Why? Why? In the name of God, why?"

According to the Archives at Tuskegee Institute, 4,743 people were lynched in the U.S. between 1880 and 1950 of which two-thirds were black. During this period, only a few Christians spoke out against this inhumane treatment. The majority remained stone silent.

It was Sunday, a little after 1:00 PM, in the year of our Lord, 1903. Jermine stood outside the small two-room jail and whispered to her 13-year-old son, "Sonny, can you hear me?" Her son immediately replied, "Yes, Mommy, I'm scared. I'm scared, Mommy, they put me in jail."

"Where's the jailer?"

"Gone to church."

"What'd you do?"

"Nothing, Mommy, nothing. I was coming out of Gracey's store with some candy when the sheriff grabbed me and asked, 'And just where'd you get 'nuff money to buy any candy?' I told him that I been picking cotton for Mr. Garvin all day, and he just paid me. He said, 'That ain't what I heard. Mr. Cole said that you stole that money from his son. Said you pulled a knife on'em and grabbed his money.' Mommy, I told him I just came from Mr. Garvin's cotton field and hadn't even seen Donnie Cole all day. But he said, 'Maybe a night in the jail will help yo mem'ry and slapped these cuffs on me.' Mommy, I'm scared. Are they gonna hurt me? I'm scared."

Just then, Jermine looked up to see that the noon service at the nearby white Grace Christian Church was ending, and the people were beginning to load into their coaches and wagons to go home. Then she heard a loud, "Let's teach the little black bastard a lesson" as a group of the churchmen had turned and were parading toward the jail.

"Oh No! No......God.....NO! Don't let them hurt Sonny. Please, God...pleeease!" Jermine pleaded.. But God did not respond, and the men kept coming. The jailer, the man with the keys to the jail, was with them...and the keys were in his hands. Several of the men carried axe handles that they must have retrieved from their wagons.

As the mob approached the jail, Cole blurted out, "Ain't no nigger gonna rob my son. We'll teach the little bastard a lesson that he won't e'r forget."

Jermine panicked. She had to do something. This was her son.... her son that she loved with all of heart. She jumped in front of the men and shouted, "Stop! Stop. This is my son. In the name of God, stop."

"Outta the way, nigger," the jailer shouted as an ax handle crashed against Jermine's head and she crumpled to the ground. She tried to get up, but a foot hit her head and then another her stomach, and another crushed her leg. They were in the building and headed towards Sonny's cell. Jermine tried again to get up but couldn't. She heard the key unlock the cell and someone shout, "There's the little bastard." She heard Sonny cry out in desperation, "Mommy... Mommy... Help me, Mommy...help me." Then she heard the unmistakable "thud" as an ax handle come down on her son.

But the ordeal was not over. Someone shouted, "I got some kerosene! Let's really teach the little bastard a lesson." Sonny cried out one more time, "Mommy, Mommy, help me."

Those would be the last words that Jermine would ever hear from her son—words that would ring in her ears for the rest of her life. In agony, she rolled over and tried again to get up, but she couldn't. Then she smelled the piercing odor of the kerosene as it was poured on Sonny, and then there was a big "WOOOOOFFF" as a match exploded into the fire that would burn her son to ashes.

As the fire began to consume the whole building, the men came rushing out and headed back to the church where their wives and children waited. They had heard a wonderful sermon teaching that "we are saved by faith, not what we do." Now they would go home and have a nice Sunday afternoon with their families.

Jermine watched in agony as the fire consumed her son, the son that she loved with all of heart. She silently mouthed the words, "I love you, Sonny, I love you."

During the years after the Civil War up until about 1930, the dominant Southern white culture, through its rigged criminal justice system continued to enslave thousands of innocent black people by leasing the prisoners to white mining, logging, and agricultural businesses. Sometimes, this oppressive culture resulted in mob murders and lynchings of innocent people. During these years, the white Christian churches in the South, with a few exception, but only a few, remained deathly quiet, choosing to concentrate on their message that "we are saved by faith alone. not what we do."

It was Saturday night in the year of our Lord, 1940. Nine-year-old Maria watched as her mother and father struggled to pack the single suitcase that they would be allowed to carry tomorrow morning. The Nazi soldiers flooding into the village had given Maria's family—her mom and dad, her sister and two brothers—just one day to prepare to leave their small Polish village.

There were only two Jewish families in town. The rest, about 1,500 people, were all Christians—about half Catholic and half Protestant. Someone had reported the Jews to the soldiers, and there had come that devastating knock on the door. That knock that would result in her father and brothers dying in the Auschwitz gas chamber only a few weeks later. Maria's mother died a few months later, and her body was thrown out into the snow along with about a hundred other bodies that would stay frozen for almost two weeks before being hauled away and tossed into a big ditch along with thousands of other Jewish bodies. Only Maria and her sister, scarred forever, would survive.

None of this, of course, she knew at this time. She knew only that they had to be at the train station the next morning at 10:30 AM with one suitcase and wearing their Star of David badges that the soldiers gave them. Two armed soldiers were stationed outside their home to make sure they did not try to escape and were on time.

Other than the one suitcase, every possession, including all money and jewelry, had to be left behind. As they packed the suitcase for all six of them, Maria's mom and dad wondered why none of their Christian friends had tried to help them or at least warn them. More devastatingly, they wondered which of their friends had reported them to the soldiers. Were their friends never really their friends at all or did they do so to protect their own lives? Maria then spoke up. "Daddy, I know that the policeman will help us tomorrow. He's my friend. I see him every day on the way to school. He'll help us." Her Dad sadly shook his head, "No, Maria, he can't. They would kill him."

Sunday morning came. Maria and her family made their final walk to the train station accompanied by their two gun-toting Nazi guards. On the way, they passed Maria's policeman friend, the Catholic priest on his way to his small church, and their Lutheran friends on their way to their Sunday morning service. No one spoke or even acknowledged that they saw Maria and her family. It was as if they no longer existed. Maria was crushed.

As she and her family continued their march to the train station, Maria thought of God and wondered, "Our friends won't help, but God will." But God, like their friends, seemed to have forsaken them. They were on their own with no friends and no God—just two Nazi guards and a waiting train.

They arrived at the station and, along with the other Jewish family in the village, were loaded into a cattle car already full of at least a hundred devastated souls. There was standing room only, and the stench was overwhelming. Mothers were trying to comfort their crying babies. Grown sons held their elderly parents. Crippled people were propped up on their walking sticks. When one person moved, all had to move. With guns aimed directly at them, Maria and her family climbed onto the train and stood together. Maria looked, and her parents were crying. This would be the last time that their family would ever be together.

The cattle car gate closed, and after a couple of jerks, the train began its trip of no return. Maria looked to see if any of their Christian friends cared enough to even wave goodbye. They didn't. They were all at their church where the preacher did not even mention the Nazi persecutions of the Jews. Instead, he was preaching that they would be saved by faith alone, not by what they did.

An estimated six million Jews were executed in Europe during the Holocaust. Except for some notable exceptions, like Dietrich Bonhoeffer who died in a Nazi prison, the Christian churches either openly supported the executions or remained supportively silent.

It was in the year of our Lord, 1958. Rev. Jim Brennon opened the door to his home with a laugh and a booming voice. "'Bout time you guys got here. 'Bout to eat without you." Ben and his wife joined in the laughter and shook hands with their new white minister. They were a little nervous because this was the first time they had ever been invited into the home of a white person for dinner. But Rev. Brennon and his wife, Christine, made them feel right at home—in fact, made them feel special.

The dinner was wonderful and the conversation even more so as they excitedly talked about the new church they were building. It would be the first racially integrated church in Decatur, Mississippi, a town of about 2,000 people, split about half and half between black and white.

"Much progress on the building yesterday?" Ben asked. "Sorry that I couldn't be there, had to finish plowing the cotton. Mr. Jordan said it had to be done 'fore the rains come this weekend."

"Went great," Rev. Brennon responded. "Five of us were able to make it, and we got two of the outside walls almost completed. The blocks for the other two walls were delivered, so we're ready to go tomorrow morning. Might even finish the outside walls by the end of the week."

"That is, if they don't get you first," Christine worriedly interjected. "We received two letters this week telling us that no church that lets coloreds worship with white folks will ever be built in this town. I'm worried, Ben…in fact, more than worried…I'm scared. Jim isn't taking this as seriously as he should."

"Ahh, that's just talk, Christine. They aren't gonna hurt us," Rev. Brennon assured her.

"Really?" Christine responded "Well, what about that Baptist preacher who came over Tuesday night? His name was Bilbo, wasn't it? You remember, Jim—don't act like you don't. He said that he was coming as a friend…doing you a real favor by letting you know that folks don't want an integrated church round here. You remember, after he quoted all that scripture, he warned you, 'You need to think a lot about what I said. I don't want you to get hurt.'"

Ben chimed in "Jim, maybe we need to rethink this thing. None of us want to be killed. They never have found those three fellas that went missing over in Neshoba County. They could do the same to us."

Rev. Brennon paused for a minute, looking at his wife and friends in dead silence. Finally, he responded. "What we are doing is right. God will protect us."

"Right, Jim. God protects those who protect themselves!" Christine firmly interjected. "Let me ask you and Ben this: Is it worth dying for?"

Ben responded "I'm not sure it is. We colored folks been getting along okay. Not great…but okay, on our own. We don't need no lives lost over this."

Rev. Brannon listened respectfully, then said, "If more of us don't speak out, this oppression and persecution of our black brothers and sisters will never go away. What we are doing is right and the time has come for us to stand up and do something."

With that, the conversation turned to talking about other things, like how much they needed the rain that was predicted for the weekend.

As Ben and his wife approached the door to leave, Ben suddenly wrapped his arms around his new white friend and held him close for a moment before saying, "I never had a white friend before." Then, close to tears, he added, "Thanks for being my first. And do be careful. I don't want to lose you."

Early the next morning, Rev. Brennon had a quick breakfast, donned his work clothes, wrote a quick note to Christine, and quietly left home before his family woke up. Like all weekday mornings, he wanted to get to the work site early to get things laid out before his other church members arrived.

The sun was just rising when he arrived. Something was wrong. The lines that showed where the other two outside walls were to be built were gone. Gaping holes had been beaten into the two finished walls. It was a wonder they were still standing at all. He touched one of them and it wobbled. There was a faint noise behind him. As he turned to look, a baseball bat crashed into his head, knocking him unconscious. He crumpled to the ground as the remaining parts of the cinder block wall fell on top of him. He laid there for over an hour before the first of his fellow church members arrived and saw his foot sticking out from under the pile of blocks. They immediately sent one of their crew for an ambulance and began setting the blocks aside. Rev. Brennon was taken to the nearest hospital where he remained unconscious for almost 30 days.

Upon being dismissed from the hospital, Rev. Brennon and his family sold their home and moved out of state. On the moving date, Ben and his wife were there to help load the van. Just before Rev. Brennon stepped into the van to leave, the two men hugged each other tightly with their tears flowing as Ben struggled to mouth, "Thanks for being the first white friend I ever had." To lighten the departure, Rev. Brennon responded, "Hope you get a better one next time."

Word of the "accident" was reported in most of the state's media, but it was never investigated by the county or state law enforcement agencies. It was just another "accident" that sometimes happened to those who didn't obey the local oppressive white Christian culture. Rev. Bilbo never even mentioned the incident in his church, choosing instead to preach that, "we are saved by faith, alone, not what we do."

During these critical years of the Civil Rights struggle, forty-one people were killed, and hundreds of others were beaten and jailed for protesting racial suppression and segregation. Except for a few brave clergy, the white Christian churches in the South either preached sermons condemning racial equality or remained silent as a church mouse because of the fear of losing members and their money.

It was in the year of our Lord, 2016. Brenda and Mary could not be happier. The U.S. Supreme Court had ruled that same-sex couples could marry. Not only were they married now, but they had also adopted two wonderful children. Ginger and Donnie were five- and seven-year-old siblings whose mother had abandoned them. Never in their lives could Brenda and Mary have imagined that they would be so blessed. Understandably reserved at first, Ginger and Donnie were now outgoing, happy children who said every day how glad they were to have two mothers who loved them. Donnie would just walk into their room and, for what appeared to be no reason at all, say with a beautiful smile, "I love you, Mommy B and Mommy M." Ginger would hop into their bed, snuggle between the two of them and say, "I'm happy."

What a contrast to the lives the two children had lived just a year ago when they were regularly beaten by their mother's boyfriend and often left alone at night when their mother and her boyfriend would go out on the town, sometimes coming in totally stoned well after midnight.

Life for the two children hadn't always been that bad. They had lived with their grandmother before she suddenly died last year, and she had shown them what love was. Now, however, there was no love from a mother who was so addicted to drugs she was out every day trying to find just one more fix. There was only fear that their mother's boyfriend would beat them while their glassy-eyed mother sat nearby and watched, doing nothing to help.

Even at his young age, Donnie tried to comfort his younger sister when they were alone, telling her that God would protect them. That is what their grandmother had always told them before she died. How they wished that their grandmother would come back and hold them just one more time.

After seeing Ginger being beaten one evening because she accidentally spilled her drink, Donnie decided that something had to be done. After his mother and her boyfriend left to party with their friends, he grabbed Ginger and said, "Let's go look for grandmother. She won't let them hurt us anymore."

Holding Ginger's hand tightly, they walked out into the dark, not knowing where they were going but knowing they had to go. An hour later they were found by a patrol car and taken to the Children's Home downtown. After hearing their story, the Home called Brenda and Mary, who had been certified as foster parents just the week before. By midnight, Donnie and Ginger were being tucked into beds by their new foster parents. Donnie smiled at Ginger and said, "I told you we'd find grandmother."

It took almost a year, but the adoptions were finally approved. They were now an official family. No one could ever take that away from them. Donnie smiled again at Ginger as the judge announced their official adoption and said, "Grandmother brought us here."

Brenda and Mary wanted their new children to know and understand God's love, so they found a church home for their family. After only a few months, Ginger and Donnie were totally involved in their church, and for the first time ever they had friends…friends that they loved to be with. Stability had finally entered their young lives as they learned about God's love for them. Both children couldn't wait until they got to church every Sunday and every Wednesday afternoon. They were now a part of a loving Christian family and literally ran to their classes.

Brenda and Mary and their two wonderful children knelt each evening in prayer to thank God for bringing them all together as one big, happy family and blessing them with a wonderful church full of loving friends. They were truly a blessed and happy family.

That was all about to change. This Sunday morning, after making sure Donnie and Ginger were safely in their classes, Mary and Brenda entered the church sanctuary for the morning service, happily greeting friends as they walked down to the pew where they usually sat. They had a new pastor and were anxious to hear his first official sermon.

Just before they reached their pew, however, a church deacon approached and asked, "Can I talk to you for a moment?" Not sure what this was all about, Brenda and Mary followed him out into a quiet corner of the foyer. Once there, he turned to them, and with a grim, almost cruel, facial expression he said, "Our new pastor met with the deacons last night, and they voted to ask all openly gay people to leave our church. They have asked me to let you know that we want you and your children to find another church. We would really appreciate this being your last service. We love you, but we just cannot condone your sin. You're a bad example for our children. You need to take your sin to another church, maybe that gay church on Meridian Road where you can be with your kind."

Mary and Brenda were totally devastated. This church had meant everything to them and their children. The previous pastor had welcomed them with the true love of Christ. They thought that they had found a church home forever. How could this be?

They tried explaining to the deacon that they had done their best to be good church members by volunteering to help in the nursery, helping serve the homeless, and leading the drive to raise funds for the children's home. Just yesterday, they had spent their entire Saturday helping an elderly member relocate to an assisted living facility.

The deacon was unmoved. "You are still sinning. The Bible is totally clear. In fact, it's more than clear. It says that the punishment for living a homosexual life is death to both parties. There's no number of good works that can make up for your sin. Our new pastor has spoken, and the deacons have voted. This really needs to be your last service in this

31

church." He then turned and walked back into the church with a look of pride on his face. He could report to his fellow deacons that he had done his job. He had faithfully obeyed the Bible.

Mary and Brenda looked down at their church bulletin and noticed that the today's sermon was titled "Saved by faith, alone, not by what we do." But in that moment, they had lost all faith and did not go back into the sanctuary. Instead, they walked down to the nearby city park, leaving their kids in their class to let them enjoy one last hour with their friends…friends that they might never see again. Once again, stability had been yanked away from Ginger's and Donnie's lives. This time by the church that they loved so much and thought loved them in return.

Brenda and Mary agonized over what to tell their children. Would it be "Never trust a Christian who says they love you?" No. They both knew that they would lie to their children to try to cover the hurt. That was what gay people had to do all of the time—lie to cover the hurt and humiliation delivered by Christians.

As they walked to the park, Mary could not help asking "Why, God, why? Why? Why? Why?" But God did not respond.

While polls show that the majority of Americans support equal rights for LGBTQs, the majority of evangelical and Catholic Christians remain fiercely opposed. The murder of transgender people is at an all-time high, and the Christian churches continue to loudly condemn homosexual relations as a sin against God and His people.

It was in the year of our Lord, 2019. Patricia was sitting in her first committee meeting with Our Savior's Baptist Church. She had been a member for a little over a year and been asked to represent the college students on the committee to nominate church officers, teachers, committee members, and deacons for the coming year. This was her first appointment to a church wide committee, and she was excited to have this opportunity to serve God and her church.

First, the committee went through the list of current teachers and committee members provided by Pastor Bob. Most had already agreed to serve another year. For those few openings, Pastor Bob had already secured suggested replacements. There were some discussions about the replacements, but after hearing from Pastor Bob, all of his recommendations were approved. Everything was going well, and Patricia was feeling good about her service. Within the first 45 minutes, all teaching and committee slots had been filled. The committee voted to send the recommendations on to the deacons and then, with their approval, to the full congregation.

The committee's final job was to nominate four new deacons to fill vacancies created by three retirements and one death. Church members had been asked to submit nominations in sealed envelopes. Pastor Bob opened the nomination box and emptied the sealed envelopes onto the table. Patricia volunteered to write the names of the nominees on a list as other committee members opened the envelopes and read the names.

Committee members began to read the names, "John Smith, Bill Sprock, Jerry Billington." Pastor Bob commented, "All good people." The names continued, "Phil Brown, Barry Green, Samuel Bonner, Wayne Gavin." "Four more good choices," Pastor Bob observed. Then one of the committee members called out "Eva Gardner."

"Scratch that one," Pastor Bob said.

"Scratch that one?" Patricia asked. "Why?"

"Because she's a woman," the pastor replied.

"What's wrong with being a woman?" Patricia asked.

"Because they aren't qualified to be deacons," Pastor Bob replied. "Everybody knows that."

"But she is the only one out of the whole group with a Doctor of Divinity degree," Patricia pointed out. "She teaches religion at the university, and I had her for my New Testament class last semester. She's a great teacher and one of the finest Christians I have ever known. She is here almost every service and serves every other Friday at the homeless shelter. She also received the Most Admired Faculty award at the university just last week. These are all good men, but none of them have the credentials that Dr. Gardner has."

"Doesn't matter," Pastor Bob explained again. "She's still a woman, and we don't care how qualified she is in the secular world. She's not qualified to serve as a deacon in our church."

Patricia should have known but didn't. She was astounded. "And just why isn't she qualified?" she asked.

Pastor Bob, getting a little irritated, responded, "Because the Bible is perfectly clear that women can't talk in church. That's why." Picking up his Bible, he added, "Here, let me read exactly what Paul says in 1 Corinthians 14:34. 'Let your women keep silence in the churches: for it is not permitted unto them to speak.' And, in 1 Timothy 2:12, Paul confirms the place of women. He says, 'But I suffer not a woman to teach, nor to usurp authority over the man, but to be in silence.'"

"So," he continued, "if you can't speak in church and can't have authority over men, you are not qualified as a deacon. It's that simple. We have to decide whether we obey the Bible or not, and our church has chosen to obey."

"Besides," he added, "you know the reason Eva is teaching at a state university is because she was fired from her seminary job a couple of years ago, don't you? The new president of the seminary discovered that she was teaching male students and let her go immediately. She knows her Bible and still willfully taught those male ministerial students. Not only is she a woman, but she actually believes that she can teach men something. What she was doing was nothing short of heresy. So, she's not nearly as biblical as you think. She really needs to find another church."

Patricia could not believe what she was hearing. She had been a member of this church for over a year but had never heard anything like this. Something was wrong. She was sure that there were women teaching men in the Sunday school classes. So, the church was speaking out of both sides of its mouth. She quickly glanced at the list of teachers that the committee had just approved, and to her astonishment, there was not a single woman teaching adult classes containing men—not a single one! The only adult classes taught by women were all-women classes.

Patricia was crushed. The oppression of women had been there all of the time, just under the surface, and it was based upon obeying the Bible because every commandment in the Bible had to be obeyed.

"Every commandment?" she wondered. "Really?"

Then, she looked up at Pastor Bob and asked, "So, when do we start putting all who work on the sabbath to death?"

Pastor Bob looked at her in confusion. "What does that have to do with women deacons?"

"Everything," she responded. "Everything...unless there is some reason other than the Bible that we can't have women deacons. If we're going to obey the Bible here, then we need to obey it everywhere, and in Exodus the Bible clearly says that anyone working on the sabbath shall be put to death. So, when do we start?"

Pastor Bob was caught in a bind and realized that he needed to soften the conversation. "Each church must decide which Biblical passages it will be faithful to," he explained. "That's the way we tell ourselves and the world what kind of Christians we are. Our church has chosen to tell the world that we are Christians who obey the Bible's laws that keep women in their biblically ordained place. But we're not the kind of church that obeys the biblical mandate that we keep the sabbath holy. Besides," he chuckled, "most of our members really don't care how we treat women, but they would care a lot if we started preaching against working on the sabbath. They like eating out after church every Sunday too much to obey that passage."

Patricia, realizing that this was a lost cause, smiled and said, "Thank you. You are right. We are shouting loud and clear what kind of Christians we are. Have you ever considered that this just might be the reason that so many people are rejecting Christianity?

Pastor Bob did not respond to her question. Instead, he suggested that, because it was getting late, the committee should adjourn and meet next Tuesday evening to complete the selection of deacon nominees. After a short prayer by one of the male members of the committee, the committee adjourned. As they were leaving, one of the members asked what the title of the Sunday sermon was going to be. Pastor Bob responded, "Saved by Faith Alone, Not What We do."

While the secular sector in America has made great progress in improving the status of women over the past several decades, evangelical Protestant and Catholic Christian churches still maintain and strongly enforce policies that tell the world that women must be subordinate to the males in their lives. Evangelical churches who choose to endorse women pastors are voted out of their state and national associations. The Pope has reconfirmed that women will always be subordinate to men in the Catholic church.

It was in the year of our Lord, 2019. Martha grabbed her five-year-old son Jimmy's hand and ran out the back door into the dark. Her husband would be back in a few minutes, and they had to be gone. She had called 911, and the operator said that a policewoman would meet them on the street behind their house in three minutes.

"Run, Jimmy, run," she whispered. Then she saw the police car turning the corner. It stopped in front of them, and the policewoman asked, "Are you Martha?" She responded, "Yes," and the lady said, "Jump in the other side." Once they were both safely inside, a feeling of pure relief overwhelmed Martha's entire body!

At that moment, the policewoman looked exactly like an angel from heaven. And in many ways, she was. "They just told me where to pick you up. What can we do to help"? the angelic lady asked. "What do you need?"

Anxiously looking up and down the street, Martha frantically said, "We need to go, or he'll find us."

"Who will find you?"

"My husband. He just went down to Quick Save for some liquor. Said that he would be right back. He has a shotgun and says he'll decide whether to shoot us when he returns."

With that, the policewoman quickly sped away. After about mile, she asked, "Where do you want to go?"

Finally able to cry, Martha sobbed, "I don't have any place to go. I don't have any family in town. I need help—can you help me? Can you help us find a place where he can't find us? I know he'll be out looking for us all night. We need a safe place where he can't find us. If he does, he'll kill us. I just know he will."

"I do know a place," the lady assured her. "They will be glad to let you stay at the Women's Refuge House, and you and your son will be safe there. The house is hidden. Only the workers and the police know where it is. Want to go there?"

"You think that they'll take us?" Martha asked.

"Sure. They'll welcome you with open arms. I can call them right now and let them know we are on our way."

"Okay. Thanks."

As they drove toward the home, going along twisting, winding streets, Martha began to share her desperation. "I knew we had to leave when he slammed Jimmy against the wall because he accidently dropped his soup bowl. Jimmy was covered with blood and was so scared that he didn't even cry. Just stood there looking at me for help. I had to help him. I'm his mother. It's my job to protect him. This just couldn't ever happen again. His whole face was covered with blood. So, I grabbed Billy, held him as close as I could, looked my husband straight in his eyes and said, 'Don't you ever do that to my son again!'"

"He shouted back, 'And don't you ever sass me again,' and slapped me right in the mouth. Busted my lips. But he didn't care, just kept on raging, 'I'm the head of this household. You understand that? Read your damn Bible. I tell you what to do. You don't tell me.'"

"He walked out of the room, and I grabbed a paper towel to wipe the blood off our faces. When I looked up, he was coming back into the room loading shells into his shotgun. He laid the gun on the table and said, 'You ever mouth off to me again I'll blow your stupid brains out. You understand that? And that brat of a son, too.'"

"I didn't respond immediately. So, he said, 'Speak, woman, speak. I wanna hear you say, 'Yes, dear. I know that you are the head of our house, and I will always do exactly what you tell me to do.'"

"I repeated his words, and he said, 'Good, now that we've got that straight, I'm going down to Quick Save for some liquor, and I want dinner on the table when I get back. Just 15 minutes—you understand that? If it ain't ready, my gun is.' With that, he picked up the gun and went out to his car."

"As soon as I heard him leave the driveway, I called 911, and they said for Jimmy and me to go to our back street, and you would pick us up. I got my purse but didn't have time to get anything else…no clothes or even tooth brushes. I know he's gonna find us and when he does, he's gonna kill us. I just know that's what's gonna happen. I just know it."

As they pulled in front of a plain, unassuming house hidden behind a fence and a dense growth of shrubs and trees, the policewoman reassured Martha that they wouldn't let that happen.

As soon as their car stopped, two really nice women came rushing out of the house. They first hugged Martha and Jimmy and then introduced themselves. "We are the two Bettys," they laughed. "So, you can't go wrong. Just say 'Betty,' and you'll have it right."

Inside the very spacious house, one of the Bettys said, "You're safe here, and you can stay as long as you need to. And don't worry. In addition to being hidden and out of the way, we have 24-hour police protection and security cameras all over the place."

The other Betty then showed them to a nice bedroom with two single beds and asked if they needed something to eat. Martha realized that she'd completely forgotten about that dinner her husband had demanded. Surely Jimmy must be starving by now.

"Maybe a couple of sandwiches?" she said. "And some tea, if you have it."

After eating, Martha and Jimmy, now feeling safe, at least for tonight, fell into their beds. Jimmy was asleep in no time, but Martha lay there thinking about all that had happened over the past few weeks.

About two weeks ago things had gotten so bad at home that she knew she had to do something. Martha had finally worked up the courage to make an appointment with her pastor to get his advice. She had expected sympathy, but she should have picked up the clue when she pulled into the parking lot. The church's large roadside sign proclaimed, "Wives submit yourselves unto your husband—Ephesians 5:22." Sympathy was not what she was going to receive.

Instead, her pastor started quizzing her about what she had done that required that her husband discipline her? Without even waiting for an answer, he asked if she had read what the Bible says about a woman's role in marriage and went on to explain that Genesis 2:18 says that she is to be "a helper suitable for him." Ephesians 5:33 says that "she must respect her husband." He went on to show how Titus 2:4 said that the wife is "to love her husband," and Ephesians 5:22-30 said that "the husband is the head of the wife and the wife subject to her husband."

The pastor then said that if she was being a good wife according to the Bible and always respected her husband's leadership, then her husband would, in turn, treat her with respect and love. It was a two-way street, but she had to start by being a good wife. He asked if she would give him that pledge—the pledge of being a good submissive wife. After reluctantly doing so, she asked, "But what if he beats me again?" To which her pastor responded, "You do your part, and he won't. I promise you that. But it has to start with you. You have got to be a good biblical wife."

As she lay there in the safety of the Refuge House, Martha remembered getting home to find that her husband had been driving by the church. He'd seen her go into the pastor's office and demanded to know what she was doing there. Caught off guard, she couldn't think of a good excuse. So, she decided to be honest. "I wanted to talk to our pastor about how you and I could have a better marriage. About how we could recapture those wonderful days when we were dating, about how we could really love each other."

"You talked to your pastor about our marriage without telling me? Did he tell you that I'm the head of the household, and you don't talk to no one without my approval? Did he tell you that? Huh? Huh? Did he tell you that? Well, I'm telling you that. Get your butt in there and fix my dinner, and we'll talk later."

She remembered how he just got madder and madder during dinner, watching in fear as he downed two shots of bourbon and three glasses of wine. What happened after dinner was too horrible for her to even recall now. And he wouldn't even let her go to the doctor. The next morning, she put on as much make-up as possible and went to work. Still, her swollen lips and black eyes showed through.

Later, Martha had a chance to talk privately with the Bettys. They talked about how she needed to put hers and her son's safety first. They assured her that marriage wasn't a one-sided deal; it was an equal partnership—no matter what anyone else said the Bible meant.

After over an hour talking with the Bettys, Martha made the decision that she should have made years ago. Her marriage was over. She would never put her and her son's lives at risk again. She would file for divorce and seek police protection. She would ask her company for a job transfer to another city. And she would never, ever, seek help from her pastor again, even though he preached great sermons about being saved by faith alone, not what we do.

The Center for Disease Control reports that 1 in 4 women are abused by their spouse. The evangelical and Catholic Churches grant their sanction and support for this abuse by continuing to teach that, according to the Bible, the wife is subordinate to the husband's commands.

It is in the year of our Lord, 2020. The short stories that you have just read are historical fiction all based on my own experiences, the experiences of personal acquaintances, documented testimonies from those to whom the tragedies happened, or direct witnesses to the tragedies. In some cases, I couldn't bear to include the very worst of what happened. In the Trail of Tears story, I simply could not bring myself to have Dandalyn's newborn son, Billy, killed by a soldier grabbing him by his feet and slamming his head against a tree. But according to documented testimonies of the Native Americans forced to march on that harrowing journey along the Trail of Tears, that is exactly what happened on many occasions. In my account, I just couldn't show that happening to Dandalyn and Billy.

Similarly, I could not bring myself to fully describe the documented treatment of Jews in the Holocaust concentration camps. The starvation, filthy living quarters, diseases, beatings, trips to the gas chambers, bullets to the back of the head, and forced disposition of the bodies of their family and friends, just to name a few, were simply too much. My failure to do so may have let you down, but I just could not do it.

I cannot close this chapter, however, without sharing with you one of the documented accounts of human cruelty that I found in my research. Mary Turner deserves that her story be told to every man, woman, and child at least a hundred times so that we will never, ever let it be repeated in any form.
In May of 1918, Hampton Smith, a 31-year-old White plantation owner in Brooks County, Georgia was shot and killed by one of his Black workers named Sydney Johnson. Hampton Smith was known for abusing and beating his workers to the point few people in the area would work for him. To solve this labor shortage, Smith turned to the debt peonage system of the day and found a ready labor pool. He used that system by bailing people out of jail, people typically arrested for petty offenses, and having them work off their debt (the bail money) to him on his plantation. Nineteen-year-old Sydney Johnson, arrested for "rolling dice" and fined thirty dollars, was one such unfortunate person.

After a few days of work on Smith's plantation, and shortly after being refused his earned wages and beaten by Smith for not working while he was sick, Sydney Johnson shot and killed Hampton Smith. What ensued after the shooting was a mob driven manhunt for Johnson and others thought to be involved in his decision to kill Hampton Smith. That manhunt lasted for more than a week and resulted in the deaths of at least 13 people with some historical accounts suggesting a higher number of persons killed. One of the people killed was a woman named Mary Turner.

"Thirty-three-year-old Mary Turner…, 8 months pregnant at the time and whose husband had been killed in this "lynching rampage" on Sunday, May 19th, publicly objected to her husband's murder. She also had the audacity to threaten to swear out warrants for those responsible. Those "unwise remarks," as the area papers put it, enraged locals. Consequently, Mary Turner fled for her life only to be caught and taken to a place called Folsom's Bridge on the Brooks and Lowndes Counties' shared border. To punish her, at Folsom's Bridge the mob tied Mary Turner by her ankles, hung her upside down from a tree, poured gasoline on her and burned off her clothes. One member of the mob then cut her stomach open, and her unborn child dropped to the ground where it was reportedly stomped on and crushed by a member of the mob. Her body was then riddled with gunfire from the mob. Later that night she and her baby were buried ten feet away from where they were murdered. The makeshift grave was marked with only a "whiskey bottle" with a "cigar" stuffed in its neck."

"Three days after the murder of Mary Turner and her baby, three more bodies were found in the area and Sydney Johnson was killed in a shootout with police on South Troup Street in Valdosta, Georgia. Once killed, the crowd of more than 700 people cut off his genitals and threw them into the street. A rope was then tied to his neck and his body was drug to Campground Church in Morven, Georgia, 16 miles away. There, what remained of his body was burned. During and shortly after this chain of events it is reported that more than 500 black people fled Lowndes and Brooks Counties in fear for their lives." [1]

At www.maryturner.org, you may find more about this story and also what the good people of Valdosta, Georgia, are doing today to honor Mary Turner and her unborn child and to keep their story alive so that it will never, ever, ever be repeated

As I read this story over and over, I couldn't help but wonder if any in that mob were Christians. My guess is that many were since

---

[1] www.maryturner.org

Christianity was the dominant religion in Georgia in those days. Then I wondered what the church pastors and leaders said the weeks after the murders. I am also guessing that they said nothing, absolutely nothing. I know for a fact that nothing was said in my Mississippi church in the 1960s after three teenage Civil Rights protestors were murdered in neighboring Neshoba County. Nothing was said after Emmet Till's murder in another part of Mississippi, or when four young black girls were killed in a church bombing in neighboring Alabama. Nothing!

WILL IT NEVER, EVER STOP? It is June 17 in the Year of our Lord, 2020, and I thought that I had finished writing this chapter. Then it happened again, and then again and then again, just like last year and the year before and the year before that, going back through the centuries. One more unarmed black man or woman murdered by white police or by some self-appointed white man or group of white men.

Just a few months ago, on February 23, Ahmaud Arbery, a young black man was out jogging through the neighborhood. He was murdered in Brunswick, Georgia, by a white father and son while a third white man videoed the murder. No arrests were made until May 7 after the video began to circulate, apparently forcing state-level law enforcement officers to step in as the local officials refused to.

On the same day of those arrests in Georgia, Breonna Taylor, a young black woman in Louisville, Kentucky, was simply sitting in her home when a white policeman, with a wrong warrant address, shot her door open and shot her to death.

Just 13 days later on May 25, in Minneapolis, Minnesota, George Floyd, a black man, was accused of trying to use a counterfeit twenty-dollar bill. He was handcuffed and then thrown to the ground by four white policemen, then suffocated to death as one of the officers pressed his knee on Mr. Floyd's neck, cutting off his breathing. In a video, Mr. Floyd can be heard crying out, "I can't breathe! I can't breathe!" until his body went limp. But even after his body went limp, the policeman continued to press his knee on Mr. Floyd's neck for a total of almost nine minutes.

A few days later, on June 4, two black teenagers in Tulsa, Oklahoma were arrested by white police officers for simply walking down a street with no sidewalk and no traffic on the street…something that I have often done. One of the teenagers was thrown to the ground and handcuffed.

A few days after that, on June 12, an unarmed, intoxicated black man who resisted arrest and tried to run was shot twice in the back and then kicked as he lay dying by the two white policemen who were trying to arrest him.

As my wife and I watched the news in horror and saw the videos of these arrests and murders, I glanced down on our coffee table and noticed a copy of Ben Crump's book, *Legalized Genocide of Colored People—Open Season*[1]. It had been given to me recently by a mutual friend, so I opened it and began to read. After only a few pages, I had to set it aside for a while. His documentation of the murders of people of color in recent decades by white men was just too much for me at that moment. And those stories were *before* the most recent murders mentioned above.

And yet, we call ourselves Christians! But when some black professional football players solemnly knelt during the national anthem before some games to humbly call attention to the prolific number of murders of their black brothers and sisters, the President of the United States called them "sons-of-bitches." What did we white evangelical Christians do? We listened only to the president and cheered. And while we cheered, our white church leaders continued to preach and teach that we are saved by faith alone, not what we do. **Does it never, ever matter how we treat others?**

---

[1] Crump, Ben, *Legalized Genocide of Colored People; Open Season*, HarperCollins Publishers, 2019

Chapter 2

How Can This Be?

How can this be? How can a people, who serve a loving God and have a long history of building hospitals to serve the sick, building schools and colleges to educate their fellow man, constructing homes for orphans and for the homeless, establishing food pantries for the hungry, ministering to refugees from wars and crimes, and praying daily for the health of their sick friends, also have a history of openly and proudly oppressing, persecuting and even murdering their fellow man? How can a people who have spent billions to send missionaries to carry the love of God to people all over the world also have such a long history of remaining totally silent while their fellow Christians oppress and persecute others, including the torture and murder of targeted groups? How can this dark, dark side of Christianity exist?

From the opening pages of *How to Read the Bible in Changing Times*, Mark Strauss states:

In How Christianity Changed the World, Alvin J. Schmidt documents the profound impact that the Bible and Christianity have had on the world. Biblical teaching and values have been the impetus behind many of the world's great social and ethical movements. These include the abolition of infanticide and advocacy for the value of human life, raising the status and dignity of women, building hospitals and promoting health care, establishing schools and broadening education, defending the rights of workers, feeding the poor and combating poverty, sponsoring the arts and sciences, and working for justice for all.[1]

---

[1] Strauss, Mark L., *How to Read the Bible in Changing Times*, Baker Publishing Company, Copyright 2011, pg. 2

On page 3, however, Strauss goes on to note that:

While the Bible is the most revered book of all time, it may also be the most misunderstood and misused, a tool of manipulation, evil, injustice, and even genocide.[1]

And on page 5, he further observes that:

The Bible has been used to promote crusades of conquest, riots and pogroms against Jews and other minorities and even subjugation of whole people groups.[2]

And the list of tragedies goes on. Frederick Douglass, the great American author and orator who escaped the humiliation, beatings, and starvation of black slavery to become a highly respected national leader of the abolitionist movement, declared in his famous 1852 July 4th speech that:

But the church of this country is not only indifferent to the wrongs of the slave, it actually takes sides with the oppressors. It has made itself the bulwark of American slavery, and the shield of American slave-hunters. Many of its most eloquent Divines. who stand as the very lights of the church, have shamelessly given the sanction of religion and the Bible to the whole slave system. They have taught that man may, properly, be a slave; that the relation of master and slave is ordained of God; that to send back an escaped bondman to his master is clearly the duty of all the followers of the Lord Jesus Christ; and this horrible blasphemy is palmed off upon the world for Christianity.[3]

Douglas observed in his autobiography that:

Were I to be again reduced to the chains of slavery, next to that enslavement, I should regard being a slave of a religious master the greatest calamity that could befall me. For all slaveholders with whom I have ever met, religious slaveholders are the worst. I have ever found them the meanest and basest, the most cruel and cowardly, of all others.[4]

---

[1] Ibid, pg. 3

[2] Ibid, pg. 5

[3] https://newsone.com/3881725/frederick-douglass-fourth-july-speech-full-text/

[4] Douglass, Frederick. Narrative of the Life of Frederick Douglass, an American Slave, Prestwick House, 1845, pg. 67.

Why is the statement by Blaise Pascal, the great French mathematician, physicist, inventor, philosopher, writer, and Catholic theologian of the 1600s, so sadly true?

Men never do evil so completely and cheerfully as when they do it from a religious perspective.[5]
How Can This Be? And at The Same Time?

How can these two sides of Christianity exist side by side at the exact same time? How could white Christians send missionaries to take the love of God to Native Americans and, at the exact same time, support the Trail of Tears which showed no mercy whatsoever? How could white Christians sit contentedly in their churches worshiping a loving God, while planning to take a teenage son from his slave family and sell him, like a cow or a horse, the following week? How could a nation of Christians worship a loving God in their churches and voice no objection when millions of their fellow Jews were being exiled and murdered? How could white Christians do so much good to help their fellow man while, at the very same time, pass Jim Crow laws that humiliated their black brothers and sisters and kept them in poverty?

How can a good, loving, dedicated pastor honestly look his congregation in the eyes and preach, "We are all equal in God's eyes," while knowing that when away from the pulpit he is leading his church to ban all literature that supports the equal treatment of women and LGBTQs?

How can a church's leaders make no comment whatsoever, other than a few short sentences to pray for the victims and their families, when a women-hating mass murderer kills two women and wounds four more just a mile or so away? On a national level, how can we "good, kind, considerate, loving" Christians sit silently in our churches and say nothing while Christian extremists (people who also sit in our Christian churches) mass murder women, Jews, LGBTQs, and immigrants? Can anything explain why we say nothing…nothing at all…about this tragic, unjust treatment of our fellow humans, choosing instead to concentrate on what we ourselves need to do to get to heaven? Is our

---

[5] *The Week*, April 22, 2022, page 17

getting to heaven totally divorced from how we treat our fellow women and men?

Perhaps, even more importantly to me personally, is the question of why have I joined my fellow Christians over the last 40+ years by saying nothing myself. What is the force that has silenced even me whose soul cries out, "Do we not even care? Is this really who God called us to be?" Am I just another "go along to get along" while others suffer every day because of my and your silence?

As I pondered all of these questions, my mind wandered back to my childhood friendship with the son of a black tenant farmer who worked for my father. We were about six or seven years old, and both of us looked forward to playing together after school most days. We were best buddies. Then one day, totally out of the blue, my mother sat me down and, as kindly as she could, told me that I could no longer play with my friend. In response to my childhood repetitive "but whys?", my mother struggled to explain. I remember she first said that it was because his family was black and ours white. To which I responded with another "why?" After struggling some more to explain, she said that it was because black people are not clean, and I might catch a disease and infect our whole family. I remember being devastated.

After more pleading on my part, my mother agreed that I could play with my friend a few more times, but she was adamant that we would have to stop soon. After that conversation, a terrible thing happened. I started to see my friend through different lens. Suddenly, he was different—he was black, and I was white. He was not quite as clean. His clothes were a little more ragged than mine. His language was not as educated as mine. My father was the boss; his father was a laborer. In short, the seed had been planted by that one conversation and my friend, who had done nothing different and was still as wonderful as he had always been, was suddenly not worthy of my friendship. I was well on my way, at that early age, to becoming a racist without even knowing it.

Later in life, as I reflected on that conversation, I wondered what forces caused my mother, who was one of the greatest mothers as well as one of the finest Christians you would ever want to meet, to have that conversation with me? What caused my loving mother to view black people as lower class, to treat them that way, and then feel obligated to teach me to treat them that way?

Whatever the reason, it quickly took root in me. As I grew up on a farm outside Newton, Mississippi in the 1940s and '50s, I joined my parents, grandparents, their friends, my friends, my pastor, my fellow church members, and our white political leaders in viewing black people as inferior people. We saw them like the "untouchables" in India, as a people who should be kept out of our white restaurants, hotels, doctors' waiting rooms and, most especially, out of our white schools, colleges and churches. When the Civil Rights movement, led by Martin Luther King, Jr., "invaded" Alabama, Tennessee, Georgia, Arkansas, South Carolina, our nation's capital, and my home state of Mississippi, I joined my family and white friends in condemning the movement.

When three teenage protestors were murdered in our neighboring Neshoba County, when the four young girls were killed in the bombing of a black church in Birmingham in neighboring Alabama, and when protestors were beaten by police and brutally attacked by their dogs during the Selma march, I joined my family and white friends in thinking and sometimes (in the "right" company) saying, "That's what they get for trying to force racial integration on 'innocent' white people. If they had just stayed home and minded their own business, none of this would have ever happened."

We were proud of Alabama Governor George Wallace when he declared:

Let us rise to the call of freedom-loving blood that is in us and send our answer to the tyranny that clanks its chains upon the South. In the name of the greatest people that have ever trod this earth, I draw the line in the dust and toss the gauntlet before the feet of tyranny . . . and I say . . . segregation today . . . segregation tomorrow . . . segregation forever.[6]

---

6   https://www.blackpast.org/african-american-history/speeches-african-american-history/1963-george-wallace-segregation-now-segregation-forever/

Governor Wallace was a highly respected Christian, having served on the Board of Stewards of the Clayton, Alabama, Methodist Church where he taught Sunday School lessons. We took what he said as the "gospel."

We felt totally vindicated when Rev. Bob Jones and many other white evangelical preachers and church leaders preached sermons and wrote editorials quoting numerous biblical passages that left no doubt in the minds of white people that racial segregation was not only ordained but mandated by God. To support racial equality and integration was a failure to obey the Bible. And while it was seldom said, it was clearly implied that it would put one in danger of going to hell when they died.

When our pastor heard a rumour that some black people were going to visit our church, he met with our deacons, and they decided to have two of the deacons guard the doors with shotguns. Fortunately, no black people arrived that day, but I have often wondered what would have happened had they visited. Would they have been murdered right there in the doors of our church by my fellow Christians for simply asking to worship with us?

As I now look back on those years, I still remember my family, my friends, and my fellow church members as very loving people who would do anything to help our fellow white friends in their time of need. Notice I said "white" friends because, at least in our community, whites helped whites and blacks helped blacks. Seldom, if ever, did we help each other. We all knew that that was the way it was supposed to be. Each to his own.

As white Christians, we were very comfortable with our wilful and adamant subordination, oppression, and persecution of our black brothers and sisters simply because their skin was darker than ours. We felt no guilt whatsoever. That was the way our God of love had ordained our roles and their roles on this earth.

All of this brings us back to the question: what can possibly explain this dichotomy? What forces exist that cause really good people— people like me (most days), my pastor, my mother, my church friends, and maybe even you, all who worship a loving God and spend lots of our time helping our fellow man, also willfully, even boastfully, oppress and persecute others? Even when we're not personally oppressing others, what forces cause us to willingly grant our support by remaining as silent as a buried rock while oppression and persecution is rampant all around us? What could possibly cause us to act as if the oppression and persecution of others is the norm, as if this is what is expected of us…what all good Christians do?

Core Christian Values

As I looked back at my own history and pondered this dichotomy, I wondered how the oppression and persecution of millions of victims over the years became part of being a good white Christian. How could this have become part of the values held by white Christians both in the past and today? So, being an amateur scholar, I conducted some very unsophisticated research. First, I researched the New Testament gospels to see what Jesus's core values were and if they included the oppression and persecution of others. Secondly, I sent an email to nine of my white Christian friends and family, asking them to send me a list of their core Christian values, using only five or six words or phrases.

In my study of the gospels, I could find no instances where Jesus oppressed or persecuted anyone. I couldn't find the smallest mention that he even advocated the oppression and persecution of any groups of people. Instead, His whole ministry was spent showing compassion for and helping those who were oppressed and persecuted by the dominant culture during His time with us on earth. The poor, the handicapped, the sick, women, Samaritans, Gentiles, those in prison, and even the prostitutes were all recipients of Jesus's compassion, love, and help. In fact, as stated in Mathew 25, Jesus made it abundantly clear that those who help the oppressed and persecuted (i.e., the least of these) will be rewarded with eternal life. Further, Jesus was most critical of those, especially religious leaders, who used their power to oppress and persecute others. There was simply no room in Jesus's teachings and actions for oppressing and persecuting others.

As I researched the gospels, I decided to think about what was not included. I promise you that I did *not* find the following statements and their principles in any form credited to Jesus in the Bible.

1. Jesus, anticipating his own death, withdrew from the crowds and began to speak only to his disciples. "I will be leaving you soon

to return to my father in heaven. It will become your responsibility to teach what I have taught you and then the responsibility of those whom you teach to teach others so that every generation will know what I have told you.

2. I know that you will succeed because my heavenly Father has blessed me with a glimpse into the future for generations to come. What I have seen gives me great pride in what you and those who follow after you and those who follow them will do to make my people powerful and wealthy.

3. I have seen that those who follow my teachings will become known as Christians. Their numbers will grow to become the largest religious group in the world, and they will become the wealthiest and most powerful people on earth.

4. I have seen that in only 400 years from now, a great ruler will order that my words, your words, the words of prophets of old, and the words of those yet to speak be put in one book and that book will be called "the Bible."

5. I have seen that the Bible will become known as the inspired word of God that is literally true and must be strictly obeyed by every true professing Christian.

6. I have seen that my people will obey the Bible to rid the world of thousands of demonic witches over several hundred years by torturing people until they confessed, and then either lynching or burning them at the stake.

7. I have seen a new land across the oceans where my people will go, carrying their Bibles with them, and then take the homes and lands of the native people and slaughter those who object.

8. I have seen that the Bible will be faithfully obeyed to generate wealth for my people by keeping millions of black people in slavery for hundreds of years. And part of that wealth will be used to spread my word to the heathen peoples in other nations.
9. I have seen that my people will use my very own words, quoted in the Bible, to exile and execute millions of Jews.

10. I have seen that my people will obey my Father's biblical racial purity laws by building a segregated society where all people of color are kept near poverty in subordinated roles for over a hundred years.

11. I have seen that my Christian men will obey the biblical words of a prophet, one who you do not yet know, to proudly oppress women and keep them in subordinated roles for thousands of years. I rejoiced when I saw men walk out when a woman stood up to preach and when churches with women pastors were expelled from church associations.

12. I have seen my people obey every word in the Bible to boastfully oppress and persecute people born homosexuals. I could not have been prouder when I saw my Christian leaders kick gay people out of their churches and churches split from associations when those associations voted to treat gay people with respect, dignity, and equality.

13. My Father has blessed me by revealing to me all of these great things that my people for generations to come will do. I now leave you knowing that what you and I have done and taught will make the world a better place for my people now and for all generations to come. So, go and do that which I have taught you, knowing that you, too, will be a part making my people powerful and wealthy."

I promise you again that I found not a single one of the above verses, or anything even vaguely close, in the gospels credited to Jesus. Yet, those verses describe exactly what Christians have done since Jesus' human time with us on earth. What I did find in reading the scriptures was a Jesus so committed to love and compassion for and service to the oppressed that he would have never condoned what we have done over the years in His name and still do today.

Now turning to the results of my informal survey of nine of my friends and family, they responded that their core Christian values were things such as "love, justice, grace, worship, forgiveness, faith, repentance, hope, joy, humility, caring, compassion, kindness, generosity, empathy, hospitality, joy, and gratitude." Not a single one listed oppression, subordination, racial segregation, persecution, condemnation, slavery, torture, execution, exile, lynching, or burning people at the stake. All of those actions, though, have been repeatedly taken by Christians at various times since Christ's death and resurrection…some of which continue to this very day in our Christian churches. Nor did any of my friends and family mention "remaining silent" when these horrible actions were (are) taken by Christians and sadly too often preached in Christian churches. (Of course, I guess that some may argue that none of my friends and family are "true Christians" who are committed to obeying the Bible.)

After reviewing Jesus's life and teachings (including what He did not say) and my friends' lists of their Christian values (and what they did not list), my layman's conclusion is that the self-claimed core values of Christians really are "love, justice, grace, worship, forgiveness, faith, repentance, hope, joy, humility, caring, compassion, kindness, generosity, empathy, hospitality, Joy, and gratitude." And so, if these truly are the core values that Christians say they hold, we come full circle back to the question of "How can this be?" What has caused Christians over the years to oppress and persecute others and, too often, do so both proudly and cruelly in God's name? And what causes that oppression and persecution to continue to this very day, even as you read these words? What causes this dark, dark side of Christianity?

Many of us will find our answer to these questions in the famous April 17, 1960, Easter radio sermon "Is Segregation Scriptural?" delivered by Reverend Bob Jones. In it he declared:

My friends, I am going to bring you today one of the most important and most timely messages I have ever brought….Now, we folks at Bob Jones University believe that whatever the Bible says is so, and we believe it says certain fundamental things that all Bible-believing Christians accept; but when the Bible speaks clearly about any subject, that settles it. Men do not always agree, because some people are dumb—some people are spiritually dumb; but when the Bible is clear, there is not any reason why everybody should not accept it.[7]

---

[7] https://www.drslewis.org/camille/2013/03/15/is-segregation-scriptural-by-bob-jones-sr-1960/

His sermon then went on at length to portray the Bible as demanding the oppression and persecution of people of color through Jim Crow racial segregation laws, although in different words, of course.

Others of us will find our answer in our core Christian values of love, justice, grace, worship, forgiveness, faith, repentance, hope, joy, humility, caring, compassion, kindness, generosity, empathy, hospitality, joy, and gratitude.

I searched for my own answer by trying to understand why I, my parents, grandparents, friends, and fellow church members were so committed to the oppression of our black sisters and brothers through racial segregation laws and customs during the Jim Crow Civil Rights era. I know for a fact that we were good people, or at least thought we were. We were committed Christians doing our best to live our lives according to our understanding of the Bible. We went to church regularly and listened intently to our pastor's sermons. We studied our Sunday School lessons and tried to live as we were taught.

So why did we not simply invite our black brothers and sisters to worship with us, and why did we not ask for the privilege of worshiping with them instead of having our deacons stand in our church doors with shotguns to keep them out? In fact, why did we even have to have our own separate church buildings? And why did I, as a teenager at the time, not personally speak out in support of racial equality?

I, of course, know the answer, and I am sure you do too. First, I believed, as my family, my school, and my church had taught me: our racially segregated society, in which people of color were held in a lower caste, was exactly as God intended. Second, and perhaps even more influential on me, I was afraid of what my parents, family, and friends would say if I did not agree with them. There were written and unwritten rules that we all understood. Racial segregation was the way that things were supposed to be, and black people, simply because their skin was a different color from ours, were supposed to be limited to low level/low pay labor jobs. They shouldn't be given access to higher paying professional jobs like policemen, accountants, lawyers, nurses, doctors, business owners and managers, and elected government officials. They had to be kept out of our white restaurants, hotels, residential communities, schools, bathrooms, swimming pools, and churches. If they entered any of these white-only facilities, they were, at a minimum, to be humiliated, but more often arrested and charged with a crime. And we could never, ever, visit each other's homes as friends. This was the norm in our white community. Anyone speaking against these norms would be ostracized, maybe even disowned by their family or fired if they were a white pastor, church leader, schoolteacher, or administrator. They might even be beaten or murdered if they actively advocated racial equality and integration.

In this environment, I did not even consider embarrassing my family by speaking out in favor of racial equality and integration. Neither did my parents and friends. In short, I, my parents, our friends, and our fellow church members and leaders were prisoners of a racial oppression and segregation culture with no honorable or safe way (in our own minds) of escaping. Now, with this insight years later, I am beginning to understand the power that the social environment within which we find ourselves governs our beliefs and behavior.

Sociologists and anthropologists refer to this social environment as "culture," and it is defined as:

...a pattern of responses discovered, developed, or invented during the group's history of handling problems which arise from interactions among its members, and between them and their environment. These responses are considered the correct way to perceive, feel, think, and act, and are passed on to the new members through immersion and teaching. Culture determines what is acceptable or unacceptable, important or unimportant, right or wrong, workable or unworkable (emphasis added). It encompasses all learned and shared, explicit or tacit, assumptions, beliefs, knowledge, norms, and values, as well as attitudes, behavior, dress, and language.[8]

None of us can escape being members of cultural groups. We are born into a family that has its own cultural values and rules. Starting as mere babies, we grow up to become members of larger cultural groups...our extended family, our church, our schools, youth sports and clubs...each of which has its own, but usually very similar, "beliefs,

---

[8] http://www.businessdictionary.com/definition/culture.html

knowledge, norms, and values" and "correct way to perceive, feel, think, and act.

As we become adults, we become members of other cultural groups such as our colleges, places of work, or maybe another church or a political party. Each again has its own but often similar "beliefs, knowledge, norms, and values" and "correct way to perceive, feel, think, and act." As adults, we have the opportunity to reject the cultures of our youth, but seldom do because of the hold that our old cultures have on us.

Although small subcultural groups almost always exist, every group has a dominant culture that both socially and legally enforces the "correct way to perceive, feel, think, and act." Sociologists describe this dominant culture as one

"that is the most powerful, widespread, or influential within a social or political entity in which multiple cultures are present. Dominance can be achieved through many different means, including economic power, force or the threat of force, or through more subtle processes of dominance and subordination. The culture that is dominant within a particular geopolitical region can change over time in response to internal or external factors, **but one is usually very resilient and able to reproduce itself effectively from generation to generation** *(emphasis added)."*[9]

Both our society at large, as well as each group (e.g., family, church, club, place of work, region of our country, etc.) of which we are a member has a dominant culture that establishes the rules, values, and customs to which we are expected to adhere. Those who do adhere are rewarded, and those who don't are punished. For those of us who are professing Christians, it is this dominant culture in our chosen churches and church associations that is so forceful and influential in shaping our "beliefs, knowledge, norms, and values" and "correct way to perceive, feel, think, and act."

While we like to think that all Christian "beliefs, knowledge, norms, and values" and "correct way to perceive, feel, think, and act" will lead

---

[9] https://www.wisegeek.com/what-is-a-dominant-culture.htm

us to treat other people with respect, dignity, and equality and to behave in a way that is kind, considerate, and loving of other people, that, unfortunately, is far from true. Some encourage, even demand, that other groups of people be oppressed and persecuted. As we saw in the historical fiction stories in Chapter 1 and the quotes from Frederick Douglas at the beginning of this chapter, history is replete with Christian cultural demands that other people be oppressed and persecuted. Historically, these cultures have demanded that others must be herded onto reservations, held in slavery, kept in ghettos, kept out of leadership roles, imprisoned, tortured and even murdered, including large scale genocides. And, sadly, as you read these words, these cultures are still demanding that white Christians oppress and persecute people of color, Jews, women, and LGBTQs.

But, still the question remains: how can such cruel and oppressive "beliefs, knowledge, norms, and values" and "correct way to perceive, feel, think, and act" exist side by side with the self-claimed core Christian values of "love, justice, grace, worship, forgiveness, faith, repentance, hope, joy, humility, caring, compassion, kindness, generosity, empathy, hospitality, joy, and gratitude?" It is as if something that does not belong has attached itself to Christianity, just like fleas or ticks or chiggers attach themselves to us when we walk in the woods. The fleas, ticks and chiggers are not a part of us, yet they attach themselves to us and derive their very lifeblood from our bodies. Similarly, these cruel, oppressive cultures seem to have attached themselves to us Christians and to our Christian institutions, deriving their very livelihood from us and our church organizations.

As I pondered this dichotomy, discussed it with both my fundamentalist and progressive Christian friends, and studied our Christian history, I slowly came to the conclusion that:

"Oppress and persecute" cultures have, for centuries until this very day, attached themselves, like parasites, to Christianity, causing us Christian hosts to willfully, and too often gleefully, oppress and persecute the cultures' victims.

To begin to understand these cruel cultures, it may be helpful for us to refamiliarize ourselves with the definitions of parasite, oppress, and persecute:

Parasite: An organism that lives in or on an organism of another species (its host) and benefits by deriving nutrients at the other's expense.[10]

Oppress: "To oppress people means to treat them cruelly, or to prevent them from having the same opportunities, freedom, and benefits as others."[11]

Please note that the definition of oppress does not have a footnote that says that people are not oppressed if the oppressor has a "good" reason for the oppression...e.g., the Bible says they should be oppressed. **Oppression is oppression regardless of the reason.**

Persecute: "To pursue in a manner to injure, grieve, or afflict; to beset with cruelty or malignity; to harass; especially, to afflict, harass, punish, or put to death for one's race, sexual identity, adherence to a particular religious creed, or mode of worship.[12]

Please also note that neither does the definition of persecute have a footnote that says that people are not persecuted if the persecutor has a "good" reason for his/her treatment of the victim...e.g., a great theologian or my pastor or my church says that that is the way these people are supposed to be treated. **Persecution is persecution regardless of the reason.**

So, what are these parasitic oppress and persecute cultures?

Oppress and persecute cultures have existed for thousands of years and consist of sets of "beliefs, knowledge, norms, and values" and "correct way to perceive, feel, think, and act" designed specifically to harm the cultures' targeted victims. That harm has historically included subordination, condemnation, ostracization, excommunication, abuse, theft, imprisonment, slavery, murder, lynching, burning at the stake and genocide.

---

[10] https://www.dictionary.com/browse/parasite
[11] https://www.dictionary.com/browse/parasite
[12] https://www.definitions.net/definition/persecute

Based on my studies, these cruel parasitic cultures attach themselves to any person, group, community, or organization willing to host them. Religious organizations, including Christianity, Islam, Judaism, Hinduism, and others have been and continue to be particularly attractive hosts. But the oppress and persecute cultures will and do attach themselves to any willing host, ranging from loving Christians like you and (hopefully) me to extremist hate groups who will do their bidding. Show even a hint of sympathy for their oppressive values and an oppress and persecute culture will attach itself to us, regardless of whether we are loving Christians or a Nazi hate group.

Based on my research and experiences, these evil cultures have no consciousness of right or wrong. They feel no guilt, but rather pride, when their victims are oppressed and persecuted. Thousands burned at the stake as "witches," millions held in slavery, generations of women held in subordination, millions of Jews executed, every LGBTQ individual damned...none of these tragedies generated one iota of guilt in the oppress and persecute cultures and their host individuals and groups. Instead, they generated the exact opposite— pride. Ask any Christian minister who is committed to oppressing women, and they will quickly tell you that their treatment of women is ordained by God and His Bible; they are obeying God and are proud that they are doing so!

These cultures will use any available means whatsoever to accomplish their evil goals. None are too cruel and none too costly. A civil war to protect the institution of black slavery claiming the lives of over 600,000 people was just fine with the oppress and persecute Blacks culture in the 1860s. The splitting of church denominations (e.g., Baptist and Methodists) prior to the Civil War was just fine with that culture. As I write these words, the splitting of the United Methodist church is welcomed by the oppress and persecute LGBTQs culture if that is necessary for this culture to maintain its cruel control over at least some of the Methodist members and churches. Today's record number of murders of transgender people is more than welcomed by this culture. The torture and murder of millions of Jews was welcomed with open arms by the European oppress and persecute Jews culture, and that culture still rears its ugly head as we see the mass murder of Jewish people even today. The subordination of women is a source of pride to the oppress and persecute women culture, which goes to great lengths to cover up the resulting thousands of cases of abuse of women and girls by the host Christian men controlled by this culture.

These cultures even cause Christians to kill other Christians. In my research, I was unable to find an estimate of how many Christians these oppress and persecute cultures have caused other Christians to kill over the past 2000 years, but the number has to be in the multi-millions. I did find an estimate that Christians have killed over 700 million people of all religions, including other Christians, over the past 2000 years. A huge dark and cruel side of Christianity that I shudder to mention.[13] Even if that estimate is double or triple or quadruple the actual number, it is still a dark and cruel side of our Christianity.

Follow-on Questions

If my conclusion that these evil oppress and persecute cultures not only exist but control our Christian lives is correct, then a whole passel of related questions immediately arises. This includes questions like:

- How are these cultures able to attach themselves so successfully to Christianity?
- Why do they select Christians?
- How are they able to get us Christians to believe, say, and do things that are in total conflict with our self-claimed core Christian values?
- Why have we Christians been such great hosts, often holding out to the very end when the broader secular culture moves on to reject the cruelty of these oppress and persecute cultures?
- What strategies do these cruel cultures use to oppress and persecute their victims?
- What roles have we Christians played, and still play today, in oppressing and persecuting the victims of these cultures?
- Can and how do these cultures transition from one human generation to the next?

---

13   www.   https://www.quora.com/How-many-people-have-been-killed-in-the-name-of-Christianity-Crusades-religious-extremism-everything-counts-Some-sources-I-found-put-the-number-around-700-million-since-the-birth-of-Christ

- Can these parasitic oppress and persecute cultures ever be removed like one removes a tick?
- What can we do if we find ourselves part of an oppress and persecute culture?

Chapter 3

Why Christianity?

As I continued to ponder my conclusion that oppress and persecute cultures have attached themselves to Christianity for generations, I could not help but wonder, "But why Christianity?" No matter how we view it, these evil, parasitic cultures are utterly inconsistent with our self-claimed Christian values and the teachings of the Christ who we claim to worship and try to follow. Yet, there is no denying that we Christians have hosted and supported these cruel, oppressive cultures for thousands of years. Even as I write these words today, we host their offspring.

But what makes Christianity such an attractive host?

Reasonable people, operating from a base of compassion and empathy, see the pain and suffering of the oppressed and persecuted. They see the horror in accusing innocent people of being witches and then murdering them. They recognize the inhumanity of slavery. They see the corruption in taking the land and homes of native Americans and forcing thousands to walk the Trail of Tears to desolate lands far away. They can identify the absolute horror of the murder of millions of Jews in the Holocaust. They see the injustice of racial segregation and oppressive Jim Crow laws. They understand the cruelty of keeping women in subordinated roles. They see the evil treatment of LGBTQs simply because they were not born heterosexuals. Reasonable people see all these atrocities.

Under ordinary circumstances, reason and human compassion, empathy and decency would quickly defeat these oppress and persecute cultures. But the cultures recognized this threat hundreds of years ago and solved it by attaching themselves to Christianity (as well as other religions). And in doing so, they have made the oppression and persecution of their victims an integral part of being a Christian.

But why Christianity?

I am not sure what thoughts come to your mind, but several occur to me.

We Christians offer a whole box of tools that the oppress and persecute cultures have become very adept at using to establish and enforce their values.

These tools include:

- God
- The Bible
- Reward of heaven
- Threat of hell
- Seminaries
- Theologians
- National and regional church associations/supervisors
- Frequently published Christian newsletters and magazines
- Weekly church worship and educational meetings
- Christian teaching literature
- National, regional, and local church creeds and policies
- Many church-sponsored schools with daily instruction
- Devoted member families, and
- Sadly, associated extremist hate groups.

Few, if any, other organizations offer so many tools to shape and influence their members. Public schools and colleges do, to some degree, but they lack five of the most critical tools: God, the Bible, reward of heaven, threat of hell, and supporting theologians. I never thought about it before, but the ability to teach their oppress and persecute values may be why these cultures are so adamant about putting the Bible and God back into our public schools or getting public funding for their private Christian schools.

But the tools listed above are not all that we Christians offer the depressed cultures.

We offer the opportunity for the oppress and persecute cultures to "look good." By associating with all of the genuine good that we Christians do for others, these cruel cultures look good and trustworthy by association. They make themselves appear to be an integral part of the "love, justice, grace, worship, forgiveness, faith, repentance, hope, joy, humility, caring, compassion, kindness, generosity, empathy, hospitality, joy, and gratitude" that Christians show every day. So, the oppress and persecute cultures "must be good and right because they are practiced by really good and holy people." For example, the oppression of women must be good because really good Christians do it.

We offer a "protective shield." We Christians provide a protective shield for these cultures so that any attempt to defeat these oppressive parasites can be portrayed as an "attack" on Christianity itself, as well as on our Christian institutions and Christian members.

Any objection to the cultures' oppression and persecution of their victims is loudly proclaimed by these cultures to be secular persecution of Christianity and a threat to our religious freedom. These cruel cultures aggressively argue that Christians must be free to oppress women and persecute gay people. For example, the underlying premise of David Brooks' New York Times Bestseller book *The Benedict Option* is that Christians are being unfairly attacked and persecuted today by the sinful secular society because of their obedience to God's word. One of the major attacks Brooks mentions is the attack on Christians who refuse to recognize and support gay relationships. Brooks concludes in his book that an attack on Christians' persecution of LGBTQs is an attack on Christianity itself and on the welfare and beliefs of individual Christians.

In my youth, our white Christian leaders in the South fought in the same way for the "freedom" to keep our black neighbors out of our churches and schools, even to the extent of using our white police to arrest those who tried to enter.

We offer our Christian brains, emotions, voices, leadership, resources, and actions. Finally, we who are members of these cultures offer the absolutely critical resource that the cultures must have to stay alive and effective: we, ourselves.

Without us, the oppress and persecute cultures would be severely crippled and might even die out. Even when we don't do the dirty work, we are the ones who keep the cultures alive and well so that they can influence others to inflict the harm. In fact, without us, they never could have tortured innocent people until they confessed to being witches and then either lynched or burned them at the stake. Without the support of us Christians, this culture could have never taken the homes and lands of Native Americans and herded them onto reservations, murdering those who objected. Without our support, the oppressive cultures never could have held millions of black people in slavery. In fact, without us Christians, these cultures could never have succeeded in getting Baptist churches in the Confederate states to leave the national Baptist association to form their own Southern Baptist Convention in support of the inhumane institution of slavery. Without us Christians, these cultures could not continue today to keep women in oppressive subordination. It is our brains, emotions, voices, leadership, resources, and actions that keep this dark side of Christianity not only alive and well, but thriving.

Chapter 4

The Model: How the Cultures Get Us to Do It

Given that these oppress and persecute cultures are heavily dependent on us to do their work, how do they get us to do it? How have these cultures, whose only goals are to hurt, subordinate, oppress, and persecute their targeted victims, been so successful in getting good, caring, and loving Christians—Christians like you and me—to treat our totally innocent fellow men and women so cruelly?

As mentioned in the previous chapter, in my case, and that of my family, friends, and fellow church members, back in the 1950s, '60s, and '70s, I understand now (I didn't back then) that it was the social pressure that we white people put on each other. Our dominant white oppress and persecute culture said that black people were inferior and had to be treated that way. Any of us violating that "rule" would be ostracized, at a minimum, and often worse. I learned later that sociologists call this pressure "social control" which has been described as:

The *lifelong process of socialization* that each person experiences is the primary way social order develops. Through this process, people are taught from birth the behavioral and interactional expectations common to their family, peer groups, community, and greater society. Socialization teaches us how to think and behave in accepted ways, and in doing so, effectively controls our participation in society. [1]

As I thought about this social control, I began to wonder about all the things that these cultures have done over the years (and still do today) to both create and maintain such complete social control over us, especially over us who call ourselves Christians. In other words, how

---

[1] https://www.thoughtco.com/social-control-3026587

do these evil parasites get us to do it? How do they get us to "toe the line?"

My curiosity finally got the best of me, and I began to recall my past experiences and to read and study books on sociology and religious history. I read books about the witch trials. I recalled my past visits to the Dachau holocaust concentration camp in Germany, the holocaust museum in Jerusalem and Anne Frank's home in Amsterdam and how I returned home each time devastated at the cruelty. I visited the African American and Native American Smithsonian museums in Washington, D.C., and I studied their exhibits showing the horror visited on them by good, caring, and loving white Christians…Christians like you and me. I bought books there, studied them and learned a lot. For example, I had no idea that the Southern states kept thousands of innocent young black men in slavery after the civil war up until about 1930 through a white-dominated, rigged, and corrupt criminal justice system. Did you? Our oppress and persecute blacks culture made sure that we did not learn that history in our white schools in my youth, and it still does the same today!

I read books on what the Southern and Northern white Christian preachers, editors, and leaders were saying and doing in the years leading up to the Civil War, and what they did, wrote, and said during and after the Civil War. I read books on what Southern white Christians were doing and saying (and not doing and saying) about racial integration and equality during the over 150 years after the civil war. I remembered my father telling me that my great uncle was a member of the KKK and had a reputation of being a really good "whupper."

I talked to some of the pastoral staff in my church and read papers written by theologians that explained why women should be kept in subordination and why LGBTQ individuals should be oppressed, persecuted, and kept out of our churches. I Googled and Googled and Googled in search of statements by Christian leaders about women, LGBTQs, and minority racial and ethnic groups. I read statements by the Pope and by Southern Baptist leaders about why women should be held in subordination by the church. I read about local churches canceling their memberships in associations because another member church welcomed LGBTQs. I learned about state church associations expelling churches with women pastors and those welcoming LGBTQ members. I exchanged letters with one of the leaders of the anti-gay group causing the world-wide split of the United Methodist church. I sought help from my Jewish and African American friends, some of whom sent me numerous references and served as my advisors.

As I waded through the mountain of information that we assembled, I began to see patterns. I began to see the same oppress and persecute cultural activities showing up century after century after century. The victims were different, but the activities and traits were the same or so similar they seemed the same. After all, if an evil culture has a successful model, why abandon it? The same strategies that enabled these evil cultures to get their Christian hosts to convict and murder thousands of innocent people as witches proved later to be just as effective in convincing Christians to hold millions of black people in slavery for centuries. It worked like a charm in convincing German Christian hosts to support the exile and murder of millions of Jews, and it works like a well-oiled machine today in keeping women in subordination. And it is perfect in getting good, loving Christians to damn, oppress, and persecute LGBTQs today at a time when the "sinful" secular culture has chosen to treat them with respect, dignity, and equality.

So, what is this oppress and persecute cultural model?

Unfortunately for the victims, the model and methods used by these oppress and persecute cultures are highly effective and are both simple and easy to implement. They consist of the following activities:

1. First, these extremely strong cultures build the case that their victims either deserve to be oppressed and persecuted or have been ordained by God to be oppressed and persecuted. Then,
2. They tell us which supporting biblical passages to obey and which to disregard,
3. They make us believe that the oppression and persecution of the victims is a part of being a good Christian,
4. They cause us to have no empathy for their victims' suffering,
5. They convince us that our own salvation is independent of how we treat others,

6. They go further to convince us that social justice is not a part of the Christian gospel.
7. They reward those of us who actively oppress, and persecute as well as those of us who support the oppression and persecution of their victims,
8. They punish those who openly object to the oppression and persecution,
9. They encourage the majority of us to be silent and do nothing,
10. They even use our friendships to perpetuate their livelihood,
11. Sadly, they cause us to create/use special organizations dedicated to oppressing and persecuting their victims
12. Finally, these cultures hide their oppressions and persecutions behind a beautiful, loving façade of our worshiping, praying, and studying the Bible and doing good things.

While, as mentioned in the previous chapter, the oppress and persecute cultures have designed and used the above strategic model (or some variations thereof) for centuries, it is us Christians who do the actual implementation. We keep these parasitic cultures that have attached themselves to us and our Christian institutions alive and thriving. We each have our assigned roles to play. One of my mother's assigned roles was to tell me that I could no longer play with my black childhood friend, and my childhood pastor's role was to place guards at our church doors to keep black visitors out.

What I, sadly, found so astounding is how powerful these cultures and their methods are. We do it because these cultures are so influential that they control our very lives. Historically, these models have dictated what we believed and didn't believe, what we said and what we didn't say, who we interacted with and who we didn't. They governed what we did and what we didn't do, where we went and where we never went, how we treated our family and friends and how we treated others. They dictated what we said in our prayers and what we never said to God, who we respected and who we disdained, and even which parts of the Bible we obeyed and which parts we ignored.

As previously mentioned, I personally experienced this control as I grew up in a racially segregated society in Mississippi in the 1950s. We were so thoroughly controlled by a white supremacist racial segregationist culture that we really did not even recognize we were being manipulated at the time. The culture made us white people trust that we were believing, acting, and behaving exactly like God wanted us to believe, act, and behave. As white people, my family, friends, and fellow church members never considered, for even one moment, supporting the Civil Rights movement.

Our culture would have exacted a huge price had we done so. We would have been socially ostracized. We would have lost close friends. The adults would have lost critically needed jobs to support their families. We would have risked visits from the KKK and maybe the burning of our homes. In short, the oppress and persecute Blacks culture in which we lived in the 1950s and 1960s had total control over our lives, and only the "trash" among us supported the Civil rights movement.

As I studied the history of how our fellow Christians oppressed and persecuted others over the years, I found repeated evidence of the very same strategies and control that I had experienced as a teenager. These cultures were so strong and influential that they caused Christians (as well as members of other religions) to be utterly inhumane in how they treated their fellowman and, sadly, to be proud of that inhumanity. And these cruel cultures are still that powerful this very day as you read these words...a dark, dark side of Christianity that refuses to go away.

Chapter 5

Building the Case

Because we Christians are good people with our self-proclaimed core values of "love, justice, grace, worship, forgiveness, faith, repentance, hope, joy, humility, caring, compassion, empathy, kindness, generosity, empathy, hospitality, joy, and gratitude," we need a reason if we are going to oppress and persecute our fellow women and men.

The oppress and persecute cultures assign the responsibility of creating and instilling those reasons to the host Christian theologians, editors, ministers, and teachers. Their job is to write the articles, books, newsletters, blogs, creeds, policies, and teaching materials that fully justify the oppression and persecution of the cultures' victims. It is their job to preach the sermons and teach the classes that carry that message to other Christians.

And, sadly, too many of us have done exactly what these cultures demanded of us. Our history is full of books, articles, newsletters, creeds, teaching materials, and sermons that fully "justify" the oppression and persecution of targeted victims.

The justifications are built, depending on the targeted group, upon "proving" that the victims are associated with the devil or by showing that they are naturally inferior or even "bad" people. At its worst, these justifications insist that the victims have been designated by God and His Bible to be oppressed and persecuted. But the justifications do not stop with simply showing that the victims deserve to be oppressed and persecuted. They go further to rationalize that they are a threat to us, our families, our children, our churches, and our Christian faith. If allowed to do so, these targeted people would (will) destroy everything for which we Christians stand. Instead of us persecuting them, these cultures demand that we believe and respond as if the victims are persecuting us.

To say that the number of books, articles, editorials sermons that attempt to "justify" the oppression and persecution of targeted victims are in the thousands is certainly safe. Hence, we will be able to look at only a small sample in this review. But if your interest is piqued, unfortunately you can find many more to read and study.

Building the Case for Executing Witches

In today's world, it is difficult for most of us to even imagine any justification for accusing innocent people of being witches and then murdering them in the name of God. But the oppress and persecute witches culture had no difficulty in getting Pope Innocent VIII to do just that in 1464 when he issued an official statement (called a "Bull") which carried the full authority of the Catholic church. That document included the following:

It has recently come to our ears, not without great pain to us, that in some parts of upper Germany, as well as in the provinces, cities, territories, regions, and dioceses of Mainz, Köln, Trier, Salzburg, and Bremen, many persons of both sexes, heedless of their own salvation and forsaking the catholic faith, give themselves over to devils male and female, and by their incantations, charms and conjurings, and by other abominable superstitions and sortileges, offences, crimes, and misdeeds, ruin and cause to perish the offspring of women, the foal of animals, the products of the earth, the grapes of vines, and the fruits of trees, as well men and women, cattle and flocks and herds and animals of every kind, vineyards also and orchards, meadows, pastures, harvests, grains and other fruits of the earth; that they afflict and torture with dire pains and anguish, both internal and external, these men, women, cattle, flocks, herds, and animals, and hinder men from begetting and women from conceiving, and prevent all consummation of marriage; that, moreover, they deny with sacrilegious lips the faith they received in holy baptism; and that, at the instigation of the enemy of mankind, they do not fear to commit and perpetrate many other abominable offences and crimes, at the risk of their own souls, to the insult of the divine majesty and to the pernicious example and scandal of multitudes.[1]

Apparently, two oppress and persecute host Christian professors of theology at the University of Salzburg, Austria, Heinrich Kramer and

---

[1] https://www.monstrousregimentofwomen.com/2015/12/according-to-their-just-deserts-witches.html

Jacobus Sprenger, needed help convincing other church leaders to believe their claims that witches actually existed and should be executed because Pope Innocent VIII's directive also stated:

And, although our beloved sons Henricus Institorus [Kramer] and Jacobus Sprenger, of the order of Friars Preachers, professors of theology, have been and still are deputed by our apostolic letters as inquisitors of heretical pravity, the former in the aforesaid parts of upper Germany, including the provinces, cities, territories, dioceses, and other places, as above, and the latter throughout certain parts of the course of the rhine; nevertheless certain of the clergy and of the laity of those parts, seeking to be wise above what is fitting, because in the said letter of deputation that aforesaid provinces, cities, dioceses, territories, and other places, and the persons and offences in question were not individually and specifically named, do not blush obstinately to assert that these are not at all included in the said parts and that therefore it is illicit for the aforesaid inquisitors to exercise their office of inquisition in the provinces, cities, dioceses, territories, and other places aforesaid, and that they ought not to be permitted to proceed to the punishment, imprisonment, and correction of the aforesaid persons for the offences and crimes above named. Wherefore in the provinces, cities, dioceses, territories, and places aforesaid such offences and crimes, not without evident damage to their souls and risk of external salvation, go unpunished.[2]

With this authoritative justification for executing witches and the endorsement of their work by Pope Innocent VIII, the most powerful Christian of that day, Kramer and Sprenger proceeded to publish their book, *Malleus Maleficarum* (usually translated as *The Hammer of Witches*). It provided guidelines to help local clergy recognize the witches in their communities, a legal guide on how to have them arrested and to torture them until they confessed (and often accused others to end the torture), instructions on how to convict them, and then how to execute them, either by burning alive at the stake or lynching.

With the publishing of *Malleus Maleficarum*, the oppress and persecute witches culture had firmly attached itself to Christianity for at least two centuries. Thirty-six editions of the book were published between 1487 and 1669, and historians credit it as being the single most important impetus for the execution of an estimated 60,000 European "witches"

---

[2] Ibid

during the period between about 1490 to 1650.[3] The parasitic oppress and persecute witches culture proudly won. Sixty thousand innocent people murdered by good Christian people who either participated in the executions or remained stone silent while their fellow Christians did the dirty work! A dark, cruel side of Christianity for several hundred years.

Building the Case for Taking the Lands and Homes of Native Americans

Imagine with me for a moment that we are European Christian explorers in the 1400s and 1500s. We now have ships capable of "sailing the oceans blue," and the world is opening up to us. We are discovering new lands, and, to our surprise, there are people already living in these lands. They are as surprised to see us as we are to see them and greet us with kindness, as evidenced by historical accounts. Reports written at that time state that the natives in San Salvador "generously presented Columbus and his men with gifts and treated them with honor" on his voyage to the Americas. Columbus described them to the King and Queen of Spain as:

So tractable, so peaceful, are these people that I swear to your Majesties there is not in the world a better nation. They love their neighbors as themselves, and their discourse is ever sweet and gentle, and accompanied with a smile; and...their manners are decorous and praiseworthy. [4]

Given these exciting new discoveries, how would we respond? Would we smile and, since we don't understand each other's language, try to communicate with smiles and gestures to show our thanks and happiness to meet them? Would we give them gifts? Would we join them in a meal or ask them to join us? Would we show them the same love that God has shown to us? Would we be God's representative to these new and wonderful people, knowing that they would see God through us? Would we do unto them as we want them to do unto us? Being good Christians, we would almost certainly look to our church leaders for guidance and Pope Nicholas V provided that very guidance.

---

[3] https://www.nationalgeographic.com.au/history/the-hammer-of-the-witches.aspx)
[4] Brown, Dee. *Bury My Heart at Wounded Knee*, Henry Holt and Company, New York, 2000, pg. 1

On June 18, 1452, he released the Dum Diversas, another papal "bull," that told King Alfonso of Portugal, as well as other Christians of that day, how these newly discovered people should be treated. Among other things, the directive stated:

We weighing all and singular the premises with due meditation, and noting that since we had formerly by other letters of ours granted among other things free and ample faculty to the aforesaid King Alfonso – to invade, search out, capture, vanquish, and subdue all Saracens and pagans whatsoever, and other enemies of Christ wheresoever placed, and the kingdoms, dukedoms, principalities, dominions, possessions, and all movable and immovable goods whatsoever held and possessed by them and to reduce their persons to perpetual slavery, and to apply and appropriate to himself and his successors the kingdoms, dukedoms, counties, principalities, dominions, possessions, and goods, and to convert them to his and their use and profit – by having secured the said faculty, the said King Alfonso, or, by his authority, the aforesaid infante, justly and lawfully has acquired and possessed, and doth possess, these islands, lands, harbors, and seas, and they do of right belong and pertain to the said King Alfonso and his successors.[5]

The directive is very clear: no Christian love, kindness, and peace was to be given. Instead, Pope Nicholas V ordered Christians ....*to invade, search out, capture, vanquish, and subdue all Saracens and pagans whatsoever, and other enemies of Christ wheresoever placed, and the kingdoms, dukedoms, principalities, dominions, possessions, and all movable and immovable goods whatsoever held and possessed by them and to reduce their persons to perpetual slavery...*[6]

And that is just what the European kings and their explorers did. Ships to Africa began routine trips to colonize the lands and establish the intercontinental slave trade that lasted for over 500 years, all not only blessed by the Pope but directed by him.

In case you are wondering, Columbus responded to the kindness of the native people on what is now San Salvador by kidnapping ten of the men and taking them back to Spain. Then, over the next four centuries, San Salvador was invaded by Spaniards who:

---

[5] https://doctrineofdiscovery.org/dum-diversas/
[6] Ibid

...scoured their islands in search of gold and precious stones....looted and burned villages; ...(and) kidnapped hundreds of men, women, and children and shipped them to Europe to be sold as slaves.[7]

Pope Nicolas V's directive, including augmentations by later popes, became known as the "Doctrine of Discovery" which was interpreted as "discover it and it is yours, regardless of who is living there." This doctrine became recognized as international law for hundreds of years. It was this Doctrine of Discovery that provided England, France, Spain, the Netherlands, Germany, Portugal, other European kings, and later the United States the "justification" for taking the lands and homes of natives in the Americas.

And these white European rulers responded just as we, sadly, might expect, in using this justification to inflict cruel and intolerable pain and suffering on the people of the Caribbean and Americas, as illustrated by the following statement issued by the rulers of Spain (written in Spanish, of course, that few, if any, of the victims, could understand):

On the part of the King, Don Fernando, and Dona Juana I, his daughter, Queen of Castille and Leon, subduers of the barbarous nations, we their servants notify and make known to you, as best as we can, that the Lord our God, Living and Eternal, created the Heaven and the Earth, and one man and one woman, of whom you and we , all the men of the world at the time, were and are descendants, and those who came after and before...
Of all these nations God our Lord gave charge to one man, called ST Peter, that he should be Lord and Superior of all the men in the world, that all should obey him, and that he should be the head of the whole Human Race...

One of these Pontiffs, who succeeded that St. Peter as Lord of the world, in the dignity and seat which I have before mentioned, made donation of these isles and Terra-firme to the afore mentioned King and Queen and to their successors, our lords...
Wherefore, as best as we can, we ask and require that you consider what we have said to you, and that you take the time that shall be necessary to understand and

---

[7] Brown, Dee. *Bury My Heart at Wounded Knee*, Henry Holt and Company, New York, 2000, pg. 2

deliberate upon it, and that you acknowledge the Church as the Ruler and Superior of the whole world…

But, if you do not do this, and maliciously make a delay in it, I certify to you that, with the help of God, we shall powerfully enter into your country, and shall make war against you in all ways and manners that we can, and shall subject you to yoke and obedience of the Church and of their Highnesses; we shall take you and your wives and your children, and shall make slaves of them, and as such shall sell and dispose of them as their Highnesses may command.[8] (Emphasis added)

And that is just what happened to millions of people in Latin America, as described in 1552 by Dominican friar Bartolome de las Casas:

We can estimate very truly and truthfully that in the forty years that have passed, with the infernal actions of the Christians, there have been unjustly slain more than twelve million men, women, and children. In truth, I believe without trying to deceive myself that the number of the slain is more like fifteen million.[9]

The Doctrine of Discovery and other statements like the above had a powerful impact on the actions of governments for centuries. Three hundred years later in 1823, when a dispute over land ownership between Native Americans and the United States government reached the U.S. Supreme Court (***Johnson v. M'Intosh***), the court ruled that the disputed land belonged to the U.S. government, not the Native Americans who had occupied it for centuries, long before there was a U.S. government. The basis for their decision? The Doctrine of Discovery.

The popes, the Christian church's most powerful leaders over the centuries, had said it and that was all the justification that was needed to establish an oppress and persecute Native Americans culture. That culture not only made it acceptable for white Christians to take the lands and homes of Native Americans, by force and murder when necessary, and then to herd them on to reservations, but it strongly encouraged those actions. And that is exactly what we did….a sad and dark, dark side of our Christianity

---

[8] McLaren, Brian D., *The Great Spiritual Migration*, New York Crown Publishing Group, 2016, pg. 80

[9] https://libquotes.com/bartolomé-de-las-casas/quote/lbm9m2a

Building the Case for Black Slavery

During the 200 years leading up to the American Civil War, there was no shortage of white Christian leaders in the Southern states who built the case that blacks should be held in slavery. The oppress and persecute Blacks culture had firmly attached itself to Southern white Christians, their churches, and their church associations, and had no trouble, whatsoever, in getting Southern white theologians, ministers, and editors to justify black slavery. In fact, these white oppress and persecute Blacks host Christians were everywhere in the Southern states and were especially vocal during the decade leading up to the Civil War.

This may sound silly to us today, but did you know that black people were ordained by God to be slaves forever because Ham saw his father, Noah, naked and laughed at him when he walked into the tent where Noah had, apparently, drunk too much and passed out without any clothes on. (Genesis 9: 20-27) According to the oppress and persecute Blacks culture, that was what the Bible said.

I will let Gus "Jabbo" Rogers, a former slave, explain it to you as he did to an interviewer years ago:

God gave it (religion) to Adam and took it away from Adam and gave it to Noah and you know, Miss, Noah had three sons, and when Noah got drunk on wine, one of his sons laughed at him, and the other two took a sheet and walked backwards and threw it over Noah. Noah told the one who laughed, "your children will be hewers of wood and drawers of water for the other two children, and they will be known by their hair and their skin being dark." So, Miss, there we are, and that is the way God meant us to be. We have always had to follow the white folks and do what we saw them do, and that's all there is to it. You just can't get away from what the Lord said.[10]

All of that would be funny if Noah's curse, as the belief became known, (also referred to as the "Curse of Ham") had not been effectively used by Christian theologians, ministers, and politicians again and again and

---

[10] Haynes, Stephen R., *Noah's Curse: The Biblical Justification of American Slavery*, Oxford University Press, 2002, page 95.

again to justify black slavery for several hundred years leading up to the Civil War.

In his 1863 book, *Pictures of Slavery and Anti-slavery*, Methodist minister John Bell Robinson explained it in simple terms:

If Ham and his son Canaan had been true to their father and grandfather, there would have been no slaves nor Negroes in this world of ours.[11]

Reverend Robinson goes on in his book to explain the sacred responsibilities of white people to hold black people in slavery:

God himself has made them for usefulness as slaves, and requires us to employ them as such, and if we betray our trust, and throw them off on their own resources, we reconvert them into barbarians, and we shall be compelled to atone for our sin towards them through all time. Our Heavenly Father has made us to rule, and the negroes to serve, and if we, through a pretended sympathy, or a false philanthropy, right in the face of all common sense and reason, set aside his holy arrangements for the good of mankind and his own glory, and tamper with his laws, we shall be overthrown and eternally degraded, and perhaps made subjects of some other civilized nation. This will be our doom as sure as God lives.[12]

Reverend Robinson was just one among hundreds (probably thousands) who used Noah's curse to justify the enslavement of Blacks. Jefferson Davis, while still a U.S. senator, joined in by stating that:

The low and vulgar son of Noah, who laughed at his father's exposure, sunk by debasing himself and his lineage by connection with an inferior race of men, he doomed his descendants to perpetual slavery.[13]

But it was not just Noah's curse that theologians, ministers, and politicians used to justify slavery in those years. Rev. Ebenezer W. Warren, pastor of the First Baptist Church of Christ in Macon, Georgia, preached a sermon on January 27, 1861, entitled "Scriptural Vindication of Slavery." His sermon was based on Ephesians 5:5-8, which reads:

---

[11] Ibid, pg. 75
[12] https://brainly.com/question/458652
[13] https://encomium.blog/2017/11/29/the-resurrection-of-jesus-christ-and-racial-strife/

5. For this ye know, that no Whoremonger, nor unclean person, nor covetous man, who is an idolater, hath any inheritance in the kingdom of Christ and of God. 6. Let no man deceive you with vain words: for because of these things cometh the wrath of God upon the children of disobedience. 7. Be not ye therefore partakers with them. 8. For ye were sometimes darkness, but are ye light in the Lord: walk as children of light.

He then went on to declare:

...slavery forms a vital element of the Divine Revelation to man. Its institution, regulation, and perpetuity constitute a part of the many books of the Bible. Both Christianity and Slavery are from Heaven; both are blessings to humanity; both are to be perpetuated to the end of time.....Slavery is right; and because the condition of the slaves affords them all those privileges that would prove substantial blessings to them; and, too, because their Maker has decreed their bondage; and has given them, as a race, capabilities and aspirations suited alone to this condition in life."[14]

Warren's sermon was apparently well received by the oppress and persecute Blacks culture of that time because it was reprinted verbatim in both the *Macon Telegraph* and *Christian Index* in the following weeks.

I guess you would have had to be there because I still don't understand how he reached his conclusions from his Biblical reference. But that is the manner in which these oppress and persecute cultures operate. In their creation of a sad and dark Christianity, these cultures can and will use anything, even vague Scripture, to justify their oppression and persecution to their believing hosts, and we Christians too often blindly agree.

Building the Case to Oppress and Persecute Jews

Not that you need reminding, but we Christians believe that God so respected the Jewish people that He chose them for the birth and upbringing of His son, Jesus Christ. You would think that alone would make every Christian hold the Jewish people in the highest regard. But

---

[14] Gourley, Bruce T., *Diverging Loyalties, Baptist in Middle Georgia During the Civil War,* 2011, Mercer University Press, pages 19-20

there was no way that the oppress and persecute Jews culture could let that happen. As soon as the early Christians began to form worship groups, the culture worked to get Christian theologians, ministers, and leaders to openly and aggressively instill the mindset that Jews are evil people who must be oppressed and persecuted. From roughly 300 A.D. to the Holocaust tragedies in the late 1930s and early 1940s, hundreds and hundreds of European Christian theologians provided "justification" through both the written and spoken word for the oppression and persecution and even murder of Jews.

And, oh how successful those theologians were, especially after the printing press was invented in the mid-1440s. This allowed books, pamphlets, and newspapers to be printed and widely distributed, carrying this hateful message to millions. History is filled with Christian sermons, speeches, books, edicts, articles, laws, and everyday conversations that condemned Jews and promoted their oppression and persecution. In fact, there are so many, dating from the earliest centuries after Christ's crucifixion, that it would probably take thousands of pages or more to simply list their names and content. So, we will only mention a few here, but you can find many, many, many more if you would like to do your own research.

John Chrysostom was the Bishop of Antioch in the eastern Roman Empire in 387 A.D. He was a highly skilled speaker, and delivered a series of eight sermons that degraded Jews and condemned Judaizers (people who supported Jews and Jewish customs and practices). His vile statements were extensive as illustrated by the following quote:

What else do you wish me to tell you? Shall I tell you of their plundering, their covetousness, their abandonment of the poor, their thefts, their cheating in trade? The whole day long will not be enough to give you an account of these things. But do their festivals have something solemn and great about them? They have shown that these, too, are impure. (VII, 1.)[15]

During the same time period, Saint Gregory of Nyssa declared:

---

[15]   https://livingarmstrongism.blogspot.com/2016/12/reading-john-chrysostoms-anti-semitic.html

Jews are slayers of the Lord, murderers of the prophets, enemies and haters of God, adversaries of grace, enemies of their fathers' faith, advocates of the devil, a brood of vipers, slanderers, scoffers, men of darkened minds, the leaven of Pharisees, a congregation of demons, sinners, wicked men, haters of goodness![16]

By the 1500s, the oppress and persecute Jews culture had firmly attached itself to the Catholic church, but it was not just the Catholic church that the oppress and persecute Jews culture controlled by then. The culture had also moved quickly to capture and control the emerging Protestant Christians as well. In 1543, Martin Luther, wrote in his treatise "On the Jews and Their Lies":

What shall we Christians do with this rejected and condemned people, the Jews?... I shall give you my sincere advice:
First to set fire to their synagogues or schools and to bury and cover with dirt whatever will not burn, so that no man will ever again see a stone or cinder of them. This is to be done in honor of our Lord and of Christendom, so that God might see that we are Christians, and do not condone or knowingly tolerate such public lying, cursing, and blaspheming of his Son and of his Christians...

Second, I advise that their houses also be razed and destroyed...

Third, I advise that all their prayer books and Talmudic writings, in which such idolatry, lies, cursing and blasphemy are taught, be taken from them...

Fourth, I advise that their rabbis be forbidden to teach henceforth on pain of loss of life and limb...

Fifth, I advise that safe-conduct on the highways be abolished completely for the Jews...

Sixth, I advise that usury be prohibited to them, and that all cash and treasure of silver and gold be taken from them and put aside for safekeeping...

Seventh, I commend putting a flail, an ax, a hoe, a spade, a distaff, or a spindle into the hands of young, strong Jews and Jewesses and letting them earn their bread in the sweat of their brow, as was imposed on the children of Adam (Gen 3[:19]).[17]

---

[16] en.wikipedia.org/Gregory_of_Nyssa)ristian world at that time.
[17] https://www.jewishvirtuallibrary.org/martin-luther-quot-the-jews-and-their-lies-quot

Ken Boutwell

The Catholic Church, of course, continued its long history of justifying the oppression and persecution of Jews. Pope Paul IV issued his Papal Bull "Cum Nimis Absurdum" on July 14, 1555, which declared:

And in spite of this truth, in spite of their utter lack of religious creativeness, they stick to their delusion of being a religious power. The truth is that modern Jewry is most certainly a power against religion; a power which bitterly fights Christianity everywhere, uproots Christian faith as well as national feeling in the people, in their stead offering them nothing but the idolatrous admiration of Jewry such as it is, with no other content but its self-admiration... Every sensible person must realize that the rule of the Semitic mentality means not only our spiritual but also our economic impoverishment... If modern Jewry continues to use the power of capital and the power of the press to bring misfortune to the nation, a final catastrophe is unavoidable. Israel must renounce its ambition to become the master of Germany. It should renounce its arrogant claim that Judaism is the religion of the future, when it is so clearly that of the past.

Since it is completely senseless and inappropriate to be in a situation where Christian piety allows the Jews (whose guilt-all of their own doing-has condemned them to eternal slavery) access to our society and even to live among us; indeed, they are without gratitude to Christians, as, instead of thanks for gracious treatment, they return invective, and among themselves, instead of the slavery, which they deserve, they manage to claim superiority: we, who recently learned that these very Jews have insolently invaded Rome from a number of the Papal States, territories and domains, to the extent that not only have they mingled with Christians (even when close to their churches) and wearing no identifying garments, but to dwell in homes, indeed, even in the more noble [dwellings] of the states, territories and domains in which they lingered, conducting business from their houses and in the streets and dealing in real estate; they even have nurses and housemaids and other Christians as hired servants. And they would dare to perpetrate a wide variety of other dishonorable things, contemptuous of the name Christian. Considering that the Church of Rome tolerates these very Jews (evidence of the true Christian faith) and to this end [we declare]: that they, won over by the piety and kindness of the See, should at long last recognize their erroneous ways, and should lose no time in seeing the true light of the catholic faith, and thus to agree that while they persist in their errors, realizing that they are slaves because of their deeds, whereas Christians have been freed through our Lord God Jesus Christ, and that it is unwarranted for it to appear that the sons of free women serve the sons of maids. [Therefore,]

84

Desiring firstly, as much as we can with [the help of] God, to beneficially provide, by this [our decree] that will forever be in force, we ordain that for the rest of time, in the City as well as in other states, territories and domains of the Church of Rome itself, all Jews are to live in only one [quarter] to which there is only one entrance and from which there is but one exit, and if there is not that capacity [in one such quarter, then], in two or three or however many may be enough; [in any case] they should reside entirely side by side in designated streets and be thoroughly separate from the residences of Christians, [This is to be enforced] by our authority in the City and by that of our representatives in other states, lands and domains noted above.

Furthermore, in each and every state, territory and domain in which they are living, they will have only one synagogue, in its customary location, and they will construct no other new ones, nor can they own buildings. Furthermore, all of their synagogues, besides the one allowed, are to be destroyed and demolished. And the properties, which they currently own, they must sell to Christians within a period of time to be determined by the magistrates themselves.

Moreover, concerning the matter that Jews should be recognizable everywhere: [to this end] men must wear a hat, women, indeed, some other evident sign, yellow in color, that must not be concealed or covered by any means, and must be tightly affixed [sewn]; and furthermore, they cannot be absolved or excused from the obligation to wear the hat or other emblem of this type to any extent whatever and under any pretext whatsoever of their rank or prominence or of their ability to tolerate [this] adversity, either by a chamberlain of the Church, clerics of an Apostolic court, or their superiors, or by legates of the Holy See or their immediate subordinates.

Also, they may not have nurses or maids or any other Christian domestic or service by Christian women in wet-nursing or feeding their children.

They may not work or have work done on Sundays or on other public feast days declared by the Church.

Nor may they incriminate Christians in any way, or promulgate false or forged agreements.

And they may not presume in any way to play, eat or fraternize with Christians.

And they cannot use other than Latin or Italian words in short-term account books that they hold with Christians, and, if they should use them, such records would not be binding on Christians [in legal proceedings].

Moreover, these Jews are to be limited to the trade of rag-picking, or "cencinariae" (as it is said in the vernacular), and they cannot trade in grain, barley or any other commodity essential to human welfare.
And those among them who are physicians, even if summoned and inquired after, cannot attend or take part in the care of Christians.
And they are not to be addressed as superiors [even] by poor Christians.

And they are to close their [loan] accounts entirely every thirty days; should fewer than thirty days elapse, they shall not be counted as an entire month, but only as the actual number of days, and furthermore, they will terminate the reckoning as of this number of days and not for the term of an entire month. In addition, they are prohibited from selling [goods put up as] collateral, put up as temporary security for their money, unless [such goods were] put up a full eighteen months prior to the day on which such [collateral] would be forfeit; at the expiration of the aforementioned number of months, if Jews have sold a security deposit of this sort, they must sign over all money in excess of the principal of the loan to the owner of the collateral.

And the statutes of states, territories and domains (in which they have lived for a period of time) concerning primacy of Christians, are to be adhered to and followed without exception.

And, should they, in any manner whatsoever, be deficient in the foregoing, it would be treated as a crime: in Rome, by us or by our clergy, or by others authorized by us, and in the aforementioned states, territories and domains by their respective magistrates, just as if they were rebels and criminals by the jurisdiction in which the offense takes place, they would be accused by all Christian people, by us and by our clergy, and could be punished at the discretion of the proper authorities and judges.

[This will be in effect] notwithstanding opposing decrees and apostolic rules, and regardless of any tolerance whatever or special rights and dispensation for these Jews [granted] by any Roman Pontiff prior to us and the aforementioned See or of their legates, or by the courts of the Church of Rome and the clergy of the Apostolic courts, or by other of their officials, no matter their import and form, and with whatever (even with repeated derogations) and with other legally valid sub-clauses, and erasures and other decrees, even [those that are] "motu proprio" and from "certain knowledge" and have been repeatedly approved and renewed. By this document, even

if, instead of their sufficient derogation, concerning them and their entire import, special, specific, expressed and individual, even word for word, moreover, not by means of general, even important passages, mention, or whatever other expression was favored, or whatever exquisite form had to be retained, matters of such import, and, if word for word, with nothing deleted, would be inserted into them in original form in the present document holding that rather than being sufficiently expressed, those things that would stay in effect in full force by this change alone, we specially and expressly derogate, as well as any others [that might be] contrary to them.[18]

The oppress and persecute Jews culture maintained its control over European Protestant and Catholic Christians throughout the 16th and 17th centuries, and it was still thriving in the 1800s as evidenced by Pope Pius IX's 1852 letter to the king of Belgium:

Your Highness is not unaware of the fact that the spirit of the Church, expressed in many dispositions and decrees … has always been to keep Catholics as much as possible from having any contact with the infidels … Otherwise, it will open the way to requests for other civil rights for the Jews and for other non-Catholics.[19]

A few years later in 1871, Pope Pius IX made a speech to a group of Catholic women, saying that Jews

…had been children in the House of God," but "owing to their obstinacy and their failure to believe, they have become dogs…We have today in Rome unfortunately too many of these dogs, and we hear them barking in all the streets, and going around molesting people everywhere.[20]

By the time of the Nazi Holocaust, the oppress and persecute Jews culture had centuries of its host Christian Protestant and Catholic theologians, preachers, and religious and political leaders building the justifications for oppressing and persecuting Jews. Christian leaders had spoken and the Christian population (except for some courageous

---

18   https://ccjr.us/dialogika-resources/primary-texts-from-the-history-of-the-relationship/paul-iv#ges:searchword%3Dsince%2Bit%2Bis%2Bcompletely%2Bsenseless%26searchphrase%3Dall%26page%3D1

19 Kertzer, David, *The Popes Against the Jews: The Vatican's Role in the Rise of Modern Anti-Semitism*, New York: Vintage Books, 2001, p. 116

20 Wills, Garry. "The Popes Against the Jews': Before the Holocaust," *The New York Times*, September 23, 2001

souls) believed. Of Germany's population of approximately sixty-eight million in 1939, approximately fifty four percent were Protestant Christians, forty percent, Catholic Christians, and six percent other, including less than one percent Jews.[21]

There is no way that the Nazi party could have taken and held control of Germany's government and executed six million Jews without the support of its Christian citizens who were under the control of a long established oppress and persecute Jews culture.

Building the Case for Jim Crow Racial Segregation, Discrimination, Oppression and Persecution

Following the Civil War, it was an easy matter for the oppress and persecute Blacks culture to retain control. The white Confederate government and armies had lost the war, but the white Southern people had not surrendered their suppression of Blacks cultural beliefs. The culture simply continued using every white Christian justification for black slavery to justify black segregation, discrimination, oppression, and persecution. All the sermons, books, speeches, editorials, and news articles that had been produced prior to the war still exerted control over white Christians in the former Confederate states (and later in other states). To almost all Southern whites, a black person was inferior to whites before the war and still inferior after the war. That had not changed, and no further justification was needed.

But the oppress and persecute Blacks culture couldn't risk that the federal reconstruction programs implemented following the war might improve the economic, social, and political status of black people in the Southern states. Just in case, the oppress and persecute Blacks culture kept its white Christian preachers, theologians, authors, teachers, and political leaders at work establishing Jim Crow racial segregation, discrimination, oppression, and persecution laws and social customs. And there was no shortage of those willing to follow their culture's calling.

---

[21] https://en.wikipedia.org/wiki/Religion_in_Nazi_Germany

Noah's (Ham's) curse, which had been used already by so many Christian theologians, preachers, and politicians to justify black slavery, was still employed after the abolishment of slavery to justify the racial segregation and suppression of black people. U.S. Senator Robert Byrd read the biblical story into the congressional record as part of his filibuster against the 1964 Civil Rights legislation.[22]

Perhaps the most infamous justification of racial segregation during the 1950-60s Civil Rights movement is the Easter radio sermon delivered by Dr. Bob Jones, the white pastor and founder of Bob Jones University. Broadcast on April 17, 1960, his forty-five minute sermon centered on the belief that God designed and demanded racial segregation. His message emphasized that the good white and colored people of the South were co-existing just fine, but that happy situation was being threatened by liberal, satanic, communist agitators. Dr. Jones declared:

My friends, I am going to bring you today one of the most important and most timely messages I have ever brought. I hope you will sit close to the radio. Do not let anything disturb you. I want you to hear this message through...

Now, we folks at Bob Jones University believe that whatever the Bible says is so, and we believe it says certain fundamental things that all Bible-believing Christians accept; but when the Bible speaks clearly about any subject, that settles it. Men do not always agree, because some people are dumb—some people are spiritually dumb; but when the Bible is clear, there is not any reason why everybody should not accept it...

For instance, we are living in the midst of race turmoil all over the world today. Look at what they are facing in Africa, and look at what we are facing in this country. It is all contrary to Scripture—it is all contrary to the Word of God...

Sometimes we have a little trouble, but then we adjust everything sensibly and get back to the established order. But the good white folks have always stood by their good colored friends, and the good colored folks have always stood by their good white friends. No two races ever lived as close together as the white people and the colored people here in the South and got along so well...

---

22 https://www.straightdope.com/21343336/what-s-up-with-the-biblical-story-of-drunken-noah-part-2

Now, what is the matter? There is an effort today to disturb the established order. Wait a minute. Listen, I am talking straight to you. White folks and colored folks, you listen to me. You cannot run over God's plan and God's established order without having trouble. God never meant to have one race. It was not His purpose at all. God has a purpose for each race...

Individually, Christian people in the South—white and black—through the years have been able to work together and to understand each other. But now a world of outside agitation has been started, and people are coming in the name of piety, but it is a false piety, and are endeavoring to disturb God's established order; and we are having turmoil all over America. This disturbing movement is not of God. It is not in line with the Bible. It is Satanic. Now, listen and understand this. Do not let people lead you astray...

I want you folks to listen—you white and you colored folks. Do not let these Satanic propagandists fool you. This agitation is not of God. It is of the devil. Do not let people slander God Almighty. God made it plain. God meant for Christian people to treat each other right. If you are a Christian white person or a Christian colored person, you will treat each other right. We Christians are children of God by faith in Jesus Christ. We are one in Christ; but let us remember that the God Who made of one blood all nations also fixed the boundaries of their habitations...

If we would just listen to the Word of God and not try to overthrow God's established order, we would not have any trouble. God never meant for America to be a melting pot to rub out the line between the nations. That was not God's purpose for this nation. When someone goes to overthrowing His established order and goes around preaching pious sermons about it, that makes me sick—for a man to stand up and preach pious sermons in this country and talk about rubbing out the line between the races—I say it makes me sick...

There has never been a time, especially in the last ten years, when the white people in the South were so eager to help the colored people build their schools and see that they get what they ought to have. All this agitation going on is not headed up by real, Bible-believing, Christian people...

These religious liberals are the worst infidels in many ways in the country; and some of them are filling pulpits down South. They do not believe the Bible any longer; so it does not do any good to quote it to them. They have gone over to modernism, and they are leading the white people astray at the same time; and they are leading colored

Christians astray. But every good, substantial, Bible-believing, intelligent, orthodox Christian can read the Word of God and know that what is happening in the South now is not of God...

After the Civil War the colored people wanted to build their schools and churches, and white friends made financial contribution to the building of these schools and churches. Back in those days it was not easy when the white folks were paying most of the taxes—don't you colored friends forget that when you are inclined to turn away from your white friends. You colored people might also remember that your ancestry in the South who were slaves breathed an atmosphere of culture back in those pre-Civil War days. Think of what your ancestors received in such an atmosphere. Think of the religion that they learned and how they found God in slavery days. Think of those old white preachers who preached to your colored ancestors when they were slaves.

Now listen, the time has come when we ought to sit down and go to thinking some things through in this country. And you colored people listening to me and you white people listening to me ought to keep your heads cool and your minds clear and your hearts warm and keep up these friendly relations we have had through the years. Do not let this outside, Communistic, Hellish influence disturb the friendly relation we have had in the South. The situation in the South had been better in recent years than it had ever been; and all of this agitation is going to set this country back in the South for twenty-five to fifty years. We are headed that way. We ought to rise up and begin to face this thing like we ought to face it as neighbors and fiends (sic). Every one of you colored people know your white friends. All you white people know your colored friends. We have some of them, and we would not let anybody mistreat them if we could help it; and they would not let anybody mistreat us. It has always been that way in the South...

But racially we have separation in the Bible. Let's get that clear. Any race has a right to come to America. We do not mean that when we came over here we wiped out the line between races. We did not do that. We should have let the Africans stay in Africa instead of bringing them here for slaves, but did you colored people ever stop to think where you might have been if that had not happened? Now, you colored people listen to me. If you had not been brought over here and if your grandparents in slavery days had not heard that great preaching you might not even be a Christian. You might be over there in the jungles of Africa today, unsaved. But you are here in America where you have your own schools and your own churches and your own liberties and your own rights, with certain restrictions that God Almighty put about you—restrictions that are in line with the Word of God...

All this agitation is a Communistic agitation to overthrow the established order of God in this world. The Communistic influence is at work all about us. Certain people are disturbing this situation. They talk about the fact that we are going to have one world. We will never really have one world until this world heads up in God. We are not going to have one world by man's rubbing out the line that God has established. He is marking the lines, and you cannot rub them out and get away with it…

When you run into conflict with God's established order racially, you have trouble. You do not produce harmony. You produce destruction and trouble, and this nation is in the greatest danger it has ever been in in its history. We are facing dangers from abroad and dangers at home, and the reason is that we have got away from the Bible of our forefathers. The best Christians who ever put foot on this earth since the Apostolic days were the men and women in America back in the old days. Some of them owned slaves, and some of them did not; and some of them were slaves, and some of them were not. Back in those days they believed the Bible, and God called this nation into existence to be a witness to the world and to be true to the Word of God. Do not let these religious liberals blowing their bubbles of nothing over your head get you upset and disturbed. Let's get back to the Word of God and be sensible.[23]

Dr. Jones closed his sermon with the prayer:

Our heavenly Father, bless our country. We thank Thee for our ancestors. We thank Thee for the good, Christian people—white and black. We thank Thee for the ties that have bound these Christian white people and Christian colored people together through the years, and we thank Thee that white people who had a little more money helped them build their churches and stood by them and when they got sick, they helped them. No nation has ever prospered or been blessed like the colored people in the South. Help these colored Christian not to get swept away by all the propaganda that is being put out now. Help us to see this thing and to understand God's established order and to be one in Christ and to understand that God has fixed the boundaries of the nations so we would not have trouble and misunderstanding. Keep us by Thy power and use us for They(sic) glory, for Jesus' sake. Amen.[24]

---

[23]   https://brucegerencser.net/2017/08/is-segregation-scriptural-by-evangelist-bob-jones-the-founder-of-bob-jones-university/
[24] Ibid

Dr. Jones's sermon confirmed the Christian beliefs of almost all of us white southern Christians in those days, and it was often referenced by other white preachers. Almost immediately following the 1961 attack on the Montgomery Freedom Riders, Reverend Henry Lyon, Montgomery's most prominent white pastor and a former president of the Alabama Baptist Convention, declared in a speech:

Ladies and gentlemen, for 15 years I have had the privilege of being pastor of a white Baptist church in this city. If we stand 100 years from now, it will still be a white church. I am a believer in a separation of the races, and I am none the less a Christian…If you want to get in a fight with the one that started separation of the races, then you come face to face with your God…The difference in color, the difference in our body, our minds, our life, our mission upon the face of this earth, is God given.[25]

The result of these and thousands more "justifications" of racial segregation (and the associated Jim Crow laws and customs) influenced me, my family, and almost all white Southern Christians to believe that our white supremacy was fully ordained by God and His Bible. The oppress and persecute Blacks culture had accomplished its mission: to continue a sad and dark chapter in the history of Christianity by using its host white Christian theologians, preachers, authors and leaders to fully and effectively build the case that black people should continue to be oppressed and persecuted.

Building the Case to Keep Women in Subordination

Just as there was no shortage of white Christian theologians, ministers, and editors who aggressively built the historic cases that slavery was ordained by God or that Jews deserved to be oppressed and persecuted, there has been, and continues to be today, no shortage of Christian theologians, ministers and editors who work to establish that women must be kept in submission. It is probably a coincidence, but most—perhaps all—of them are men.

One of the many men building the justification for keeping women in submission in Christian churches is Dr. Owen Strachan, a professor

---

25   https://brewminate.com/the-historical-roots-of-white-supremacist-ideas-in-u-s-christianity/

and theologian at Midwestern Baptist Theological Seminary in Kansas City. Below are two short excerpts from his many publications, this one entitled "Divine Order in a Chaotic Age: On Women Preaching."

There is physical order in the cosmos; there is also social order, and spiritual order. There are things that are right based on God's creative design, and there are things that are wrong. It is right for **men to lead their homes,** *and put their lives on the line when their family members are endangered, and work hard to be the financial pillar of their loved ones. It is right for* **women to be distinctively feminine, bear and raise children as God allows, submit to and support their husbands** *per 1 Peter 3, and serve their churches in ways that use their gifts. Living out these realities is good and glorious, and shows us the beauty of the Christian worldview over against secular conceptions of the sexes. (emphasis added)*

In terms of local church polity, God does not tell us to select leaders according to gifting and talent. The Lord working through the Spirit calls only godly men to provide spiritual leadership, shepherding, and teaching for the gathered assembly of God's people (see 1 Corinthians 14:34-35). All this, as we have said, is spiritual and ecclesial order. It is dependent on God's making of the sexes: Ἀδὰμ γὰρ πρῶτος ἐπλάσθη εἶτα Εὕα–"for Adam was formed first, then Eve," Ἀδὰμ being the first word in the Greek text of 1 Timothy 2:13. Men preach in the church, Paul teaches, because Adam was made first, and Adam was not deceived by the serpent (1 Tim. 2:14). The verse flow mirrors the flow of thought: the breakdown of creation order in the garden of Eden led to the deception of the woman and the fall of humanity. The stakes are terrifyingly high when it comes to the design of God in the world of men."[26] (emphasis added)

In other words, there is social and spiritual order in the world and that order requires that men be head of the household and women be "feminine, bear and raise children as God allows, (and) submit to and support their husbands." Why? Because Adam was created first and Eve was the one first deceived.

Out of curiosity, I looked up the definition of feminine and one of the meanings is "delicacy and prettiness." So, the roles assigned to women by God, according to Strachan, are to be delicate and pretty, have

---

[26] https://www.patheos.com/blogs/thoughtlife/2019/05/divine-order-in-a-chaotic-age-on-women-preaching/

children, and obey the men in their homes and church, but never, ever lead or preach.

But it is not enough for Dr. Strachan that the world's social and spiritual order demands that women be held in submission. He goes on to explain that bad things will happen if they are not held in submission:

*For a woman to teach and preach to adult men is to defy God's Word and God's design. **Elders must not allow such a sinful practice; to do so is to bring the church body into disobedience against God.**[27] (Emphasis added)*

End of Discussion. To many Christians controlled by the parasitic oppress and persecute women cultures, the subordination of women is so common as to seem self-evident. Reverend Pat Robertson, the highly respected host of *The 700 Club* television show, which reaches millions each year, stated plainly:

I know this is painful for the ladies to hear, but if you get married, you have accepted the headship of a man, your husband. Christ is the head of the household, and the husband is the head of the wife, and that's the way it is, period.[28]

Not only is the subordination of women "the way that it is, period," Reverend Robertson goes further to tell us what those women seeking equality are really trying to do to us, to our children and to our nation:

The feminist agenda is not about equal rights for women. It is about a socialist, anti-family political movement that encourages women to leave their husbands, kill their children, practice witchcraft, destroy capitalism and become lesbians.[29]

Danvers Statement. Perhaps the most comprehensive Christian "justification" for oppressing women was written when a group of leading evangelical theologians and ministers came together in

---

[27] Ibid
[28] https://www.cnn.com/2013/07/09/us/pat-robertson-facebook-remark/index.html
[29] https://www.nytimes.com/1992/08/26/us/robertson-letter-attacks-feminists.html

Danvers, Massachusetts, in December 1987, to produce the following joint statement:[30]

Rationale

We have been moved in our purpose by the following contemporary developments which we observe with deep concern:

1. *The widespread uncertainty and confusion in our culture regarding the complementary differences between masculinity and femininity;*

2. *the tragic effects of this confusion in unraveling the fabric of marriage woven by God out of the beautiful and diverse strands of manhood and womanhood;*

3. *the increasing promotion given to feminist egalitarianism with accompanying distortions or neglect of the glad harmony portrayed in Scripture between the loving, humble leadership of redeemed husbands and the intelligent, willing support of that leadership by redeemed wives;*

4. *the widespread ambivalence regarding the values of motherhood, vocational homemaking, and the many ministries historically performed by women;*

5. *the growing claims of legitimacy for sexual relationships which have Biblically and historically been considered illicit or perverse, and the increase in pornographic portrayal of human sexuality;*

6. *the upsurge of physical and emotional abuse in the family;*

7. *the emergence of roles for men and women in church leadership that do not conform to Biblical teaching but backfire in the crippling of Biblically faithful witness;*

8. *the increasing prevalence and acceptance of hermeneutical oddities devised to reinterpret apparently plain meanings of Biblical texts;*

---

[30] http://www.grbc.net/wp-content/uploads/2015/09/The-Danvers-Statement-on-Biblical-Manhood-and-Womanhood.pdf

9. *the consequent threat to Biblical authority as the clarity of Scripture is jeopardized and the accessibility of its meaning to ordinary people is withdrawn into the restricted realm of technical ingenuity;*

10. *and behind all this the apparent accommodation of some within the church to the spirit of the age at the expense of winsome, radical Biblical authenticity which in the power of the Holy Spirit may reform rather than reflect our ailing culture.*

Purposes

Recognizing our own abiding sinfulness and fallibility, and acknowledging the genuine evangelical standing of many who do not agree with all of our convictions, nevertheless, moved by the preceding observations and by the hope that the noble Biblical vision of sexual complementarity may yet win the mind and heart of Christ's church, we engage to pursue the following purposes:

1. *To study and set forth the Biblical view of the relationship between men and women, especially in the home and in the church.*

2. *To promote the publication of scholarly and popular materials representing this view.*

3. *To encourage the confidence of lay people to study and understand for themselves the teaching of Scripture, especially on the issue of relationships between men and women.*

4. *To encourage the considered and sensitive application of this Biblical view in the appropriate spheres of life.*

5. *And thereby*
   —to bring healing to persons and relationships injured by an inadequate grasp of God's will concerning manhood and womanhood,
   —to help both men and women realize their full ministry potential through a true understanding and practice of their God-given roles,
   —and to promote the spread of the gospel among all peoples by fostering a Biblical wholeness in relationships that will attract a fractured world.

Affirmations

Based on our understanding of Biblical teachings, we affirm the following:

1. Both Adam and Eve were created in God's image, equal before God as persons and distinct in their manhood and womanhood (Gen 1:26-27, 2:18).

2. Distinctions in masculine and feminine roles are ordained by God as part of the created order, and should find an echo in every human heart (Gen 2:18, 21-24; 1 Cor 11:7-9; 1 Tim 2:12-14).

3. Adam's headship in marriage was established by God before the Fall, and was not a result of sin (Gen 2:16-18, 21-24, 3:1-13; 1 Cor 11:7-9).

4. The Fall introduced distortions into the relationships between men and women (Gen 3:1-7, 12, 16).

5. In the home, the husband's loving, humble headship tends to be replaced by domination or passivity; the wife's intelligent, willing submission tends to be replaced by usurpation or servility.

6. In the church, sin inclines men toward a worldly love of power or an abdication of spiritual responsibility, and inclines women to resist limitations on their roles or to neglect the use of their gifts in appropriate ministries.

7. The Old Testament, as well as the New Testament, manifests the equally high value and dignity which God attached to the roles of both men and women (Gen 1:26-27, 2:18; Gal 3:28). Both Old and New Testaments also affirm the principle of male headship in the family and in the covenant community (Gen 2:18; Eph 5:21-33; Col 3:18-19; 1 Tim 2:11-15).

8. Redemption in Christ aims at removing the distortions introduced by the curse.

9. In the family, husbands should forsake harsh or selfish leadership and grow in love and care for their wives; wives should forsake resistance to their husbands' authority and grow in willing, joyful submission to their husbands' leadership (Eph 5:21-33; Col 3:18-19; Tit 2:3-5; 1 Pet 3:1-7).

10. *In the church, redemption in Christ gives men and women an equal share in the blessings of salvation; nevertheless, some governing and teaching roles within the church are restricted to men (Gal 3:28; 1 Cor 11:2-16; 1 Tim 2:11-15).*

11. *In all of life Christ is the supreme authority and guide for men and women, so that no earthly submission-domestic, religious, or civil-ever implies a mandate to follow a human authority into sin (Dan 3:10-18; Acts 4:19-20, 5:27-29; 1 Pet 3:1-2).*

12. *In both men and women a heartfelt sense of call to ministry should never be used to set aside Biblical criteria for particular ministries (1 Tim 2:11-15, 3:1-13; Tit 1:5-9). Rather, Biblical teaching should remain the authority for testing our subjective discernment of God's will.*

13. *With half the world's population outside the reach of indigenous evangelism; with countless other lost people in those societies that have heard the gospel; with the stresses and miseries of sickness, malnutrition, homelessness, illiteracy, ignorance, aging, addiction, crime, incarceration, neuroses, and loneliness, no man or woman who feels a passion from God to make His grace known in word and deed need ever live without a fulfilling ministry for the glory of Christ and the good of this fallen world (1 Cor 12:7-21).*

14. *We are convinced that a denial or neglect of these principles will lead to increasingly destructive consequences in our families, our churches, and the culture at large.*

Through the Danvers Statement, the male supremacist oppress and persecute women culture spoke loudly and clearly. Women must be held in subordinated roles in both homes and churches. Men are the head of both, and women must be submissive to that male dominance. Why? Because:

- That is what the Bible demands.
- Equality for women will destroy "our families, our churches and the culture at large."

Ken Boutwell

And there you have another one of hundreds, maybe thousands, of "justifications" written by male Christian theologians and ministers for keeping women in submission.

To the delight of the oppress and persecute women culture, the Danvers Statement is the basic "creed" of the national Council on Biblical Manhood and Womanhood. It has been adopted by several evangelical churches, church associations, and seminaries, including Southwestern Baptist Theological Seminary, Southeastern Baptist Theological Seminary and Midwestern Baptist Theological Seminary who have always taught that women must be held in submission both in the home and the church.

Building the Case to Oppress and Persecute LGBTQs

Up until the last few decades, the dominant oppress and persecute LGBTQ culture that most of us lived in had almost no difficulty in getting us host heterosexual Christians to fully commit to the Bible's oppression and persecution of LGBTQ victims. I don't know about you, but we did not personally know any gay people during my youth. I now assume that was because they all stayed "closeted," no matter how painful it may have been for them. I learned years later that one of my wife's high school classmates who committed suicide was gay. To our shame today, I am confident that we would have ridiculed, ostracized and made life miserable for my wife's classmate if he or others had come out. I am sure that the classmate knew that all too well, and that it was the oppress and persecute gays culture we strongly supported that killed him.

Everything we learned about gay people during my youth came through our churches which were totally controlled by our oppress and persecute LGBTQ culture. You can be sure that that culture gave no room whatsoever for treating LGBTQs with respect, dignity and equality. No justification was needed, although it was sometimes given from our pulpits, Sunday School classes, and publications. Our powerful culture had spoken, and we dared not oppose. Had any of us voiced support for gay people, we would have definitely been ridiculed and ostracized ourselves and perhaps even subjected to personal counseling. So, it never even entered our minds to do so.

As is almost always the case, the movement to confront the oppress and persecute LGBTQ culture came not from us loving Christians but from the victims themselves. Like the Israelites in Egypt and the African Americans during the Civil Rights movement, the LGBTQ community finally grew tired of suffering and mounted their own protests that continued for several decades. Slowly, but consistently, their protests picked up support from the secular sector. Some local communities and then some states adopted ordinances and laws both prohibiting discrimination based on sexual orientation and granting equal rights. This awareness and commitment to fairness gradually took hold and grew, reaching the federal level in July 2015 when the US Supreme Court rendered an opinion granting LGBTQs equal rights to marry the person they loved.

This secular LGBTQ victory, however, was a "call to arms" for Christians hosting the oppress and persecute LGBTQ culture. Just as it created justification from Scripture for killing witches, holding Blacks in slavery, executing Jews, and keeping women in submission, it created justifications for damning all LGBTQs. Christian theologians, editors, and ministers all over the nation rushed to use biblical messages to condemn the Supreme Court decision.

Franklin Graham, the head of Samaritan's Purse and the Billy Graham Evangelistic Association (both highly respected national and international Christian service and mission organizations), weighed in immediately after the Supreme Court decision. Not only did he condemn LGBTQs, but he also portrayed the decision as an attack on Christianity:

Today the U.S. Supreme Court enacted a new law that adds sexual orientation and gender identity to the 1964 Civil Rights Act as "protected classes." As Justice Alito has pointed out, the majority went too far—he called it a "brazen abuse of our authority." The Supreme Court exists to interpret the law, not to make new laws—making laws is the job of our Representatives in Congress, elected by the people.

I believe this decision erodes religious freedoms across this country. People of sincere faith who stand on God's Word as their foundation for life should never be forced by the government to compromise their religious beliefs. Christian organizations should never be forced to hire people who do not align with their biblical beliefs and should not be prevented from terminating a person whose lifestyle and beliefs undermine the ministry's purpose and goals.

As a Bible-believing follower of Jesus Christ, my rights should be protected. Even if my sincerely held religious beliefs might be the minority, I still have a right to hold them. The same holds true for a Christian organization. These are the freedoms our nation was founded on.

The Supreme Court does not override and will never overturn the Word of God. One day we will all have to stand before God, the Righteous Judge, whose decisions are not based on politics or the whims of culture. His laws are true and are the same yesterday, today, and forever.[31]

At another time Graham declared, in reference to homosexuality:

We have allowed the enemy to come into our churches. I was talking to some Christians and they were talking about how they invited these gay children to come into their home and to come into the church and that they were wanting to influence them.

And I thought to myself, they're not going to influence those kids, those kids are going to influence those parents' children. What happens is we think we can fight by smiling and being real nice and loving. We have to understand who the enemy is and what he wants — he wants to devour our homes. He wants to devour this nation.[32]

Mike Huckabee, the former Baptist minister, Arkansas governor and candidate for U.S. president also jumped in immediately after the court decision to advise all Christians to resist the decision:

The Supreme Court has spoken with a very divided voice on something only the Supreme Being can do-redefine marriage," Huckabee said in the statement. "I will not acquiesce to an imperial court any more than our Founders acquiesced to an imperial British monarch. We must resist and reject judicial tyranny, not retreat.[33]

---

[31] https://www.facebook.com/FranklinGraham/posts/ 3381726081883549
[32] https://www.lgbtqnation.com/2016/01/rev-franklin-graham-gay-christians-are-the-enemy/
[33] https://talkingpointsmemo.com/livewire/mike-huckabee-gay-marriage-decision

Huckabee called the ruling "unconstitutional."

This ruling is not about marriage equality, it's about marriage redefinition.... This irrational, unconstitutional rejection of the expressed will of the people in over 30 states will prove to be one of the court's most disastrous decisions, and they have had many. The only outcome worse than this flawed, failed decision would be for the President and Congress, two co-equal branches of government, to surrender in the face of this out-of-control act of unconstitutional, judicial tyranny.[34]

In reference to the Supreme Court decision, Ronnie Floyd, President of the SBC, declared:

The Supreme Court of the United States is not the final authority nor is the culture itself. The Bible is God's final authority about marriage and on this book we stand.[35]

The progress that LGBTQs made in gaining support from the secular community was based upon their position that sexual orientation is a "born with," not a "chosen" trait that can be easily altered by a conversion experience. As more and more gay people came out and we, their heterosexual family, friends, and neighbors, got to know them on a personal basis, we realized that their claim was true. Except for their sexual orientation, they were just like everybody else in every way, with the same capacity for and commitment to being kind, loving people.

This meant that the Christian oppress and persecute LGBTQs culture, having already lost its control over the secular society, was in danger of also losing its control over its Christian hosts. In fact, by the time of the Supreme Court decision in 2015, some Christians were already openly and happily accepting LGBTQs into their churches. The oppress and persecute LGBTQs culture absolutely had to defeat this idea that sexual orientation is a "born with" trait. In fact, it had to replace that idea with the concept that sexual orientation is a "chosen" lifestyle that can be easily altered. And, as always, host Christians stepped forward to comply.

---

[34] Ibid
[35] http://www.ontopmag.com/article/21069/Southern_Baptists_Ronnie_Floyd_Compares_Supreme_Court_To_Nazi_Regime_On_Gay_Marriage

I mentioned earlier in Chapter 4 that I wrote a letter to one of the leaders of the United Methodist anti-gay movement. In my letter, I pleaded with him to join with those of his Methodist brothers and sisters who supported treating LGBTQ people with respect, dignity, and equality.

Because we are all influenced by the cultures of which we are a part, I knew that the chances of his speaking against his culture were nil. But I had to try. As expected, he kindly rejected my request, noting that he was on the "side of the great theologians." (That made me wonder what makes a theologian "great" and I still don't know, but I assume that such scholars are deemed "great" if they write papers or deliver sermons or speeches that agree with "my" culture.) Anyhow, the very kind Methodist leader included with his responding letter a paper written by Dr. James V. Heidinger II, the former president and publisher of *Good News*, a conservative ministry of the United Methodist Church. His paper was entitled "Reflections on the Science of Homosexuality."

The paper is well written and concentrates exclusively on building the case that our LGBTQ brothers and sisters and sons and daughters are living a chosen lifestyle that can be easily changed through therapy and conversion experiences. Interestingly, Dr. Heidinger never says in his article that being gay is a sin. Instead, he starts by condemning a Methodist bishop who supports the equal treatment of LGBTQs, and he credits the bishop and those who agree with him as being one of the reasons that a 2010 consultant's report found there was a "pervasive lack of trust" in the United Methodist denomination.

Dr. Heidinger then attempts to prove emphatically that homosexuality is neither an innate (born with) or immutable (can't be changed) human trait, but rather a chosen lifestyle that can be easily reversed by therapy. He quotes court cases in the 1990s that ruled that homosexuality is neither innate or immutable. He summarizes studies, papers, and books prepared by other theologians finding that homosexuality is a lifestyle choice, as well as studies conducted by carefully selected professional psychologists that produced similar conclusions. He then ridicules the comparison of LGBTQ civil rights to racial civil rights, quoting black civil rights leader Bishop Andrew Merritt of Straight Gate Ministries as saying such a comparison is "abhorrent."

But what about the progress that the secular sector has made in treating our LGBTQ brothers and sisters with respect and dignity, including the equal rights to marry the person they love? And what about medical conclusions that sexual orientation cannot be altered via therapy and the state and local laws that prohibit 'conversion therapy" because of both its ineffectiveness and its potential harm to the patient? Heidinger dismisses these acts as political, not biblical or scientifically, based.

Dr. Heidinger's conclusion is:

What we have seen in this brief study is that the supposed "consensus of the scientific community"—that homosexuality is inborn and unchangeable, that is, innate and immutable—is (at least thus far) without scientific documentation. It is more "supposed," mythical claim kept alive by endless, non-critical repetition. It is not the "scientific consensus" many claim it to be. However, many sincere and well-meaning, compassionate people across America and in our churches believe it is. **And that, unfortunately, has had an immeasurably negative impact on American society and behavior for well over thirty years.** *(emphasis added)*

A phase heard by a number of the therapists…was that change could take place "if the person were strongly motivated." It is unfortunate that the climate in America will not encourage the needed motivation. Homosexuality is being granted political (if not privileged) status. A number of churches are giving official ecclesiastical endorsement, the medical community is increasingly viewing it as normative, pro-homosexual activists are aggressively hostile toward those seeking therapy for homosexual attraction and practice, and the media and pop culture are affirming it non-stop. Unfortunately, many persons have bought into the supposed "science says" argument claiming it is both innate and immutable.

I read Dr. Heidinger's paper several times because something simply did not seem right. Then it dawned on me—something was missing. That something was personal testimonies from LGBTQ people to confirm Heidinger's claims. Every reference and quote in his paper was from heterosexual people stating their own conclusions about homosexual people.

You would think that if all these heterosexuals were right in their conclusions, there should be dozens, if not hundreds or maybe even thousands of previously homosexual people who would be anxious to endorse Dr. Heidinger's conclusions. Surely there would be at least one included in his paper. Instead, his entire paper consists of a whole cadre of heterosexual people making claims about homosexual people...claims that not a single one of them had ever personally experienced.

But in this case, as all the ones before, logic and experience don't matter. Heidinger's paper delivered exactly what his oppress and persecute LGBTQs culture demanded of him, a strong "justification" in his own mind and that of his fellow supporters for oppressing and persecuting our homosexual brothers and sisters and sons and daughters. And he did such an effective job of building that justification that the Methodist anti-gay leader with whom I corresponded chose his paper to send to me. And, as I write these words, Heidinger and others have done such a successful job that the United Methodist church is splitting over this very issue.

Who Builds the Justifications?

If we now go back and review the above justifications for the oppression and persecution of these millions and millions of innocent people over the years, we see a common thread. That thread is that the "justifications" are all made by members of the dominant cultures who do the oppressing and persecuting. The cultures demand that these "justifications" be produced from within its followers, and the cultural hosts have been happy and willing to create them. The victims are never listened to by the hosts of these oppressive cultures. No one in these cultures cared what the victims said...and still don't care today.

- It was the Christian hosts of oppress and persecute witches cultures who gave the justification for the murder of the innocent people falsely accused of being witches. My research found no case where an elderly woman accused of being a witch thought that it was a good idea herself.

- It was the white immigrating European Christians who justified stealing the land and homes of Native Americans and marching them on the Trail of Tears. I found no case where Native Americans eagerly volunteered to give up their homes and land and march the Trail of Tears.

- It was white Christians who wrote the editorials and stood up in our church pulpits to preach the justification of black slavery. Maybe you have, but I found no testimonies of black slaves praising the institution of slavery.

- It was Christians who justified the exile and execution of millions of Jews. I was unable to find a single Holocaust victim's testimony which supported the horror and cruelty of the genocide.

- It was the white Christians who justified the Jim Crow laws that kept black people in subordinated poverty for over a hundred years after the civil war. I found no reports where African Americans expressed their support and appreciation for those suppressive laws and customs.

- It is male Christians who write the papers, preach the sermons, and establish the church bylaws, policies, and creeds that keep women suppressed. I found no cases where women who had been called to Christian ministry praised the church creeds, policies, and sermons that prevent them from fulfilling their call.

- It is the heterosexual Christians who write the blogs and church literature, preach the sermons, and establish the church creeds and policies that dogmatically condemn the equal treatment of homosexuals. You may have, but I found no blogs or editorials or speeches or anything else created by gay people supporting these beliefs, positions, and publications.

It has always been the dominant white, and mostly male, Christian cultures that have built the justifications, never the victims themselves. And, as we have already seen and will see even more vividly in subsequent chapters, when the victims cried out for mercy, the Christian hosts of these cruel oppress and persecute cultures called them every vile name in their arsenal: devil worshipers, bitches, sons of bitches, thugs, savages, communists, socialists, fascists, sinners, niggers, feminists, fags, and other names that are more vulgar than I want to write, but you have probably heard. A dark, dark side of Christianity that continues on today.

Chapter 6

Which Bible Passages to Obey

As I am sure you may already suspect, the Bible is critical to the oppress and persecute cultures' strategies being successful. It is, in fact, one of the most effective weapons they have to manipulate us Christians to do their will. Unfortunately, justification for almost any cruel thing we want to do to others can be found in the Bible, and every one of these oppressive cultures have used the Bible to justify their cruelty.

They have done this by using their host Christian theologians, editors, ministers, Bible teachers, and lay leaders to tell (actually, dictate to) us exactly which biblical passages to obey and which must be ignored. And, sadly, we have believed exactly what our cultures tell us to believe. In doing so, we have enabled these cultures to build historical precedent for using the Bible, not as a guide on how we can "do unto others as we would have them do to us," but as a dagger to stab the very hearts and souls of millions of innocent people who were (and are) the victims of these evil oppress and persecute cultures.

As I shared previously, when I was growing up during the Civil Rights movement, my surrounding culture was quite clear that we had to obey biblical passages that prohibited racial integration and interracial marriages. We knew because our white leaders, schoolteachers, newspapers, friends, and family, as well as our church newsletters, Sunday school lessons, and pastor's sermons said so. The messages were often not direct but, rather, hidden within more "loving" messages...messages like "God loves us all equally, but wants us to worship with our own people" or "God made us separate races and wants to keep us that way."

Scriptures like Acts 17:26 (God wants each race to stay where he put us) and Deuteronomy 23:2 (God forbids interracial marriages) were referenced and always lurking in the back of our minds (at least, my mind).

The chief way in which this method is successful is by establishing the supreme, unquestionable authority of the text of the Bible, specifically as interpreted by these oppress and persecute cultures. Do as I say, the cultures demand, even when it conflicts with the very nature of God.

This was made very clear to me when I attended a religious retreat at the Methodist Epworth by the Sea conference center on St. Simons Island, Georgia a couple of years ago. During a break, I met a nice gentleman from Canada. After a few minutes, our conversation, somehow, drifted to the role of women in the church. He said that his Canadian church was a "complementarian" church which meant that women cannot hold pastoral positions.

I remarked that the subordination of women had always bothered me. He quickly responded, "So, you don't believe in the authority of the Bible, do you?" Thinking quickly, I looked at my watch and responded, "Good grief. I was supposed to meet my wife five minutes ago (which, fortunately, was true.) Catch up with you later."

I don't know about you, but the issue of citing the "authority of the Bible" as an absolute and then choosing which biblical laws and moral guides to obey has troubled me for years. As I walked away from my brief conversation, I wondered if he meant the authority of just the New Testament or the whole Bible. He cited the authority of "the Bible," which for Christians would include both the Old and New Testaments. That made the question even more difficult because there are some truly cruel biblical guidelines in the Old Testament, many of which would never be condoned today. But that didn't seem to be a problem for him at all.

That conversation crystallized for me that the "authority of the Bible" is absolutely critical to the ability of oppressive cultures to get us Christian hosts to obey their cruel demands. Every oppress and persecute culture in our Christian history, from the time of the witchcraft trials to black slavery to the modern suppression of women and persecution of gay Christians, has used this "biblical authority" to exert social and religious pressure on us to oppress and persecute the cultures' victims.

Interestingly, we (or, at least, I) very rarely, if ever, hear the phrase, authority of the bible, used to promote the good biblical moral guides like "do unto others as you would have them do unto to you" or "love your neighbor as yourself," or "serve the least of these."

How tragic it is that the Bible itself is used to motivate Christians to kill those they believed to be witches, to murder the Jews or remain silent in complicity, keep Blacks in slavery, subordinate women, and damn the LGBTQs. So, at least based on my experience, whenever you see or hear a Christian rely on the term "authority of the Bible" to support their position, you can be almost certain that the oppression and persecution of some victim group will follow.

But for the moment, let's play along with the concept of the "authority of the Bible" and see how these cultures have used the moral guides and laws that fill both testaments in the Christian Bible to justify their cruel treatment of their targeted victims. I believe we can agree that it's no small task to try to follow each and every one of the thousands of laws, commands, and moral guides in the Bible. This is evidenced by the overwhelming number of books that have been written on how to interpret and understand the Bible.

Even beyond books written independently, our churches and church associations adopt statements designed to guide the personal application of Scripture. For decades I've attended Southern Baptist churches belonging to the Southern Baptist Convention. Those churches have adopted the following statement:

The Holy Bible was written by men divinely inspired and is God's revelation of Himself to man. It is a perfect treasure of divine instruction. It has God for its author, salvation for its end, and truth, without any mixture of error, for its matter. Therefore, all Scripture is totally true and trustworthy. It reveals the principles by which God judges us, and therefore is, and will remain to the end of the world, the true center of Christian union, and the supreme standard by which all human conduct, creeds, and religious opinions should be tried. All Scripture is a testimony to Christ, who is Himself the focus of divine revelation.[1]

---

[1] https://mbcpathway.com/2022/05/17/article-i-of-the-bfm-the-scriptures/

Unfortunately, it's not clear to me whether this statement requires that I obey absolutely all of the biblical laws or not. By using the word "all," however, the statement clearly implies that. However, that simply can't be true because we, thank goodness, no longer murder every man, woman and child who has a religion different from ours (Deuteronomy 7:1-2). So, clearly there is a disconnect here between citing the authority of "all" of Scripture and actually following through with each and every command.

Ultimately, however, each of us must make our own choices as to which biblical passages we will obey and which we will ignore or, maybe, even condemn. However, when we Christians allow the oppress and persecute cultures to make those decisions for us, they will take every opportunity to use the "authority of the Bible" to make sure it is those biblical messages, the ones that rationalize and justify their own agenda of oppression and persecution, that are at the top of the list of what must be obeyed.

The following is a small sample of biblical laws and morale guides that illustrates the complexities we face in choosing which biblical passages to obey. It also clearly shows how the oppress and persecute cultures have been intentional in selecting those passages which advance their agenda of persecution and power, while ignoring those which would undermine their own authority over the Christians who carry out their agenda.

- *"Thou shalt not suffer a witch to live." Exodus 22:18*
- *"A man or woman who is a medium or spiritist among you must be put to death. You are to stone them; their blood will be on their own heads."* Leviticus 20:27
- *Remember the sabbath day, to keep it holy.* Exodus 20:8
- *"Six days work shall be done, but on the seventh day you shall have a Sabbath of solemn rest, holy to the LORD. Whoever does any work on it shall be put to death." Exodus 35:2*
- *"One day while the people of Israel were out in the wilderness, one of them was caught gathering wood on the Sabbath Day. Numbers 15:32…Then the Lord said to Moses, 'The man must die. All of the people shall stone him to death outside the camp.' So, they took him*

outside the camp and killed him as the Lord had commanded." Numbers 15:35-36

- *Wives, submit yourselves unto your own husbands, as unto the Lord. Ephesians 5:22*

- *"Love the Lord your God with all your heart and with all your soul and with all your mind and with all your strength. The second is this: 'Love your neighbor as yourself.' There is no commandment greater than these." Mark 12:30-31*

- *"There is neither Jew nor Greek, there is neither bond nor free, there is neither male nor female: for ye are all one in Christ Jesus." Galatians 3:28*

- *"As in all of the churches of the saints, women should be silent in the churches. For they are not permitted to speak, but should be subordinate, as the laws also say. If there is anything they desire to know, let them ask their husbands at home. For it is shameful for a woman to speak in church." 1 Cor. 14: 33-35*

- *"A bastard shall not enter the congregation of the Lord; even to his tenth generation shall he not enter the congregation of the Lord." Deuteronomy 23.2 (Note: In this case, "bastard" means the child of a mixed-race couple.)*

- *"And he [God] made from one man every nation of mankind to live on all the face of the earth, having determined allotted periods and the boundaries of their dwelling place." Acts 17:26:*

- *"Then I, the king, shall say to those at my right, 'come, blessed of my Father, into the kingdom prepared for you from the founding of the world. For I was hungry, and you fed me; I was thirsty, and you gave me water; I was a stranger and you invited me into your homes, I was naked and clothed me; sick and in prison and you visited me." Mathew 25; 34-35*

  - *"Now therefore kill every male among the little ones, and kill every woman that hath known man by lying with him. But all the female children, that have not known a man by lying with him, keep alive for yourselves." Numbers 31:18*

  - *"The Jews, who killed both the Lord Jesus and the prophets, and have persecuted us, do not please God, and they are adversaries to all men, prohibiting us from speaking to the Gentiles that they may be saved, to fill up their sin always: for the wrath of God has come upon them to the end." I Thessalonians 2:14-16*

- *For by grace you have been saved through faith; and that not of yourselves, it is the gift of God; Ephesians 2:8*

- *Jesus speaking to the Jewish leaders: "For you are the children of your father the devil and you love to do the evil things he does…" John 8:44*

- *"The penalty for homosexual acts is death to both parties…." Leviticus 20:13*

- *"Treat others as you want them to treat you." Luke 6:31*

- *"When Noah awoke from his drunken stupor, and learned what had happened and what Ham, his young son, had done, he cursed Ham's descendants: 'A curse upon the Canaanites,' he swore. 'May they be the lowest of slaves to the descendants of Shem and Japheth.' Then he said. 'God bless Shem, and may Canaan be his slave. God bless Japheth and let him share the prosperity of Shem, and let Canaan be his slave.'" Genesis 9: 24-27*

- *"However, you may purchase slaves from foreign nations living around you, and you may purchase the children of foreigners living among you, even though they have been born in your land. They shall be permanent slaves for you to pass on to your children…" Leviticus 25: 44-45*

- *"Slaves, obey your masters, be eager to give them your very best. Serve them as you would Christ. Ephesians 6.5*

- *"…For a pastor must be a good man whose life cannot be spoken against…" (Timothy 3: 2)*

- *"Give freely to the poor person, and do not wish that you didn't have to give. The Lord your God will bless your work and everything you touch." Deuteronomy 15:10*

The above sample of biblical laws and guidelines reveals that some are essential to living a confident, happy and caring personal life; some are essential to creating loving communities; and some are essential to understanding our relationship to God and our role as a part of His creation. Others, however, are just plain cruel and inhumane.

It is this latter group where the oppress and persecute cultures have, historically, invoked the "authority of the Bible" to tell us host Christians to believe and obey. As a result, there is a long, dark history of using these verses to hurt other people, including slavery, torture, murder, genocide, subordination, ostracization, condemnation and excommunication.

Witches

During the European witch trials, host theologians, ministers, and lay people of the Christian church fully complied and even eagerly carried out those biblical verses calling for the death of witches (e.g., Exodus 22:18 and Leviticus 20:27). The Bible demanded their death, and the host Christians obeyed the Bible as interpreted by their oppress and persecute cultures.

Native Americans

It may be hard to believe today, but according to the Puritans, God ordained the taking of the lands of the Native Americans as His gift to mankind as stated in Genesis. European settlers took for themselves the promise given to Abraham for the Jewish people, that God's intent was to give them a permanent homeland and that a great people would live there.

The Lord had said to Abram, "Go from your country, your people and your father's household to the land I will show you. I will make you into a great nation, and I will bless you; I will make your name great, and you will be a blessing. I will bless those who bless you, and whoever curses you I will curse; and all peoples on earth will be blessed through you. (*Genesis 12:1-3, NIV*)

With this verse, the white oppress and persecute Native Americans culture of that day provided all the biblical justification needed for the white European Christians to take the lands of Native Americans and murder them when they objected.

The Governor of the Massachusetts Bay Colony expressed his appreciation for God sending the smallpox disease to give the new American land to the immigrating white Europeans when he wrote in 1634, "For the natives, they are near all dead of the smallpox, so as the Lord hath cleared our title to what we possess." [2]

---

[2] www. ExChristian.Net - Articles: How many people have been killed by Christians since Biblical times?

Slavery

During the antebellum slavery years in America, white Southern Christian pastors, editors, and political leaders fervently obeyed the oppress and persecute Blacks culture's demand that those biblical scriptures supporting slavery be fully obeyed. Host Christians faithfully preached and quoted the multitude of biblical scriptures supporting the enslavement of millions of black women, men and children (e.g., Leviticus 25: 44-45 and Ephesians 6.5). They even twisted the account of Noah and his sons to mean that God himself had condemned blacks to be slaves to whites. (Genesis 9:24-27).

Jim Crow Racial Segregation

The Confederates lost the Civil War, but the oppress and persecute Blacks culture was not defeated. It simply regrouped and used the same pro-slavery biblical scriptures plus others (e.g., Acts 17:26:) to justify the oppression and persecution of blacks through racial segregation. Jim Crow subordination laws and customs were created with the cruelest of care and deliberation to keep blacks in a legalized form of economic and social slavery, and we host white Christians were obedient, chapter and verse.

Holocaust

In one of the most evil and cruel atrocities in the history of the world, the oppress and persecute Jews culture was able to convince millions of German host Christians to ignore the brutalities being committed within their own towns, churches, and neighborhoods. It swayed those under its authority that that biblical scriptures like John 8:44 (which says Jews are the children of the devil) fully justified the exile and murder of millions of Jews.

With some notable exceptions (e.g., Dietrich Bonhoeffer), host German Christians bought the oppress and persecute Jews culture's biblical claims "hook, line and sinker" and either participated in the exile, torture and murder of their Jewish friends and neighbors or closed their eyes and silenced their voices while others performed the horrors.

One of the saddest parts of this historic tragedy is that the anti-sematic scriptures in the Bible are vague, at best. Yet, the oppress and persecute Jews culture was able to convince German (and other European) Christians to believe that those vague scriptures required that millions of Jews be murdered.

Women

While major progress has been made over the past century in the equal treatment of women outside of the church (e.g., women's suffrage, expanded career options, comparable compensation, representation in corporate executive and elected governmental positions), the oppress and persecute women culture has been very effective in preventing any progress within the churches hosting this culture. This continued suppression of women is based almost entirely on scriptures like Timothy 3: 2 (a pastor must be a man), 1 Corinthians 14:34 (a woman should be silent in church) and Ephesians 5:22 (wives submit yourself unto your husbands).

All these verses are cited as authority, even as Scripture is filled with other examples of women in strong leadership roles, e.g., Judges 4:4, 2 Chronicles 34:14-33, John 20:16-18, and Romans 16:1. Again, the oppress and persecute cultures will ignore and redefine that which does not support its agenda.

LGBTQs

Similar to the situation of women, our LGBTQ brothers and sisters and friends and neighbors have made significant progress in achieving equality in our secular culture over the past few decades. However, no progress has been made in achieving that same status in evangelical churches that keep oppress and persecute gays cultures alive and well based on scriptures such as Leviticus 18:22-24 (homosexual relationships are detestable), Leviticus 20:13-15:.(homosexual relationships shall be punishable by death), and Romans 1:26-27 (homosexual relationships are shameful sins).

You might ask yourself for a moment, "How are we Christians so easily misled? Why have we complied with things that are patently against the nature of our faith as shown by Jesus, Himself?"

The reason lies in what I shared about my own experience growing up under the influence of this culture. When a child is taught by trusted figures such as parents, and those parents themselves learned from those before them, and then those messages are reinforced by those in great authority, it's very hard to question those messages. The oppress and persecute cultures perpetuate themselves by preserving the lie that it is the final authority, and it uses Scripture as one of its chief tools.

There is absolutely no question that the Christian hosts of oppress and persecute cultures are correct in many of their statements about what the Bible says about how victims are to be treated, especially within more ancient cultures. The Bible does clearly say that witches should be killed (Exodus 22:18) and that slaves can be held and passed on to our children (Leviticus 25: 44-45). It says that women are to be submissive to men in both their marriages and their churches, and that homosexual relationships are sinful.

As I reflected back, however, on my biblical beliefs, I realized that I, like every other person, was choosing to believe and obey some parts of the bible, while conveniently ignoring other parts.

It was at that point in my spiritual journey that I realized that when I chose to ignore any part of the Bible, I had lost the "right" to claim that I was justified in oppressing and persecuting other people because the Bible told me to do so. No matter what we tell ourselves or others, not a single one of us obeys every message in the Bible. We have to choose those messages we will obey and those we will ignore. That is what every one of us does.

For example, in addition to the verses used in the case of witchcraft, slavery, the persecution of Jews and other tragedies, the Bible also says that it is permissible to raid a neighboring city and kill every man, woman and child, except for the young virgin girls who can be kept for yourselves. (Numbers 31:18) (I hope that this does not mean what I am afraid that it means.) The Bible also says that every person with a different religion must be killed (Deuteronomy 17:2-5). And, although, often tried to explain away, the Bible also says that a girl must marry the man who rapes her (Deuteronomy 22: 28-29). But, over the centuries, thank goodness, we ignore these and many other similar verses.

The Bible is filled with laws and guidelines concerning physical appearance and how people should dress. Virtually all of those stipulations are not followed in church today. Next Sunday, look around the sanctuary and ask yourself how many women have short hair, braided hair, or gold wedding rings? (1 Timothy 2:9-10) How many of the men have trimmed sideburns and beards? (Leviticus 19:27) If you checked the laundry tags in their garments, are any of them wool and linen blends? (Deuteronomy 22:11) All of these things are prohibited by scripture, and yet the oppress and persecute cultures totally ignore these biblical guides and none of us obey them.

And then there are the Ten Commandments, one of which, is to "remember the sabbath day to keep it holy." The Bible goes even further to say that those who work on Sundays should be killed (Exodus 35:2). In my youth, we took this biblical guide seriously. The Southern Baptist 1963 Statement of Baptist Faith and Message stated:

VIII. THE LORD'S DAY

The first day of the week is the Lord's Day. It is a Christian institution for regular observance. It commemorates the resurrection of Christ from the dead and should be employed in exercises of worship and spiritual devotion, both public and private, and by **refraining from worldly amusements, and resting from secular employments,** *work of necessity and mercy only being excepted. (Emphasis added)*

The Bible was clear on this subject and so were the Southern Baptists, quoting the authority of the Bible. Sundays were days of rest and worship back in those days. Our pastor preached sermons about not working on Sundays. State and local governments all over the nation, especially the southern states, had "blue" laws that prevented businesses from operating on Sundays. On our farm, we could milk the cows and feed the animals, but that was all. We couldn't plow or harvest the crops or build fences or cut timber or bale hay or do anything else that was not critical, e.g., "ox in the ditch." All of those non-critical activities were forbidden on Sundays, and we understood that doing them could affect whether we went to heaven or hell when we died.

119

But something has changed from those days. Today, biblical authority no longer applies to working on Sundays. The business blue laws are gone, voted away by Christian voters. Almost every retail business is open on Sundays, and we Christians are fully supportive with our Sunday lunches after church services. Even our Southern Baptist churches have dropped their "no working on Sundays" stance. Our SBC 2000 Statement of Faith and Message now says:

VIII. THE LORD'S DAY

"The first day of the week is the Lord's Day. It is a Christian institution for regular observance. It commemorates the resurrection of Christ from the dead and should include exercises of worship and spiritual devotion, both public and private. **Activities on the Lord's Day should be commensurate with the Christian's conscience under the Lordship of Jesus Christ."** *(Emphasis added)*

This change in the authority of the Bible over what we do on Sundays makes me wonder: if our culture now allows us to use our conscience to disobey one of the Ten Commandments, why can't we also use our conscience to treat people of color, women and LGBTQs with respect, dignity and equality instead of oppressing and persecuting them as required by other biblical verses that our church oppress and persecute cultures say we must obey?

Chapter 7

Oppressing and Persecuting Others Is Part of Being a Good Christian

Wonder why European Christians were so afraid of witches rather than the people killing the witches?

Anonymous

I have to admit, I wish that the title of this chapter were not true. But, sadly, although it is contrary to all that Jesus taught and to all that we tell others we believe, that is our Christian history, and part of my own history. Somehow, once these oppress and persecute cultures attach themselves to us and our churches, they take control of our beliefs and actions, making us think that oppressing and persecuting others is an integral part of being a good Christian…what we are supposed to do.

Good Christians Torture and Kill Witches

The oppress and persecute witches culture during the European witch trial centuries was emphatic. Being a good Christian meant both believing in witches and supporting their torture and execution. Any Christian not supporting this cruel and inhumane treatment of innocent people was not a good Christian. In fact, they were not Christians at all, as Reginald Scot discovered in the 1580s. Scot wrote and self-published his book *Discovery of Witchcraft*, which argued that witches did not exist and that the church was murdering innocent people, mostly elderly women who could not defend themselves. The book was highly controversial and was quickly condemned by many Christian theologians of that time as being non-Christian. King James the First (remembered today for the King James version of the Bible) ordered that all copies of Scot's book be confiscated and burned.[1]

---

[1] https://www.controverscial.com/Reginald%20Scot.htm

Being a good Christian of his day, King James, of course, wrote his own three volume book, *Daemonologie,* that advocated the persecution of witches because, among many reasons, they were tools of the devil who had left his evil mark on their bodies.[2]

And these cruel cultures hold on forever. Over 400 years later, in 1930, Scot's Christianity was still being questioned. Montague Summers, a Catholic scholar wrote:

Upon a careful investigation it appears that the flaw in Scot's argument is not that admitting the existence of evil spirits he declared that we know nothing of them or in relation to them save that they do not and cannot intermingle with the affairs of men, a sufficiently illogical position, but rather that although for caution's sake covering his atheism with the thinnest veneer, in fact he wholly and essentially denies the supernatural.

Accordingly, we are not surprised to encounter a heap of irrelevant matter in his treatise. **Surely the first chapter of his Eighth Book is a clear announcement of atheism:** *That miracles are ceased… Yet the treatise is valuable; it gives us the complete armoury(sic) of the atheist. But, Good Lord! what feeble rusted weapons.*[3] *(Emphasis added)*

Good Christians Oppress and Persecute Jews

Over the 1114 years (756-1870) that the Catholic pope was both the religious leader and the King of the papal states (what, for the most part, is Italy today), the Church was able to use the Pope's legal authority to keep Jews oppressed in walled-in, poverty-stricken ghettos. Periodically, the Jews would seek relief and even protest. When this happened, the Church would place even more restrictions on them and execute them from time to time on trumped up charges like alleged ritual murders of Christian children to get their blood for Jewish religious celebrations.

During this time period of papal rule, periodically, a "good" Christian would sometimes baptize a Jewish child (sprinkle some water on their

---

[2] https://en.wikipedia.org/wiki/Daemonologie
[3] https://skullsinthestars.com/2009/09/22/the-discoverie-of-witchcraft-by-reginald-scot-1584/

head and repeat the words "I baptize you in the name of the Father, the Son, and the Holy Ghost") without permission of the child's parents. Whenever the Church learned of this event, whether immediately or years later, the Christian police would take the child from her/his parents and send them to a home for "rescued" Jewish children. That is what "good" Christian officials did because the child could now go to heaven when they died, as opposed to hell, if they died a Jew.[4]

It is interesting that our secular societies are often more "Christian" than Christians in terms of "doing unto others as you would have them do unto you." After the popes lost their kingship powers in September 1870, the secular government began to release the Jews in the papal state ghettos and treat them with more respect, dignity, and equality, allowing them to attend universities, open businesses, become doctors, professors and governmental workers and socialize with Christians. As you might expect, many Jews had successful careers, becoming business, professional, governmental and social leaders. This was devastating for the oppress and persecute Jews culture that had controlled the Catholic church (and many Protestant churches) for centuries. The culture had lost its legal authority to oppress and persecute Jews but was not about to concede defeat.

Through its control over the Catholic church, the culture launched an all-out media campaign against Jews, not only in the previous papal states but all over Europe, in the latter part of the 1800s and early 1900s. The communications were designed to convince church, business and governmental leaders and the Christian population, as a whole, that the oppression of Jews was part of being a good Christian. David Kertzer's extensive research of Vatican archives revealed that Catholic popes, editors, cardinals, priests, and theologians produced hundreds and hundreds of messages that condemned Jews through books, news articles, pamphlets, reports, letters, sermons and directives. There was no let up. The communications came month after month after month and year after year through Catholic newspapers such as:

---

[4] Kertzer, David I., *The Popes against The Jews*, Vintage Books, 2001. page 45,

- *L'Osservatore Cattolico* (the Vatican's own newspaper),
- *L'Unita' Cattolica,*
- *Civilta' Cattolica* (a Jesuit biweekly that kicked off a series of 36 anti-Semitic articles over forty weeks in 1880).
- *Le Bloc Catholique*
- *La Croix* (a French daily newspaper published by the religious order of the Assumptionist fathers)
- *Pro Christo* (Polish Catholic periodical)
- *L'Univers* (highly respected Catholic French newspaper with close ties to the Vatican)
- *L'Osservatore romano* (a Jesuit journal)

News articles were re-enforced by Christian books such as:

- *The Jew: Judaism and the Judaization of Christian People* by Henri Gougenot des Mousseaux, (a French Catholic scholar) Note: The Nazis reprinted his book in 1921
- *The Talmud Jew* by August Rohling (a Catholic priest)
- *The Jews Before the Church and History* by a French Dominican friar
- *Mystery of the Blood Among the Jews* by Father Henri Desportes, alleging Jewish ritual murders
- *Killed by Jews* by Father Desportes, also alleging Jewish ritual murders

Kertzer summarizes the constant anti-Semitic Church messages over several decades beginning in the 1870s:

There is a secret Jewish conspiracy; the Jews seek to conquer the world; Jews are an evil sect who seek to do Christian harm; Jews are by nature immoral; Jews care for money and will do anything to get it; Jews control the press; Jews control the banks and are responsible for the economic ruination of untold numbers of Christian families; Jews are responsible for communism; Judaism commands its adherents to murder defenseless Christian children and drink their blood; Jews seek to destroy the Christian religion; Jews are unpatriotic, ever ready to sell their country out to the enemy; for the larger society to be properly protected, Jews must be segregated and their rights limited.[5]

These were the messages with which all Catholic leaders and followers were constantly bombarded month after month and year after year beginning in the 1870s and continuing into the 1930s. So, by the time the Nazi party was formed in the 1920s and came into power in the early 1930s, the Christian church had firmly established the oppress and persecute Jews culture in not only Germany, but in most of the other European countries. The oppression and persecution of Jews was an integral part of being a good Christian.

(Note: Fortunately, there were a few strong, courageous Christians who risked their own lives to save the lives of Jews. But they were few and far between. The vast majority of Christians were strong oppress and persecute Jews supporters or cared so little that they remained totally silent.)

Good Christians Take the Lands and Homes of Native American

Although the Europeans migrating to America in the seventeenth and eighteenth centuries came from many European nations, two of the most influential (at least early on in the first part of the seventeenth century) groups were the Pilgrims and the Puritans. Both were devout Christian groups who migrated from England. The Pilgrims were the smaller, more tolerant group seeking to separate from the rigorous controls of the Church of England. For the most part, the Pilgrims were poor people who were grateful to the Native Americans for their charity in helping them survive in the new world. The Puritans, on the other hand, were the more elite and wealthier who wanted to reform the worship restrictions and requirements of the Church of England but continue to force adherence to their own revised restrictions and requirements. The Puritans, in particular, saw America as a gift from God, a land where they could create an ideal Christian society, "the city

---

[5] Ibid, pg. 206

upon the hill," as their leader, John Winthrop, called it, that "the world would be watching."[6]

In the beginning, the Puritans and the Native Americans got along well, both learning from and trading with each other. Rather than seizing the lands of the Native Americans, the Puritans bought the land, paying what now seems like trinkets, but, nevertheless, paying for the land. Part of the problem was that, initially, the Natives did not understand the European concept of "owning" land. The Natives thought that they were simply giving rights to hunt, fish and gather nuts and fruits from the land, not own it in the sense that others could not also hunt fish and gather on the same land. As more and more Europeans migrated to the new world, the natives found that their sources of food and clothing were being depleted by these new white immigrants.

Additionally, these newcomers were ridiculing the natives' god, telling them that the only true god was Jesus and His Father, God. Soon, the Puritans and the Native Americans found themselves in conflict with the Puritans continuing to claim the lands of the natives and the natives trying to protect their homes and lands from the escalating invasion of white men. Isolated violence began to occur, and then larger confrontations occurred as the Natives tried to protect their homelands.

But the masses of immigrating Europeans felt strongly that America was a promised land that had been given to them by God to inhabit and build a new world. Native Americans, like the Canaanites who occupied the Jews' promised land, were simply people who had to be dealt with in whatever way necessary to take their lands and homes.

Good Antebellum Christians Strongly Supported Black Slavery

During the years leading up to the civil war, the white, southern Christian oppress and persecute Blacks culture recognized only two types of Christians: good Christians who supported slavery and bad

---

[6]   https://www.thoughtco.com/city-upon-a-hill-john-winthrop-735137#:~:text=John%20Winthrop%20used%20the%20phrase%20%22City%20upon%20a,certainly%20represented%20a%20new%20destiny%20for%20this%20land.

Christians who were against slavery. Actually, that is an understatement. To the oppress and persecute Blacks culture that controlled the white Christian churches in the South in those days, racial abolitionists were not Christians at all; they were atheists, as explained by the renowned white New Orleans pastor, Rev. B. M. Palmer, in his famous 1860 Thanksgiving sermon supporting slavery:

Last of all, in this great struggle, we defend the cause of God and religion. **The abolition spirit is undeniably atheistic.... This spirit of atheism,** *which knows no God who tolerates evil, no Bible which sanctions law, and no conscience that can be bound by oaths and covenants, has selected us for its victims....[7] (Emphasis added)*

Ten years earlier, another white Presbyterian minister, Rev. Ferdinand Jacobs, explained that slaveholders are good Christians who are given "intimate communion with God," when he wrote:

Slavery has existed in the Church from the earliest ages; has been recognized under every dispensation, as one of the permanent relations of life; has been treated as properly a subject of rule; the **holders of slaves are recognized as the servants of God, are spoken of in the highest terms of approbation, and are admitted to intimate communion with God.**[8]*(Emphasis added)*

During the same time period, yet another white Presbyterian minister, Rev. John T. Hendrick, explained how great slavery had been for the slaves themselves:

No truth is clearer to my mind than that the hand of God is in all this matter, and that great and glorious results will follow from the existence of slavery in the United States.... How amazing and how gracious the overruling providence of God, in making use of the slave trade, as a means, indirectly, of saving more souls than all the combined missionary operations of all Christendom, within the last three hundred years....[9]

---

[7] Website: **Benjamin Morgan Palmer's "Thanksgiving Sermon" November 29, 1860.**
[8] Website: A Rhetorical Analysis of Selected Pro-Slavery Sermons by Presbyterian Clergy in the Antebellum South. Russell Pepper LSU Historical Dissertation, 1994, pg. 155
[9] Ibid, pg. 166

Hundreds more white Christian ministers in the South provided similar support for black slavery, making it clear that those Christians who supported black slavery were indeed servants of God, doing what God asked of them.

Good Christians Forcefully Condemn LGBTQs and Their Supporters

Our oppress and persecute LGBTQs culture leaves no room for doubt here. Oppressing and persecuting LGBTQs is an absolute requirement of that culture to be a good Christian. We hear it in our sermons, read it in our church literature, and experience it with our fellow church members.

1. Condemn our LGBTQ Family and Friends. You may recall that in 2020, Pete Buttigieg, the mayor of South Bend, Indiana, was one of the top ten candidates for the Democratic Party's U.S. presidential nomination. What made Mayor Buttigieg special was that he was happily married to his gay partner. In addition, he was a professing Christian. But was that possible? Can an openly gay person also be a good Christian? Of course not, says the oppress and persecute LGBTQ culture. Openly gay people cannot be good Christians, and we genuinely good Christians should take every opportunity that comes our way to forcefully tell them and the world. That is what our culture tells us we are supposed to do and exactly what Reverend Franklin Graham, a national "good Christian role model," did when he wrote:

Presidential candidate & South Bend Mayor @PeteButtigieg is right—God doesn't have a political party...But God does have commandments, laws & standards He gives us to live by. God doesn't change. His Word is the same yesterday, today & forever.

Mayor Buttigieg says he's a gay Christian. As a Christian I believe the Bible which defines homosexuality as sin, something to be repentant of, not something to be hlaunted, praised or politicized. The Bible says marriage is between a man & a woman—not two men, not two women.[10]

In other words, Reverend Graham was saying there was no way that Mayor Buttigieg could be a good Christian because good Christians do what Reverend Graham was doing…attack, ridicule, oppress, and persecute openly gay people.

But our oppress and persecute LGBTQs culture does not stop with just oppressing and persecuting gay people, it demands more…more like showing how our gay brothers and sisters are not only sinning but hurting others. I wrestled for weeks as whether to include the quote below from Reverend Ronnie Floyd, the long-term pastor of a mega church in Northwest Arkansas, past president of the Southern Baptist Convention and author of the book *The Gay Agenda*.

If you are a member of the LGBTQ community or the parents of an LGBTQ child who you love or a brother or sister or friend, I apologize for the hurt that you will feel as you read the quote below. But, ultimately, I felt that it needed to be included because it shows how cruel and insensitive the oppress and persecute LGBTQs culture can make us be. I have never met Reverend Floyd but am sure that, in many respects, he is a good man. He has certainly had a very successful career, earned a highly respected national reputation, and is viewed by many as being a good Christian role model. What he says matters to a lot of Christian people and carries great weight for them. But, he, like me and maybe like you, can become a victim of a culture that forces us to say and do things that cause others to hurt and that is exactly what his words below did for me.

I do not rise to speak on this issue with my own agenda, but I do rise to speak on this issue with God's agenda. I do rise to speak on this issue out of brokenness, realizing the many families in our own church who have lost family members to the homosexual lifestyle. I have seen them weep, grope and beg God for divine intervention. I have sat in a circle with them, their faces drooped, so burdened with

---

[10] https://www.cbsnews.com/news/franklin-graham-says-pete-buttigieg-should-repent-for-being-gay/

something that is beyond words. I have had some say to me, "Pastor Floyd, it would have been easier to have lost my child to death than to homosexuality. It is killing me." With this same burden, I have attempted to assist those who are in that lifestyle who want out but are so blinded by their sin they do not think there is a way out.

This burden translated into challenging one of our families to begin a ministry that would assist and minister support to other families who have lost sons, daughters, moms, dads, brothers, sisters, uncles and aunts to the homosexual lifestyle. This ministry is called "HOPE," meaning, Heal Our Pain El Shaddai. Due to our commitment to helping these families receive assistance, our own church and this ministry has come under attack from other churches and Christians because we even minister to these families. Well, we do believe there is hope. Through the years our ministry has also ministered to those in the gay lifestyle, attempting to see them receive what they want so desperately — deliverance.

…It appears now that everywhere you look, everything you read and everything you hear is about the gay lifestyle. Satan has taken his tool of homosexuality, a gross and evil sin, and done a con job on the American culture, making it seem like all is okay when you are gay. I hope you are aware that what was once subtle has now turned into the rage of a lion as brazen and threatening as anything in our culture. I must sound the trumpet loud and clear, praying that we do not run in retreat, but march in the truth of God valiantly. This is not a skirmish or a conflict or a disagreement, but it is a war. The war they have declared against our culture has an agenda and we need to be aware of it.[11]

Because of the hurt, I hesitate to suggest that you do so, but I do suggest that you re-read Reverend Floyd's quote because it is a classic example of how these cruel cultures work. In fact, it is almost identical to the way that the previous oppress and persecute cultures convinced Christians to murder thousands of innocent people as "witches" and millions of Jews. In your rereading, notice how this modern-day evil culture:

- Uses a highly recognized national Christian leader to encourage the evil treatment of the gay victims, very similarly to the way

---

[11]   https://www.glaad.org/blog/new-southern-baptist-convention-pres-claims-homosexuality-satans-con-job

that the previous oppress and persecute witches and Jews cultures used the Catholic popes,

- Portrays the real victims (our gay family members and friends) as villains out to destroy our Christian families,

- Portrays the real villains (Christians) as the victims who are suffering at the hands of their gay family members and friends,

- Associates gay people with Satan,

- Portrays Christians' oppression and persecution of gay people as something good ...acts of war against Satan, and

- Creates an image of emergency, calling all Christians to rise up against gay people now or lose this battle with Satan who is using gay people to destroy our religion.

Yes. That is what our oppress and persecute LGBTQs culture tells us: good Christians must defend our religion against Satan's war by ridiculing, oppressing, and persecuting gay people...and that is what too many of us do...a dark, dark and sad side of Christianity promoted by us Christian hosts of this parasitic oppress and persecute culture.

2. Condemn Those Who Support Gay Rights. The oppress and persecute LGBTQ culture does not stop with oppressing and persecuting openly gay people. Already, too many people in the secular culture and in some Christian churches are treating their LGBTQ family and friends just like anybody else...with respect, dignity, and equality. This cruel culture absolutely cannot let this trend expand into those Christian churches that it controls. It had to get the word out that "Good" Christians not only oppress and persecute LGBTQs, but also oppress and persecute the heterosexuals who treat LGBTQs with respect and dignity.

So, how do they do that? Simple: if a church becomes an LGBTQ open and confirming church, you immediately classify the members as sinners and kick them out of your association. At least, that is what the Mississippi Pine Belt Baptist Association did to University Baptist church in Hattiesburg in 2015. In explaining the excommunication, the Association leaders proclaimed:

...we, the Executive Committee, are unashamedly confident that churches affirming the homosexual lifestyle are not seeking to follow the teaching of Scripture and are not in friendly cooperation with the mission and purpose of the Mississippi Baptist Convention.[12]

In other words, the members of University Baptist Church were not good Christians (maybe not Christians at all) because good Christians condemn, oppress, and persecute openly gay people. And if you are not a good Christian, you can't stay in our association because the rest of us are all "good Christians."

3. **Good Christians Ridicule, Harass, Oppress and Persecute People of Color.** When my wife and I lived in Washington, D.C., the pastor of my Mississippi home church visited with us. This was the pastor who baptized me years earlier and who preached in our church while our deacons stood in its doors with shotguns to keep any visiting blacks out.

During my pastor's visit with us, we went downtown to see the capital on a Saturday afternoon. We parked in the Capitol parking lot and were walking up the sidewalk towards the Capitol building. On a nearby sidewalk that would soon merge with our sidewalk, walked a young mixed-race couple, having fun, laughing and holding hands. As our two sidewalks came together, my pastor suddenly jumped in front of the couple, put his hands on his hips and with a condescending voice that I had never before heard, almost shouted, "You should be ashamed of yourselves." He then just stood there with a cold glare, blocking their walk. Fortunately, the couple ignored his harassment, walked around him, and continued their walk to the Capitol steps. My pastor then looked at my wife and me with a sense of pride as if he had just done something really good.

To our shame today, neither my wife nor I confronted my pastor about his harassment. I am sure, however, that the couple's happiness for the

---

[12] https://www.wdam.com/story/30365721/hattiesburg-church-dismissed-from-baptist-association-for-affirming-homosexual-lifestyle/

day, and maybe for several weeks, was damaged because they had the misfortune of meeting a "good" white Christian. They were no longer laughing happily as they continued their walk.

We continued our walk to the Capitol steps as if nothing had happened. But what had actually happened was that my pastor had just done what his oppress and persecute Blacks culture told him that all good Christians do: denigrate and harass both black people and those who treat them with respect and dignity. And my wife and I had just done what our oppress and persecute Blacks culture told us that good Christians do: give our approval by remaining as silent as a church mouse. I know that you would have done better.

Chapter 8

Removal of Our Empathy

I have often wondered if the feeling of empathy is the greatest virtue that we can have. Could it be that when we get to the point in our lives where we can, deep within our souls, feel and understand the problems, issues, pains, barriers, and circumstances that others face as if those problems, issues, pains, barriers, and circumstances were our own, it is at that time we become a soul worthy spending eternity with God?

Roger Ebert, the famous American film critic, historian, journalist, screenwriter, and author, captured my feelings exactly with his statement:

"I believe empathy is the most essential quality of civilization".[1]

So did Melinda Gates with her statement that:

There is no morality without empathy.... Morality is loving your neighbor as yourself, which comes from seeing your neighbor as yourself, which means trying to ease your neighbor's burdens — not add to them.[2]

And so did William Blake in this poem from *Songs of Innocence and of Experience*:

Can I see another's woe,
And not be in sorrow too.
Can I see another's grief,
And not seek for kind relief.

And, of course, so does Jesus, who, in Mark 22:31, says:

---

[1] http://www.rogerebert.com/rogers-journal/cannes-7-a-campaign-for-real-movies
[2] Gates, Melinda. *The Moment of Lift: How Empowering Women Changes the World.*

… You shall love your neighbor as yourself. There is no other commandment greater than these.

It is this empathy that we Christians hold so dear to our hearts. When we see those in need, we have empathy and respond. When one of us is sick, we feel their pain and pray for them, visit them, and take them food. We feel the suffering of the homeless and contribute to our local homeless shelters, often personally cooking and serving the food. We understand the problems of the elderly and the handicapped and help repair their homes. We have food drives for our local food pantries. We make special efforts to help orphans because we feel for them. When a fellow church member has needs, we care and are there to help.

The same was true in the church of my youth and all other churches of which my wife and I have been members over the years as our careers took us to different cities. I am sure that it is true in your church. At our core, we Christians are and always have been good people who genuinely care for others, feel their pain when they hurt, and try to serve the loving God we worship.

Where Did Our Empathy Go?

So, I am sure that you join with me in looking back at our history and wondering:

- How in the world could we good Christians watch an innocent woman accused of being a witch be burned to her death and not feel her dying pains when she cried out in anguish?

- How could we Christians possibly watch a son or daughter being torn from their crying slave mother's arms and sold at an auction block and not feel the suffering and humiliation of both the child and the mother?

- What could possibly cause us Christians to have no compassion and empathy for Native Americans when our white government forcefully took their homes and lands and

Ken Boutwell

marched them hundreds of miles to new lands where they would be confined?

- How was it even possible that we German and other European Christians could watch our Jewish friends and neighbors loaded onto train cars and sent to their deaths in gas chambers and have no compassion and empathy whatsoever?

- How could I, my family and white friends and neighbors during my youth watch as our black brothers and sisters were held in cruel submission and poverty in a Jim Crow society and have no empathy whatsoever for them?
- What could possibly cause us caring Christians to have no feelings of empathy at all when a young woman who graduated at the top of her seminary class is denied a pastoral job simply because she is a woman? What happened to our human decency?

- How is it even conceivable that we Christians, who worship a loving God, cannot understand how our LGBTQ brothers and sisters feel when we ridicule and condemn them? What happened to our "do unto others as we would have them do unto us"?

What in the world happened to our empathy? Do we not see or feel this suffering and pain? Why do we have so much compassion and love for those around us who are like us, but none for those who seem even the slightest different? I wish that I knew your thoughts on these questions.

The answer, of course, is that the oppress and persecute cultures that control our lives have robbed us of our love, compassion, and empathy for these others. Instead, the cultures make us oppress and persecute, taking from us the very values that we committed to when we became a Christian...and the very values that we try to tell the world we hold today.

These cultures steal our empathy by:

- Redefining evil as good,
- Hiding the oppression and persecution under "nice" names,
- Convincing us that oppression and persecution is something good and even mandated by God.

Redefining Evil as Good.

Oppress and persecute cultures have been especially good at portraying the cruel treatment of others as something really good…something that makes both us and God feel good. In other words, redefining evil as good. These evil cultures convinced us that we were doing the "right thing" when we executed witches, took the homes and lands of Native Americans, held millions of Blacks in slavery, and executed millions of Jews. We are doing something really good today by oppressing people of color and suppressing women and LGBTQs. These cruel cultures tell us all this, and we, unfortunately, believe. And the sad, sad fact is that the cultures carry out their evil deeds through our Christian churches.

Yielding to the demands of the antebellum slavery culture of their time to make evil look good, Robert Breckinridge and Henry Ruffner, two highly respected Presbyterian ministers in the mid-1800s, wrote in an article in the *North Carolina Presbyterian* in 1858 that:

Slavery is justifiable in the sight of man and God; that system has yielded untold and inconceivable blessings to the negro race;[3]

Breckinridge and Ruffner had redefined the evil of slavery as something good which meant that when we white Christians subjected millions of black men, women, and children to slavery, we were doing something really good for them. Hence, no empathy was warranted, and, for the most part, no empathy was given by white Christians in the slaveholding states.

Also, yielding to the oppress and persecute women culture of his time, Dr. Owen Strachan, the acclaimed Midwestern Seminary theologian,

---

[3] cited in Richard J. Carwardine, *Evangelicals and Politics in Antebellum America* New Haven: Yale University Press, 1993, page 286.

wrote as to why women should be submissive to men in the home and the church. He declared that:

Biblical teaching on the sexes is not bad. It is not harmful to women. It is good—thunderously good—for women and men.[4]

With that statement, he redefined the evil of the male domination of women as something good. More than that, it was "thunderously good." And when women are being treated "thunderously good," no empathy is needed. Instead, women should be thankful when they are denied a job because that is good for them.

Hiding our oppression and persecution under nice names. Another way that our culture steals our empathy is by hiding the oppression and persecution under polite, socially acceptable names...names like:

- ✓ Separate but equal
- ✓ Complementarian
- ✓ Love the sinner but hate the sin
- ✓ Law and order

Separate but equal. As already discussed, after the Civil War and during the first half of the 1900s, the dominant Southern white culture created two separate social, economic, religious, and justice systems—an inferior, suppressive one for Blacks and a superior, dominant one for Whites. Perhaps to sooth our white consciences or, at least, to keep us from appearing as evil as the two-tier system really was, our culture created the "nice" name of "separate but equal."

I know that I, my family, and my white friends living in Mississippi during the racial segregation years firmly believed that the phrase "separate but equal" actually existed. We believed that people of color had the exact same opportunities as we did to a good education, access to health care, successful careers, stable families, crime free neighborhoods, and justice in the courts. Their poverty, poor health,

---

[4] Strachan, Owen. "Divine Order in a Chaotic Age: On Women Preaching." https://www.patheos.com/blogs/thoughtlife/2019/05/divine-order-in-a-chaotic-age-on-women-preaching/

low level/low paying jobs, and disproportionate representation in prisons were all due to their own poor work ethics, low moral values, and lack of family stability. That is what our white culture demanded that we believe, and we believed as it demanded.

We never saw that a segregated "separate but equal" system was a lie, not even when contrary facts stared us in the face. Ibram Kendi reported in his book, *How to be an Antiracist* that in 1930, Alabama was spending $37 per white student per year and $7 per black student in their "separate but equal" public schools. Georgia was spending $32 per white student and $7 per black student, and South Carolina spent $53 per white student and only $5 per black student.[5] P.D. East, a Petal, Mississippi, editor, reported in his book *The Magnolia Jungle* that in 1954 Washington County, Mississippi, was spending approximately $185 per white student per year and $50 per black student.[6]

Phrases like "separate but equal" were simply untrue. There was no equal education, no equal access to health care, no equal career opportunities, no equal justice, and no equal living conditions. But our oppressive culture kept us white Christians from seeing all those things. We had no feelings that we were oppressing people of color. We had no empathy, whatsoever, for the devastating lot in life that we had forced on them. Our culture had totally robbed us of any empathy and had, as intended, embedded almost insurmountable barriers to the economic and social success of our black brothers and sisters for generations to come.

Sadly, that same oppress and persecute Blacks culture still exists today. Too many of our white churches and communities don't believe that oppression exists, and no empathy is felt. If you don't believe me, ask some of your white evangelical friends if they feel that people of color are being oppressed today. In fact, as mentioned earlier at the end of Chapter 1, when some courageous professional football players chose to protest the oppression and persecution of their black brothers and sisters by kneeling during the national anthem, the President of the United States called them "sons of bitches," and most of us white evangelical Christians applauded. We saw no oppression and

[5] Kendi, Ibram., *How to be an Antiracist*, Penguin Random House, copyrighted 2019, pg. 175.
[6] East, P.D., *The Magnolia Jungle*. Simon and Schuster, Inc., copyrighted 1960, pg. 129.

persecution and felt no empathy. Our culture had not only robbed us of our compassion and empathy, but it went so far as to replace that compassion and empathy with contempt for the kneeling players.

Complementarian. I am not sure when the "nice" name "complementarian" was first used to describe the role of women and men in the church. Some writers credit the Council on Biblical Manhood and Womanhood (CBMW) with the first use of the term being in The Danvers Statement released by the Council in 1988. (See Chapter 5 for the full statement.)

In its simplest form, Christian complementarianism claims that men and women are equal in God's eyes but have been given different roles by the Bible both in the home and in the church. Men are given the dominant leadership roles and women the support roles, meaning that in both the church and the home, the woman must be submissive to the authority of the man. By using the term "complementarian," hosts of oppress and persecute women cultures can feel good because they have declared first that men and women are "equal" in God's eyes. That declaration, of course, hides the second demeaning "male supremist" part of the term.

But the nice name "complementarian" works like a charm in removing all empathy that we might feel for women denied professional careers in our churches and dominated in their Christian homes by the males in their family. When I asked a friend if he and his fellow complementarian Christians had any empathy for the women who are prevented from becoming ordained ministers, he responded with a quick and absolute, "No". I was sadly astounded.

When I asked why, he explained that the Bible mandates that women be submissive to men both in the home and in the church and that is their God-given role. Hence, no empathy is warranted. Still seems to me that the complementarians could have just a smidgen of empathy, maybe just enough that they could say to the women, "So sorry that the Bible mandates that you be submissive to me and my fellow men, but I hope that you understand, we absolutely must all obey every single verse in the Bible."

Since that conversation with my complementarian friend, I have wondered if today's complementarians would have any empathy for an elderly woman being burned alive after having been convicted of being a witch because their same Bible commands that witches be killed. I am guessing that you would have empathy for the elderly woman, no matter what the Bible says. I am sure that I would. In fact, I had a hard time writing the short story about the lynching of Jeremy's grandmother at the beginning of Chapter 1, even though I was only writing historical fiction.

Love the sinner but hate the sin. This is another term I am sure you've often heard applied to our LGBTQ brothers and sisters and sons and daughters. You may have even used it yourself a few times. It is a "nice" term that our culture has created to enable us to feel that we are being really kind and considerate to our LGBTQ brothers and sisters, even as we oppress and persecute them. We claim to love them as individuals, just not their "sin" as the Southern Baptist website states:

"Christians can, and should, minister to homosexuals in a kind, yet firm manner. The church should never turn its back on homosexuals who are searching and seeking to heal the hurts within their lives. ... While God hates the sinner in his sin, **we are called to love the sinner and hate the sin.** *In doing so, Christ can work through our lives to touch those lost in a world of confusion and darkness."* (Emphasis added)

"We affirm God's plan for marriage and sexual intimacy – one man, and one woman, for life. Homosexuality is not a 'valid alternative lifestyle.' The Bible condemns it as sin. It is not, however, unforgivable sin. The same redemption available to all sinners is available to homosexuals. They, too, may become new creations in Christ."[7]

In other words, by ridiculing homosexuals and, if necessary, kicking them out of our churches, we are showing our love by providing the motivation they need to reject the "sin" of loving their same gender partner...which, if not repented of, guarantees them eternity in hell. No man has more love for his fellow women and men than to do

---

7   https://www.hrc.org/resources/stances-of-faiths-on-lgbt-issues-southern-baptist-convention

everything we can, including tough love, to keep them out of hell. At least, that is what our oppress and persecute LGBTQs culture tells us... "love the sinner but hate the sin." And with that one simple phrase, we eliminate any empathy that we might have when our LGBTQ family and friends are oppressed, persecuted, and condemned by us and our churches, promoting the dark, dark side of Christianity.

Law and order. Unlike the other nice names, "law and order" is more than just a stock phrase behind which we can hide our oppression and persecution. The concept itself is essential to a functioning society. We have to have laws that govern how we treat each other, and we need law enforcement officers and courts to enforce those laws. Otherwise, we would have anarchy with our lives and possessions being in danger at all times. I am sure that we can agree that no society can function without law and order. It is essential.

However, co-opting that term which is meant to describe the essential requirement for law and order in society at large, gives oppress and persecute cultures the openings that they need. And these cultures take full advantage of these opportunities by:

- Making themselves look good by claiming that they strongly support "law and order," and
- Getting us hosts to establish and enforce laws that oppress and persecute cultural victims.

We are all familiar with the Ku Klux Klan and the horror that it thrust upon innocent non-white and non-Protestant Christian victims for decades. But did you know that it hid its terror behind the nice name of law and order, telling its members and the world that its mission was to ensure law and order in its communities? In fact, the preamble to Knights of the Ku Klux Klan's 1922 constitution states:

*To the lovers of **Law and Order**, Peace and Justice, we send greeting; and to the shades of the valiant, venerated Dead, we gratefully and affectionately dedicate the KNIGHTS OF THE KU KLUX KLAN.[8] (Emphasis added.)*

---

[8] *https://archive.org/details/ConstitutionLawsKnightsOfKKK/page/n1/mode/2up*

The Klan's membership recruiting materials were based on attracting people who wanted to contribute to maintaining law and order. For example, the Klan's November 13, 1920, advertisement in the Virginia newspaper *The Richmond News Leader* (that included a drawn picture of a hooded Klan member) read:

If you are 100% American, believe in doing things, and want to get with a real bunch of Americans who love **law and order***, and will protect the pure womanhood, our constitution and enforce its principles, Address State Secretary, P.O. Box 1874, Richmond, Va.*[9] *(Emphasis added.)*

By hiding behind the socially responsible term "law and order," the KKK was able to (or, at least, tried to) look good and respectable and yet still be an organization dedicated to terrorizing non-whites and non-Christians.

But oppress and persecute cultures aren't simply interested in reasonable societal laws. Through the use of "law and order," these cultures get us hosts to enforce their laws that oppress and persecute, all the while portraying ourselves as good "law and order" people. Nazi Germany enacted over 2,000 anti-Semitic laws that included:[10]

- Prohibiting Jews from serving in governmental jobs, as an attorney, as a tax consultant, as a newspaper editor and as a public schoolteacher
- Requiring that the letter "J" be stamped on Jewish passports
- Closing all Jewish-owned businesses
- Requiring that Jews surrender all personally owned gold, silver, diamonds, and other valuables to the government without compensation
- Prohibiting Jews from attending plays and concerts, owning telephones, having drivers licenses, and owning cars
- Prohibiting Jews and non-Jews from marrying.
- Forcing companies to fire Jewish workers and managers.

---

[9] https://www.lva.virginia.gov/exhibits/mitchell/jimcro.htm
[10] https://encyclopedia.ushmm.org/content/en/article/anti-jewish-legislation-in-prewar-germany

After enacting these oppressive laws, the Nazi government then used the nice name "law and order" to enforce them, ultimately leading to the Holocaust and execution of over six million Jews.

During my youth, thousands of state and local laws were passed with the specific purpose to segregate, subordinate, humiliate, oppress and persecute people of color and our white policeman and white judges enforced them. We had "law and order."

George Wallace, the segregationist candidate for president in 1968, ran on a "law and order" platform…a platform that made him seem like a nice man dedicated to maintaining peace and harmony in our neighborhoods. Of course, every one of us back in those days, both black and white, knew exactly what Wallace's "law and order" meant. It was a widely understood, but seldom expressed, code that meant keeping and enforcing every single one of the state and local Jim Crow laws that kept Blacks in their subordinated places and prevented them from protesting their oppression.

Although I have no idea who would want them today, you can still buy Wallace's Law and Order campaign posters, buttons, T-shirts, and mugs on the internet. The culture lives on.

Sadly, while a lot has changed since 1968, too much has not changed. The oppress and persecute Blacks culture that had control of us white evangelical Christians in the 1960s still uses the "law and order" term to subordinate people of color today. The culture still shapes the feelings and attitudes of law enforcement agencies and personnel, leading some officers to shoot unarmed black people in moments of crises. For example, between 2015 and 2021, 135 black unarmed men were killed by police in the United States.[11]

And when people across the nation took to the streets to protest these shootings, a majority of us white evangelical Christians responded with demands for "law and order." President Trump ran for re-election in 2020 on a "Law and Order" platform, and the polls showed that he had the support of over 80 percent of those of us identifying ourselves

---

[11] https://www.npr.org/2021/01/25/956177021/fatal-police-shootings-of-unarmed-black-people-reveal-troubling-patterns

as white evangelical Christians. Just as it did in the 1960s, our oppress and persecute culture still tells us that "law and order" means keeping Blacks and others in their place.

Convincing us that the oppression and persecution is something good mandated by God

After redefining evil as good, and then giving oppression and persecution "nice" names to make us feel that we are really being kind to those who we oppress and persecute, these cruel cultures deliver the final blow. They tell us that when we oppress and persecute the cultures' victims, we are doing exactly what God, through His Bible, tells us to do. That is what the really nice gentleman who I met at the Epworth by the Sea conference was saying when he responded to my concern about the subordination of women with "So, you don't believe in the authority of the Bible?" He was telling me that I should do what he and his church culture were doing: use the Bible to keep women in submission. And, when that is done, no empathy for women held in submission is needed.

And, sadly, it was the same for Christians who lived during the European witch trials, the taking of the homes and lands of Native Americans, antebellum slavery, the holocaust, and the Jim Crow racial segregation times of our history. By convincing us that we were doing what God wants us to do, our oppress and persecute cultures destroyed any feelings we might have had for the victims' pains and losses, even while the heartbreaking suffering was happening all around us.

Cole Todd may have gotten it right when she said in her book *Burn Out of a Fairy Godmother:*

Money is not the root of all evil. A lack of empathy is.

145

Chapter 9

Separating Our Own Salvation from How We Treat Others

The New Testament talks a lot about salvation...what we must do to avoid hell and get to heaven when we die. In Mathew 25, Jesus lays the requirements out in clear and simple terms:

Then I, the king, shall say to those at my right, 'come, blessed of my Father, into the kingdom prepared for you from the founding of the world. For I was hungry, and you fed me; I was thirsty, and you gave me water; I was a stranger and you invited me into your homes, I was naked and you clothed me; sick and in prison and you visited me. Mathew 25; 34-35

But Jesus does not stop with what we must do to get into heaven. He goes on to explain, again in easily understood terms, what happens to us if we do not serve the least of these:

Then I will turn to those on my left and say, "Away with you, you cursed ones, into the eternal fire prepared for the devil and his demons. For I was hungry and you wouldn't feed me; I was thirsty and you wouldn't give me anything to drink; a stranger, and you refused me hospitality; naked, and you wouldn't clothe me; sick and in prison and you didn't visit me." Mathew 25: 41-43

In addition, Jesus said in Mathew 22: 37 that the second of the two greatest commandments is "Love your neighbor as yourself" and in Mathew 7:12 "Do unto others as you would have do unto you." And in response to the question of "What must I do to inherit eternal life?" Jesus told the story in Luke 10: 25-37 of the Samaritan (a people despised, suppressed, and persecuted by Jews in those days) who stopped along the road to help a Jew who had been robbed and beaten. In the story, Jesus clearly says that eternal life depends on helping those in need.

To be perfectly clear, according to the gospels of Mathew and Luke, these messages about how our salvation is connected to how we treat others came not from Paul, or one of Jesus's disciples, or from one of the Old Testament writers, but directly from Jesus. So, I don't know about you, but it seems very clear to me that we have to love our neighbors as ourselves, do unto others as we would have them do unto us, and serve the least of these (those who are suffering) to be welcomed into heaven. And that probably means not lynching them or keeping them in slavery or murdering them in gas chambers or stealing their homes and lands or keeping them in poverty or denying them respect, dignity, and equality.

It did not matter, however, that these criteria for our salvation were given directly by Jesus himself. There was no way that the parasitic oppress and persecute cultures that have attached themselves to and taken control of our Christian institutions for centuries could let how we treat others become the basis for our salvation. It would be impossible to get us to stack the wood to burn an innocent "witch" woman alive, or to buy a slave, or to force our Jewish neighbors into cattle cars headed to their deaths if we understood those actions would mean spending our eternity in hell. We Christians couldn't be led to write papers and preach sermons to keep women in submission or to expel gay members from our churches if doing so meant that we wouldn't be entering heaven. In fact, I am almost a hundred percent sure that the deacons who stood in the doorway of the church of my youth with shotguns to keep African Americans out would not have done so had they thought that their actions would reserve an eternal home for them in hell. I know for sure that I would have spoken out a lot quicker against the oppression and persecution of my black brothers and sisters if I had thought in those days that it was required for me to join God in heaven someday.

No. In order to achieve their goals, Christian oppress and persecute cultures absolutely had to replace Jesus's criteria for who goes to heaven and who goes to hell with their own criteria that divorces our own salvation from how we treat other people, and that is exactly what these cultures did. In fact, the criteria are designed to make us host Christians actively want to oppress and persecute other people or at a minimum be silent when our fellow Christians commit such horrors, without any fear, whatsoever, that it will affect our own salvation.

Fortunately for the oppress and persecute cultures, other books in the Bible provided the needed alternative passages and it's these substitutes that the cultures latched onto. Since I am not a religious historian, I am not sure when this alternative became the perceived dominant path to salvation, but it appears to have grown out of the Protestant reformation led by Martin Luther, John Calvin, and others in the 1500s.

The way to heaven established by the oppressive cultures is "by the grace of God through our faith." But just to make sure that the criteria stated by Jesus in Mathew and Luke do not slip back in, the culture's chosen path to salvation added "not by works." In other words, we cannot get to heaven by serving the "least of these," no matter what Jesus says, because that is work. So, the way established by the oppressive cultures became "saved by the grace of God through faith, not by works."

Then to make doubly sure that Jesus's message about the importance of helping others does not creep back into our beliefs, the culture added the word "alone." In this way, according to the oppressive cultures in which we Christians have lived for centuries and many of us live today, our salvation is granted "by the grace of God through our faith, <u>alone</u>, not by works." How we treat others, including helping the "least of these" is utterly beside the point, as if Jesus had never even mentioned it in Mathew 25. It is "our faith through the grace of God, alone, not by works" that grants our salvation and has become the pillar of our Christian belief.

This message is written by our theologians, taught in our seminaries, preached in our churches, taught in our Sunday school classes, included in our creeds, written in our hymns, printed in our newsletters, and often repeated by us. Sadly, how we treat others plays no role. According to the oppress and persecute cultures in which we and our Christian ancestors lived, we could kill the witches, keep blacks in slavery, murder the Jews, steal the lands of Native Americans, keep our black brothers and sisters in poverty, subordinate women, and forcefully condemn LGBTQs but still, by the grace of God through our faith, alone, be welcomed into heaven with open arms.

I know that when I publicly professed my faith in Christ in my early teens at a summer church revival meeting and was baptized in Henry Lay's stock pond (after running the cows out), it was with the full understanding that in that moment I was guaranteed a place in heaven when my life on earth was finished. There was nothing else that I had to do. My home in heaven had been fully secured by my faith and God's grace alone.

It, of course, was not said at the revival, although it was understood by all of us, that when we left our baptism on that hot Sunday afternoon (letting the cows have their pond again), we were expected to continue our culture's mission. We were to oppress and persecute Blacks by keeping them in an oppressive, segregated Jim Crow society and most especially keeping them out of our white churches, even if it required shotguns to do so. It was okay to use the "n" word at church, and we often did. Also, we were expected to keep women in submission and to condemn all our homosexual brothers and sisters (all of whom tried to keep their sexual orientation hidden in those days). Actually, these were more than expectations. They were unspoken, but fully understood, mandates established by our white Christian oppress and persecute culture, and no one in our white church dared violate them. We seldom, if ever, talked about them. We just did them because that was what we were supposed to do.

I am sure that those passages in Matthew and Luke where Jesus clearly stated the criteria for going to heaven must have been mentioned by my church during my youth at some point in time, but I do not recall it. Other messages about my salvation being based on faith alone were far more prevalent . In fact, now that I think about it, I do not recall ever hearing a sermon or reading a Sunday school lesson during my entire life based on Jesus' declaration in Mathew 25 that we go to hell if we don't serve the least of these and go to heaven if we do. Out of curiosity, I asked ten of my Christian friends and acquaintances if they had ever heard a sermon about Jesus' Mathew declaration, and they all said "no." Clearly, our oppress and persecute cultures have been highly successful in keeping this message under wraps. I hope, however, that you have heard and read Jesus's message because it seems pretty important.

Even the jokes that we white Christians told each other back then ignored Jesus' commandment to have empathy for others and treat them with respect and dignity. I remember one that we Whites thought was really funny back then. I share it here to help you understand just how firm a hold the oppress and persecute Blacks culture had on us at the time:

A young black boy had unexpectedly died, gone to his final judgement, and was being interviewed by Saint Peter, who asked him to give a quick summary of his life. So, the young boy explained that he had worked hard to help his people achieve equality by overcoming racial segregation. He had participated in Civil Rights protests, had been one of the first black students to enroll in a white public school, and had just become the very first black person to join a white Baptist church. Saint Peter was very complimentary and immediately admitted him to heaven. As the young boy stood to leave the room, St. Peter asked if he had any questions. The boy responded, "I do have one. How long are they supposed to hold your head under water when they baptize you?"

The fact that that joke was hilarious to us white Christians back in those days (but I hope not to you in these days) tells you all you need to know about what we "good" Christians who believed that we had been saved by the grace of God through faith alone—were thinking, saying, and doing to others. In our minds, how we treated our black brothers and sisters played no role, whatsoever, in our salvation. Not only did we not speak out when people of color (and their white supporters) were beaten and murdered for protesting their oppression and persecution, we actually told and laughed at jokes where good white Christians murdered Blacks.

Historically, we know what the world looks like when the "saved by the grace of God through faith, alone, not by works" path to salvation is prevalent, and it's not pretty. In fact, it is horrible. It has resulted in millions held in poverty and slavery. Millions murdered, and millions more oppressed and damned…all in God's holy name! And this dark, dark Christian oppression and persecution continues to this very day.

What do you think the world would look like if our culture had allowed us to take Jesus' Mathew 25 criteria for our final destination seriously? What would we Christians have done differently over the years if we had believed and acted in accordance with Jesus's words, that our salvation depends on how we treat other people...that we go to heaven if we serve the least of these and hell if we don't? Of course, we know that the "authority of the Bible" that demands that certain biblical verses be used to oppress and persecute other people does not apply to Jesus's declaration in Mathew 25. He was just flat out wrong. Our culture has already told us that.

But, just for a moment, let's ask ourselves what if Jesus were right in Mathew 25? Would we live in peace with each other and without war? Would we spend our time helping each other instead of hurting each other? Would people of all races and ethnicities be joined together in harmony to worship our God? Would there have been no slavery, no lynching, no Jim Crow laws, no holocaust, no subordination of women, and no condemnation of our gay brothers and sisters? Would church associations not expel churches with women pastors and those who openly confirm gay rights? Would there be no need for professional football players to kneel during the national anthem to call attention to the brutal treatment of their black brothers and sisters? Would they not have been called "sons of bitches" when they kneeled? Would women not be called "____ bitches" when they occupy positions of leadership? **Would all of these evil, horrible, and frankly ungodly things that we Christians have done to others over the years been replaced by peace, harmony, love, respect, service, compassion, and empathy if our salvation depended on how we treated other people?**

Unfortunately, we will never know because our oppress and persecute cultures have total control over our beliefs about how we get to heaven, and it is "by the grace of God through our faith, alone, not by works." And with this belief, based on our history, we are free to, and do, treat other people as cruelly as we want without any fear that it will affect our salvation.

I hope that you will forgive my attempt at satire at this point, but I keep envisioning my standing in front of God on my judgement day and hearing God say, "I don't see any record of your having helped any of the 'least of these.'" I respond as my culture taught: "I know, God, but that was work, and I know that we can't be saved by works. But I have faith, and I know that Your grace will save me. That, alone, is all that I need." That vision is followed by one of God turning to Lucifer and saying, "Another one for you."

Chapter 10

Absolute Rejection of Social Justice as a Part of the Christian Gospel

Over the past several decades, the social justice movements in the secular sector that have treated minorities, women and LGBTQ people with respect, dignity and equality has begun to threaten the very foundations of the white Christian oppress and persecute cultures. Even some mainline Christian churches have begun to preach that Jesus' teachings on how we treat others matters. Marcus Borg, the highly respected and widely published theologian says in his book *Days of Awe and Wonder*:

Jesus was...filled with a passion for justice..........It set him against a politically oppressive and economically exploitive system that had been designed by wealthy and powerful elites in their own narrow self-interests and then legitimized by religion.......God's justice is social justice.[1]

However, no matter what Marcus Borg says or the secular culture is doing or the mainline churches are beginning to teach and do, the evangelical Christian oppress and persecute cultures have gone beyond separating our salvation from how we treat other people (salvation by faith alone) to try to kill the idea that social justice is a part of the Christian church and gospel in any way. Otherwise, the cultures risk how we treat other people becoming an important part of our Christian responsibilities.

Fortunately for the oppress and persecute cultures, thousands of their white Christian hosts have stepped forward to remove social justice from Christian beliefs or, at least, do their very best to do so. These cultures demand that social justice not only be condemned as a part of being Christian, but that social *injustice* actually be ordained as being a

---

[1] Borg, Marcus J. *Days of Awe and Wonder*, HarperCollins Publishers, copyright 2017, pgs. 136-137.

part being a Christian, i.e., God actually demands through His Bible that Christians oppress and persecute others.

Removal of Social Justice from the Christian Gospel

Led by Georgia Baptist pastor and founder of G3 Ministries, Rev. Josh Buice met along with fourteen preachers and theologians at a Dallas restaurant on June 19, 2018, to discuss the secular encroachment of social justice into the Christian gospel. That meeting eventually resulted in the production of *The Statement on Social Justice and the Gospel.*

Those participants included Florida Baptist pastor and now President of Founders Ministries, Rev. Tom Ascol, who drafted the first document and Dr. John MacArthur, a renowned national author, Christian speaker, and highly respected pastor-teacher at Grace Community Church in Sun Valley, California. By the latest count that I can find on the internet, the statement has been signed by over 10,000 Christian churches and individuals.[2] I was unable to verify that all of the signers were white male Christians, but we can be sure that most of them were, given the messages in the statement. The statement begins with:

In view of questionable sociological, psychological, and political theories presently permeating our culture and making inroads into Christ's church, we wish to clarify certain key Christian doctrines and ethical principles prescribed in God's Word. Clarity on these issues will fortify believers and churches to withstand an onslaught of dangerous and false teachings that threaten the gospel, misrepresent Scripture, and lead people away from the grace of God in Jesus Christ.

*Specifically, we are deeply concerned that values borrowed from secular culture are currently undermining Scripture in the areas of race and ethnicity, manhood and womanhood, and human sexuality. The Bible's teaching on each of these subjects is being challenged under the broad and somewhat **nebulous rubric of concern for "social justice."** If the doctrines of God's Word are not uncompromisingly reasserted and defended at these points, there is every reason to anticipate that **these dangerous ideas and corrupted moral values will spread their influence into other realms of biblical doctrines and principles.**[3] (Emphasis added)*

---

[2] https://en.wikipedia.org/wiki/Statement_on_Social_Justice_and_the_Gospel#History
[3] https://statementonsocialjustice.com/

The statement very clearly declares the Christian oppress and persecute cultures' beliefs that the secular culture's increasing movement toward treating people with respect, dignity and equality (e.g., social justice) are "dangerous ideas" based on "corrupted moral values" that could "spread their influence."

As illustrated by the following excerpts, the Statement then goes on to set out 14 affirmations and denials that not only reject social justice as being an integral part of the Christian gospel but actually ordain social *injustice* as a required part of that gospel.

SCRIPTURE

WE AFFIRM *that the Bible is God's Word, breathed out by him. It is inerrant, infallible, and the final authority for determining what is true (what we must believe) and what is right (how we must live). All truth claims and ethical standards must be tested by God's final Word, which is Scripture alone.*

WE DENY *that Christian belief, character, or conduct can be dictated by any other authority, and we deny that the postmodern ideologies derived from intersectionality, radical feminism, and critical race theory are consistent with biblical teaching. We further deny that competency to teach on any biblical issue comes from any qualification for spiritual people other than clear understanding and simple communication of what is revealed in Scripture.*

This statement is a critical part of the white oppress and persecute cultures which have attached themselves, like parasites, to us Christians and our organizations. Their strategy totally rejects the "postmodern ideologies" that social justice is "consistent with biblical teaching." In other words, the ways that the dominant groups oppress and persecute marginalized groups through racial and gender relations do not even exist and, even if they did, this is "consistent with scriptural teachings." It puts forth that we white Christians are not going to listen, not even for one moment, to the concerns of our minority brothers and sisters that systemic discrimination against people of color still exists within our nation's laws, regulations, economic activities, educational system, criminal justice system, and social customs (critical race theory). Those suffering can complain all they want, but we white Christians refuse to hear them and deny that their concerns have any validity.

Ken Boutwell

GOSPEL

WE AFFIRM *that the gospel is the divinely-revealed message concerning the person and work of Jesus Christ—especially his virgin birth, righteous life, substitutionary sacrifice, atoning death, and bodily resurrection—revealing who he is and what he has done with the promise that he will save anyone and everyone who turns from sin by trusting him as Lord.*

WE DENY that **anything else, whether works to be performed or opinions to be held, can be added to the gospel without perverting it into another gospel.** *This also means that implications and applications of the gospel, such as the obligation to live justly in the world, though legitimate and important in their own right, are not definitional components of the gospel. (Emphasis added)*

So, the statement declares that helping other people ("works to be performed and opinions to be held") perverts the gospel "into another gospel." In other words, how we treat other people not only has absolutely nothing to do (*"not definitional components of"*) with the Christian gospel but is, actually, totally contrary to the gospel.

SALVATION

WE AFFIRM *that salvation is granted by God's grace alone received through faith alone in Jesus Christ alone. Every believer is united to Christ, justified before God, and adopted into his family. Thus, in God's eyes there is no difference in spiritual value or worth among those who are in Christ. Further, all who are united to Christ are also united to one another regardless of age, ethnicity, or sex. All believers are being conformed to the image of Christ. By God's regenerating and sanctifying grace all believers will be brought to a final glorified, sinless state of perfection in the day of Jesus Christ.*

WE DENY that salvation can be received in any other way. *We also deny that salvation renders any Christian free from all remaining sin or immune from even grievous sin in this life. We further deny that ethnicity excludes anyone from understanding the gospel, nor does anyone's ethnic or cultural heritage mitigate or remove the duty to repent and believe. (Emphasis added)*

This statement reaffirms the Christian oppress and persecute cultures' position that social justice plays no role in a Christian's salvation, no matter what Jesus says in Mathew 25. Instead, salvation is a grant from God by His grace alone, leaving Christians free to subordinate, oppress, and persecute other people at will. In fact, as we will see in the statements below, the subordination, oppression, and persecution of others is even required by the Bible according to this group of believing Christians.

THE CHURCH

WE AFFIRM *that the primary role of the church is to worship God through the preaching of his word, teaching sound doctrine, observing baptism and the Lord's Supper, refuting those who contradict, equipping the saints, and evangelizing the lost. We affirm that when the primacy of the gospel is maintained that this often has a positive effect on the culture in which various societal ills are mollified. We affirm that, under the lordship of Christ, we are to obey the governing authorities established by God and pray for civil leaders.*

WE DENY that political or social activism should be viewed as integral components of the gospel or primary to the mission of the church. *Though believers can and should utilize all lawful means that God has providentially established to have some effect on the laws of a society, we deny that these activities are either evidence of saving faith or constitute a central part of the church's mission given to her by Jesus Christ, her head. We deny that laws or regulations possess any inherent power to change sinful hearts. (Emphasis added)*

As demanded by the oppress and persecute cultures that caused this statement to be written and signed by thousands of evangelical Christians, the statement reaffirms, one more time, that social justice has no role in the Christian church. Based on that, historically, the Christian church had no responsibility to intervene in the killing of innocent women as witches, keeping blacks in slavery, executing millions of Jews, and keeping Blacks in an oppressive, segregated society. And it has no role, today, in seeking social justice for our fellow men and women.

SEXUALITY AND MARRIAGE

WE AFFIRM *that God created mankind male and female and that this divinely determined distinction is good, proper, and to be celebrated. Maleness and femaleness are biologically determined at conception and are not subject to change. The curse of*

157

sin results in sinful, disordered affections that manifest in some people as same-sex attraction. Salvation grants sanctifying power to renounce such dishonorable affections as sinful and to mortify them by the Spirit. We further affirm that God's design for marriage is that one woman and one man live in a one-flesh, covenantal, sexual relationship until separated by death. Those who lack the desire or opportunity for marriage are called to serve God in singleness and chastity. This is as noble a calling as marriage.

WE DENY *that human sexuality is a socially constructed concept. We also deny that one's sex can be fluid.* **We reject "gay Christian" as a legitimate biblical category.** *We further deny that any kind of partnership or union can properly be called marriage other than one man and one woman in lifelong covenant together. We further deny that people should be identified as "sexual minorities"— which serves as a cultural classification rather than one that honors the image-bearing character of human sexuality as created by God. (Emphasis added)*

Through this statement, the oppress and persecute LGBTQs culture makes it clear: the condemnation, oppression and persecution of our gay brothers and sisters by Christians is not social injustice and will never be recognized as such. Instead, as demanded by their culture, the signing Christians proudly announce their commitment to continue the condemnation, oppression, and persecution of every last one of our LGBTQ brothers and sisters, plus all of us who affirm and support them.

COMPLEMENTARIANISM

WE AFFIRM *that God created mankind both male and female with inherent biological and personal distinctions between them and that these created differences are good, proper, and beautiful. Though there is no difference between men and women before God's law or as recipients of his saving grace, we affirm that God has designed men and women with distinct traits and to fulfill distinct roles.* **These differences are most clearly defined in marriage and the church, but are not irrelevant in other spheres of life. In marriage the husband is to lead, love, and safeguard his wife and the wife is to respect and be submissive to her husband in all things lawful. In the church, qualified men alone are to lead as pastors/elders/bishops and preach to and teach the whole congregation.** *We further affirm that the image of God is expressed most fully* *and beautifully in human society when men and women walk in obedience to their God-ordained roles and serve according to their God-given gifts. (Emphasis added)*

WE DENY *that the God-ordained differences in men's and women's roles disparage the inherent spiritual worth or value of one over the other, nor do those differences in any way inhibit either men or women from flourishing for the glory of God.*

The 10,000+ evangelical Christian churches and individuals who signed the document have spoken clearly through their support of this statement. As demanded by their oppress and persecute women culture, the suppression of women in the home, in the church and in **"other spheres of life"** is not social injustice. The gospel actually demands that women be suppressed, and every male Christian must treat women accordingly.

You can treat your wife that way if you want. I choose to treat my wife as my equal or better.

RACE/ETHNICITY

WE AFFIRM *God made all people from one man. Though people often can be distinguished by different ethnicities and nationalities, they are ontological equals before God in both creation and redemption. "Race" is not a biblical category, but rather a social construct that often has been used to classify groups of people in terms of inferiority and superiority. All that is good, honest, just, and beautiful in various ethnic backgrounds and experiences can be celebrated as the fruit of God's grace. All sinful actions and their results (including evils perpetrated between and upon ethnic groups by others) are to be confessed as sinful, repented of, and repudiated.*

WE DENY *that Christians should segregate themselves into racial groups or regard racial identity above, or even equal to, their identity in Christ. We deny that any divisions between people groups (from an unstated attitude of superiority to an overt spirit of resentment) have any legitimate place in the fellowship of the redeemed.* **We reject any teaching that encourages racial groups to view themselves as privileged oppressors or entitled victims of oppression. While we are to weep with those who weep, we deny that a person's feelings of offense or oppression necessarily prove**

that someone else is guilty of sinful behaviors, oppression, or prejudice.[4] (Emphasis added)

The denial is clear. This group of all, or almost all, white evangelicals totally reject the idea that racial "victims of oppression" should feel any right to relief from their oppression. Their feelings of oppression do not, in any way, mean that they are or were oppressed, and it should not make those who committed the oppression feel any guilt whatsoever. The murder of millions of Jews does not make those who murdered them guilty of sinful behaviors, no matter what the Jews say. The holding of millions of black people in slavery for several hundred years does not make those who held them in slavery guilty of any sinful behavior, no matter what the slaves said. Subjecting millions of black people to Jim Crow laws that kept them in a poverty-stricken, segregated society for over a hundred years does not make those who kept them in that society guilty, no matter what the victims say. It is we white Christian oppressors, not the victims, who get to decide if we are "guilty of sinful behaviors, oppression, or prejudices." We may "weep" a little when they weep, but our oppress and persecute culture will never, ever let us feel any guilt when they cry out for mercy, much less actually help.

And so, thousands of white evangelical Christians have spoken as demanded by their oppressive culture: How we treat other people has absolutely nothing to do with our salvation. As we white Christians have done throughout our history, we can and will continue to oppress and persecute other people as long as our Christian heart's desire and will never feel any guilt......A dark and sad side of Christianity of which the oppress and persecute cultures are proud.

Social Justice is Communism

But a belief in social justice is not only not Christian, it is communism and fascism, as explained by the oppress and persecute culture host, Glen Beck, the acclaimed radio and television host:

---

[4] https://statementonsocialjustice.com/

Where I go to church, there are members that preach social justice as members—my faith doesn't—but the members preach social justice all the time. It is a perversion of the gospel….

Social justice was the rallying cry-economic justice and social justice-the rallying cry on both the communist front and the fascist front. *That is not an American idea. And if we don't get off the social justice economic justice bandwagon, if you are not aware of what this is, you are in grave danger. All of our faiths—my faith your faith—whatever your church is, this is infecting all of them…. (Emphasis added.)*

I beg you, look for the words 'social justice' or 'economic justice' on your church Web site. If you find it, run as fast as you can. Social justice and economic justice, they are code words. Now, am I advising people to leave their church? Yes! …

If you have a priest that is pushing social justice, go find another parish. Go alert your bishop and tell them, "Excuse me are you down with this whole social justice thing?" If it's my church, I'm alerting the church authorities: "Excuse me, what's this social justice thing?" And if they say, "Yeah, we're all in that social justice thing"—I'm in the wrong place.[5]

Church Literature that Supports Social Justice Must Be Banned

National rhetoric statements like the above are highly effective in promoting Christian cultural beliefs and behaviors, but it is at the local level where these evil cultures are most effective in carrying out their cruel deeds. This is where we Christians teach the biblical messages and values that guide our lives and those of our children. It's where these cruel cultures have been most effective in removing social justice from the gospel. Accordingly, it is at the local level where these cultures seek to ban all literature that suggests that the way that we treat others is a critical part of the gospel.

Banning (most often, actually burning) books and teachings has, of course, been a long-standing trait of oppressive cultures. History has recorded hundreds and hundreds of such burnings which most often

---

5 https://sojo.net/articles/glenn-beck-responds-social-justice-perversion-gospel

seemed to burn books proposing justice for those being persecuted. A few quick examples are:

- In perhaps the first recorded banning of literature, Babylon King Jehoiakim's burned Jeremiah's scroll, as described in Jeremiah 36:23.

- As a part of oppressing and persecuting Jews in the mid-1200s, Christian officials in France denounced Hebrew books as "blasphemous" and ordered that twenty-four carts of the confiscated books be delivered to a public burning.[6]

- In 1497, the Christian church in Florence, Italy, had public book burnings that included books written by celebrated authors such as Dante, Boccaccio and Savonarola, after declaring the authors heretics.[7]

- Martin Luther's books were burned in St. Paul's churchyard in England in 1521.[8]

- In 1596, King James of England ordered that all copies of Reginald Scott's book, *Discovery of Witchcraft,* which argued against the execution of witches, be burned.[9]

- The "Slave Bible" published in England in 1807 for use by white missionaries witnessing to slaves in the West Indies banned (i.e., excluded and left out) all biblical support for social justice in the form of "references to freedom and escape from slavery, "and retained only those "passages encouraging obedience and submission…" The result was that ninety percent of the Old Testament and half of the New Testament were excluded.[10]

- In 1859, Christians all over the South, including churches, held public burnings of copies of the abolitionist sermons preached

---

[6] https://www.enotes.com/topics/book-burning
[7] Ibid
[8] Ibid
[9] https://salemwitchmuseum.com/product/the-discoverie-of-witchcraft/
[10] https://en.wikipedia.org/wiki/Slave_Bible#:~:text=The%20slave%20Bible%20is%20an%20edition%20of%20the,of%20the%20British%20Empire

and published by London, England, pastor, Rev. Charles Spurgeon, that advocated social justice in the form of freedom for antebellum slaves. The Southern culture had to absolutely ban any ideas that social justice for slaves was a part of the Christian gospel.[11]

- One of the largest book burnings in history occurred in 1933 when the Nazis launched a nationwide banning of books deemed to be "un- German." On just one of many nights, May 10, over 25,000 books, including books written by Thomas Mann, Erich Maria Remarque, Ernest Hemingway, André Gide, Jack London, Upton Sinclair, and Margaret Sanger were taken from public libraries and burned. High on the list of burned books were those written by Jews as well as those supporting the equal treatment of Jews. Through these book burnings, the oppress and persecute Jews culture of that time was able (or, at least, was making a major attempt} to remove the teachings that social justice, especially justice for Jews, was a critical part of human relations.[12]

- During my youth in the 1950s and '60s, many white churches in Mississippi banned Sunday morning study guides (published by national church organizations) when the literature started mentioning that social justice in the form of racial integration and equality was the Christian thing to do. Why? The Board of Deacons at the Moss Hill Baptist Church explained it quite simply: the literature failed to "systematically teach the Scriptures" and gave too much attention "to racial issues— which we believe communistically influenced."[13] There was no way that the oppressive cultures in those dogmatic white segregated churches could allow their members to read such "heretical" ideas that violated the Bible's commandments that the races be kept separate and pure. Although I do not recall my own church during my youth specifically banning any literature,

---

[11]   https://www.thegospelcoalition.org/article/why-american-south-would-have-killed-charles-spurgeon/

[12] https://www.enotes.com/topics/book-burning

[13] Dupont, Carolyn Renee, *Mississippi Praying*. New York University Press, Copyrighted 213, pg. 110

> I do know that our pastor and church leaders did not tolerate, for even one moment, a lesson supporting social justice for people of color. That was our culture and we obeyed it.

After living through that experience as a youth and knowing of the many book burnings throughout history by tyrannical regimes, I never thought that I would see the same thing happen again, especially in the twenty-first century. But these oppressive cultures never give up and are always out there seeking to make sure that we Christians never, ever allow how we treat others become a part of the gospel. They act boldly whenever they find an accepting host.

Ironically, just as I was writing this chapter, the pastoral staff in my predominately white Southern Baptist Tallahassee church did exactly what our church's oppress and persecute culture required of them. Like Babylon King Jehoiakim in the Old Testament, like the Church leaders in France in the mid-1200s and Italy in the 1497, like King James in 1596, like the Slave Bible in 1807, like the Nazis in Germany in 1933, and like the Mississippi churches of my youth, they mounted a campaign to banish teachings in our church that promoted social justice as a part of the Christian gospel. Our pastoral staff spent days reviewing the Smith and Helwys' (a church literature publishing company) study guides used by three of our adult study classes and produced a scathing twenty-page critique.

The critique began by describing the theological background of past authors, being very careful to point out that:

- Several of them were women.
- Some of them were associated with other, more liberal organizations (i.e., the Seattle School of Theology & Psychology, "a progressive, multi-denominational institution.")
- One of them worked for a seminary that served other denominations, including "African Methodist Episcopal" churches,
- Some of them are known for writing about "…racial issues, but no genuine gospel."

- In addition to being a woman, one of them is an associate pastor with the United Church of Christ that "boast of their LGBTQ+ affirmations."

At a church wide meeting to discuss the banning of the literature, the pastoral author of the critique added that people of the United Church of Christ are not Christians. This meant, among other things, that in his culture, the suppression of women and condemnation of LGBTQs, which United Church of Christ people do not do, is required to be a Christian. Individuals not doing so are simply not Christians.

This, of course, is a common trait of oppressive cultures. They make their Christian hosts believe that those who support social justice as a part of the Christian gospel are not only not good Christians, they are not Christians at all. You will recall from earlier chapters that this same allegation was made by Christian ministers and theologians against those who objected to the murder of women accused of being witches and against those who opposed ante-bellum slavery. Those people were not Christians at all.

The critique placed a great deal of emphasis on the fact that several of the authors supported LGBTQ rights, some wrote on racial issues, and some promoted the equality of women….all absolutely unacceptable and heresy beliefs in our church culture. The critique went on to damn the literature for failing to teach the truth and authority of the Bible, and then stated:

"When the gospel is mentioned, it is treated more as a matter of social justice and action than as the good news of reconciliation of sinners to a holy God through Jesus Christ's death and resurrection."

The critique alleged that the Smith and Helwys literature is closely aligned with a national church organization that has a personnel policy allowing the employment of gay people and has a publicly stated belief that women should be treated equally to men. The critique specifically pointed out that one of the stated beliefs of the national organization is:

"...the participation of women and men in all aspects of church leadership and Christian ministry."

In short, the critique damned the Smith & Helwys literature for not being true to a literal interpretation of the Bible and for supporting the idea that social justice is an important part of being a Christian. There was no way that our church's dominant oppress and persecute women and LGBTQs culture could allow these teachings to continue. Accordingly, our pastoral staff did exactly what their culture demanded of them: recommended that our church ban the use of all Smith and Helwys literature. When I facetiously asked, in a church wide meeting, if those of us who wanted to continue to use the literature could purchase our own books, the response was "No, if our recommendation is accepted by the congregation, that literature will not be allowed within the church building."

The pastoral staff's recommendation was passed on to a pastoral selected committee and then to the church's deacons, and both groups did exactly what our culture wanted...approved the literature ban. The issue was then carried to the church congregation who voted three to one to ban the literature.

And just like that, the dominant oppress and persecute culture in our church removed all "heretical" teaching that social justice is a part of the Christian gospel, eliminating (or, at least, attempting to eliminate) any potential opposition within our church to its suppression of women and damnation of our LGBTQ friends and family members. It was a sad and dark, dark day at our church, but one that our culture loved and will hold on to as long as possible.

Replacing Social Justice with Murder

As a side note, I guess that I should consider myself fortunate. I, of course, spoke and voted against the literature ban in our church. The good news is that I was able to leave the meeting with no physical harm for my "heresy." Michael Servetus was not so fortunate in 1553 when he theologically disagreed with John Calvin, a now highly regarded theologian in many Christian Protestant churches. With Calvin's strong support (actually, Calvin wanted him beheaded), Servetus was burned at the stake along with some of his publications on October

27, 1553, by the local city council who convicted him of "heresy."[14] In fact, in many ways, Servetus' murder was premeditated by Calvin because he wrote in a letter to a friend in 1546:

"Servetus offers to come hither, if it be agreeable to me. But I am unwilling to pledge my word for his safety, for if he shall come, I shall never permit him to depart alive, provided my authority be of any avail."[15]

Clearly, John Calvin did not believe that social justice had anything to do with the Christian gospel and one's salvation, including his own salvation. In fact, the oppress and persecute culture of his day had not only removed social justice from the Christian gospel but replaced it with social <u>injustice</u> in the form of murder as a part of being a Christian. That may help explain why Calvin preached so strongly that we are saved "by our faith and God's grace alone, not by works." Like all Christians who choose to oppress and persecute others, he had to find a way to heaven that, in his own mind, did not depend on how he treated other people. That is how strong these horrible cultures can become...so strong that they destroy everything in us that Christ stood for during His human time with us...a sad and dark, dark side of our Christianity.

Victims See Injustice Different from Us White Christians

While dominant white Christian cultures rid the gospel of all social justice requirements and release us from all guilt, the victims of our oppression and persecution see it totally different, as illustrated by the following excerpt from Howard Thurman's book *Jesus and the Disinherited:*[16]

...chopping cotton beneath the torrid skies, the slave said to his mate:

I got shoes.
You got shoes
All God's children got shoes

---

[14] https://en.wikipedia.org/wiki/Michael_Servetus
[15] https://www.reenactingtheway.com/blog/john-calvin-had-people-killed-and-bad-bible-interpretation-justified-it
[16] Thurman, Howard, *Jesus and the Disinherited,* Beacon Press, Copyrighted 1976, pg. 51

Ken Boutwell

When we get to heaven
We're goin' to put on our shoes
An' shout all over God's heaven
Heaven! Heaven!

Then, looking up to the big house where the master lived, he said:

Everbody talkin' bout heaven
Ain't goin' there!

Chapter 11

Rewarding Those Who Actively Oppress and Persecute Others

A well-known adage in organizational management is, "Be careful what you incentivize because that is what you will get." These oppress and persecute cultures take this principle seriously and know exactly what to incentivize to get us to oppress and persecute their victims.

Reward for Executing Witches. Heinrich Kramer and Jacobus Sprenger, the theologians who wrote *Malleus Maleficarum*, were rewarded handsomely for their brutal treatment of innocent people, mostly women, accused of being witches. They were appointed as prestigious agents of the church by Pope Innocent VIII, given extensive preaching opportunities, and between 1487 and 1669 thirty-six editions of their book were published.[1]

I wonder if Kramer and Springer ever thanked God for their tremendous success in life? I am sure that the hosts of the oppress and persecute witches culture were thrilled. So, maybe they thanked God. I doubt that the murdered women and men and their families did.

Rewards for Taking the Lands and Homes of Native Americans

The rewards promised to the white Christian settlers arriving in droves from Europe in the 1500 to 1900 years were nothing short of astounding. In 1500, what is now the United States and Canada was home to an estimated 7 to 18 million Native Americans which were organized into an estimated 600 tribes who spoke diverse languages. The combination of these factors essentially eliminated their ability to speak and act as one political body. While the tribes occupied lands on which they lived, hunted and grew their food, no formal laws of land

---

[1] https://en.wikipedia.org/wiki/Malleus_Maleficarum

ownership existed. In fact, as Alan Eckert explains in his exhaustively researched book *That Dark and Bloody River*, the Native Amerocan tribes:

...knew that land belonged to no one; it was a gift of their god... to His...children, but not a possession. Rather, it was a treasure in trust, given to them only to use wisely and well and then to pass on to future generations in as natural a state as when they received it. They could not comprehend the ownership of land as whites owned things. They were merely the guardians of a deeply revered trust and they had no intention of meekly turning away from it.[2]

If a tribe lived on a land, they "owned" it in "trust" until such time that they elected to move to another land which they then occupied and "owned" in "trust" again. The setting was perfect for the arriving Europeans with their completely different beliefs about land ownership. Under the religious and legal cover of the Doctrine of Discovery issued by the Catholic Popes (discussed earlier in Chapter 5), European kings began granting American lands to elite white settlers and companies, no matter who was occupying them at the time, and carefully documenting their new ownership in written records. After all, as Increase Mather, a highly respected Puritan clergyman and twenty-year president of Harvard, described, this was a land occupied by:

Heathen People amongst whom we live, and whose Land the Lord God of our Fathers hath given to us for a rightfull Possession.[3]

The rewards, of course, were the lands themselves and all that they contained (i.e., gold, silver, game, fertile valleys, beautiful plains, streams of pure water, and majestic mountains). The fact that they were also the ancient homelands of Native Americans and their communities, as well as their sources of food, water, and clothing, was just an inconvenience that had to be dealt with in whatever way necessary. With such huge rewards "granted by God, Himself," dangling in front of wave after wave of immigrating Europeans, a culture of oppressing and persecuting Native Americans quickly took

---

[2] Eckert, Akan, *That Dark and Bloody River*, Bantam Books, Copyrighted 1995, page xxxvii
[3] Mather, Increase, A Brief History of the Warre with the Indians in New-England (Boston, 1676)

control and still thrives today. All methods of oppression and persecution were permissible, including murder, scalping, killing their livestock and crops and driving them out of their fertile homelands onto barren reservation lands.

In 1863, General Carlton in New Mexico, wrote out the following words for Major Carlson to exactly say to the captured Navahos:

Go to the Bosque Redondo (a designated barren reservation), or we will pursue and destroy you. We will not make peace with you on any other terms.... This war shall be pursued against you if it takes years, now that we have begun, until you cease to exist or move. There can be no other talk on the subject.[4]

About the same time General Carlton wrote the War Department Headquarters asking for additional troops because of a new gold strike just west of the Navaho country. The additional troops were needed, he wrote:

...to whip the Indians and to protect the people going to and at the mines....Providence has indeed blessed us....the gold lies here at our feet to be had by the mere picking of it up![5]

As General Carlton explained to his superiors, the rewards were clearly worth taking the lands and homes of the Navahos and feeding them rations:

These six thousand mouths must eat, and these six thousand bodies must be clothed. When it is considered **what a magnificent pastoral and mineral country they have surrendered to us—a country whose value can hardly be estimated**—*the mere pittance, in comparison, which must at once be given to support them, sinks into insignificance as a price* **for their natural heritage.**[6] *(Emphasis added)*

These huge rewards existed all over the Americas as this story was repeated for almost all of the approximately six hundred Native

---

[4] Brown, Dee, *Bury My Heart at Wounded Knee,* Henry Holt and Company, Copyrighted 1970, page 25
[5] Ibid
[6] Ibid

American tribes…at least for those tribes that were not totally eradicated by the invading white Christians and the diseases they brought with them.

And what were the white Christian preachers and theologians saying during these years? Instead of speaking out in defense of the Native Americans, they were busy helping to build this inhumane oppressive culture where the Natives were viewed as worthless individuals.

Cotton Mather, Increase's son and highly respected clergyman and author in his own right, declared in a 1698 Thanksgiving sermon:

The Indians are Infamous, especially for Three Scandalous Qualities: They are Lazy Drones, and love Idleness Exceedingly! They are also most impudent Lyars, and will invent Reports and Stories at a strange and monstrous rate; and they are out of measure Indulgent unto their Children, there is no Family-Governance among them.[7]

In a speech to New England militiamen fighting French and Indian belligerents in King William's War (1688-97), Mather quoted the Bible and exhorted:

At the first Appearance of the Tawny Pagans, then Courage brave Hearts; Fall on! Fall on Couragiously, with that Appearance in Psal. 3.6,7. I will not be afraid of ten thousands of the people that have set themselves against me. O my God, thou hast smitten all mine Enemies. Yea, when once you have but got the Track of those Ravenous howling Wolves, then pursue them vigorously; Turn not back until they are consumed: Wound them that they shall not be able to Arise; Tho' they Cry Let there be none to Save them; But beat them small as the Dust before the Wind, and Cast them out, as the Dirt in the Streets.[8]

Reward for Supporting Black Slavery

Imagine for a moment that you are the pastor of a white Presbyterian church in New Orleans in 1860. You know that the city has multiple trading "blocks" where slaves are sold like cattle almost every week.

---

[7] Mather, Cotton, The Wonderful Works of God Commemorated, Boston, 1690
[8] Corrigan, John and Neal, Lynn S., *Religious Intolerance in America: A Documentary History*, Chapel Hill, 2010, pgs. 32-33.

These "blocks" are where children are frequently stripped from their grieving mothers' arms and sold to new masters. You have seen desperate slave mothers, who would not let go of their children, beaten until they lost their grip. You know that wives and husbands are sometimes sold to different masters, never to see each other again; after all, they are simply "breeding stock." In fact, you knew that to accommodate the splitting of married slaves by their masters, the white marriage vows stating *"til death do us part"* was revised for slave couples to *"til death or buckra (the white man) part you"* or *"til death or distance do you part."*[9]

You know that some of the white members of your church own slaves and others are involved in the slave trade. You know that your salary depends on the donations of those white slave traders and owners. You know that if you support slavery, you will be rewarded, and you know just as surely that if you oppose such cruel treatment of God's black children you will be disgraced and lose your job. You know that there is a real chance that the growing "atheist abolitionists" in the northern states may lead Congress to abolish slavery. What would you have done? What would I have done?

I cannot answer for you but based on what I did in my youth during the Civil Rights era, I am afraid that I would have thought about numero uno—me and my family. I would have strongly supported the cruel, inhumane institution of slavery. And that is exactly what Reverend Benjamin Palmer, the white New Orleans Presbyterian minister, (mentioned earlier in Chapter 7) did when he preached his famous November 29, 1860, Thanksgiving sermon advocating that the slaveholding states succeed from the United States federation. In his sermon, he declared:

As keepers of a providential trust, it is our supreme mission to conserve and to perpetuate the institution of slavery as now existing....

This argument (for slavery)...touches the four cardinal points of duty to ourselves, to our slaves, to the world, and to almighty God. It establishes the nature and solemnity of our present trust, to preserve and transmit our existing system of

---

9   https://en.wikipedia.org/wiki/Marriage_of_enslaved_people_(United_States)#Quasi-marriages

domestic servitude, with the right, unchanged by man, to go and root itself where Providence and nature might carry it. This trust we will discharge in the face of the worst possible peril.[10]

Palmer was rewarded handsomely by the white culture within which he lived. His sermon was so well received that it was published by newspapers throughout the South and even printed and distributed in pamphlets. In fact, he is credited by historians as playing a significant role in encouraging southern states, especially Louisiana, to secede from the Union.

And just like Palmer, thousands of white ministers, politicians, theologians, plantation and business owners, lawyers, accountants, government and law enforcement officials...in fact, almost all white people in the southern slave states were rewarded for supporting slavery. The white supremacist oppress and persecute culture in which they lived clearly controlled their lives, rewarding many of them handsomely for their cruelty, while removing all Christian love and empathy for the victims. A dark, dark and cruel side of Christianity.

Rewards for Oppressing and Persecuting Jews

A careful reading of David Kertzer's book *The Pope Against the Jews*[11] reveals that during the almost 1100 years leading up to the Holocaust, the powerful oppress and persecute Jews culture maintained a consistent requirement that career promotions within the ruling Catholic Church depended on a record of actively promoting the oppression and persecution of Jews. Kertzer frequently describes a priest or bishop's oppression and persecution of Jews, and then notes the priest's or bishop's promotion to a higher-level position such as archbishop, cardinal, seminary president, editor of a Catholic journal or newspaper, or some position on the pope's Vatican staff. There were other requirements, of course, but a strong record of oppressing and persecuting Jews was a common trait. The result, of course, was that through its reward system, the oppress and persecute Jews culture

---

[10] Palmer, B. M., The South: Her Peril, and her Duty. A Discourse, delivered in the First Presbyterian Church, New Orleans, on Thursday, November 29, 1860 (New Orleans, Prints at the office of the True Witness and Sentinel, 1860
[11] Kertzer, David, *The Pope Against the Jews,* Random House, 2001

was firmly established within and controlled the Catholic church for centuries. Almost all cardinals in those days had long histories of keeping Jews in their ghettos of poverty. And when it came time for the cardinals to name a new pope, it was a foregone conclusion: someone who had a record of oppressing and persecuting Jews.

The result was that for over 1,100 years, the Jews in the Catholic-controlled European countries were kept in poverty-stricken ghettos, excluded from higher education, prevented from holding professional positions like physicians, bankers and government workers, and from owning and operating businesses. Additionally, they were periodically subjected to Christion riots that resulted in mass murders and the burning of their homes, all enabled by a powerful oppress and persecute Jews culture...1,100 years of a dark and cruel Christianity.

Rewards for Jim Crow Racial Segregation and Oppression

During my youth in Mississippi in the 1950s and '60s, rewards for white racial segregationists were enormous. If you wanted to be elected to a public office, you had to be a white racial segregationist. If you wanted a job teaching in a white school, or a post as a white church pastor, or to be a professor in a white university, or an administrative role with city or county government, you had to be a white segregationist. If you wanted a job as a law enforcement officer or a judgeship with the courts, you had to be a white segregationist. If you were an accountant or a lawyer, you only got the bigger white clients if you were a segregationist. Even a small hint of empathy for the day-to-day burdens fostered on our black neighbors by our segregated society and economy would almost certainly prevent you from getting the job. The same went for promotions. Any white church pastor hoping for a larger church knew that he (no women pastors in most churches in those days) had to be a segregationist.

Not only did all of the rewards go to the segregationists, but we saw what happened to those who supported the equal treatment of our black friends and neighbors, and it was not good. Even as a teenager, I knew all that. We heard it in our conversations with adults. It was sometimes explicit, and always implicit, in the news that we read and heard. It was spoken by our church teachers and ministers. It was woven throughout our social conversations. It was lived out every day as black and white people went to separate schools and churches, swam in separate pools, used separate bathrooms, ate in separate restaurants, and drank from separate water fountains. It was present every day when Blacks had to always say "yes, sir and no, sir" or "yes, ma'am and no, ma'am" to white people, and they were always sure to let the white people go through doors first. It was enforced in our laws and court systems. It was our culture, and we all knew the reward system.

So, guess what we did? We strongly supported racial segregation so that we could reap the rewards. That was the norm, and that is what we white people did without giving it one thought. We refused to see the resulting cruelty for our black neighbors, only the big rewards for us white people.

Rewards for Oppressing Women

The oppress and persecute women culture has established a strong and active reward system for those who suppress women. Many (maybe, most) evangelical Christian seminaries in the nation have either formally adopted the Danvers Statement (discussed earlier in Chapter 5) or, at least, chosen to abide by its demands. Although hidden under the nice name of "complementarian," you will recall that that statement "justifies," in fact, demands, the suppression of women within the church. Now, guess who gets rewarded with the professional jobs in these seminaries? And who gets promoted to higher level positions when vacancies arise? You're right. It is those men who strongly support the oppression of women. Women, of course, can occupy the lower, support level jobs where they work under the direction of men.

Now, guess who gets rewarded with jobs as pastors and pastoral staff in evangelical churches? You're right, again. These positions are reserved for those who most fervently follow the cultural requirements that women cannot serve in any role where they might supervise or even teach men.

Now guess which lay leaders get to serve as members of the governing boards of evangelical churches? You are batting a thousand. Those leadership positions are reserved for men who strongly support the suppression of women.

And who gets rewarded with the speaking invitations at evangelical conventions and retreats? Who gets their evangelical books published? Who are asked to serve on association committees and boards? Who get the presidential, vice presidential, and dean jobs at the seminaries? Who gets elected to officer positions in evangelical associations? This list could go on for many more pages, but I think you see the pattern clearly.

The oppress and persecute women culture has total control over who gets the rewards, and it is not women or men who support the equal treatment of women. It's those hosts who follow the culture's call. If you are a woman, it does not matter how strongly you feel that God has called you to His service as a pastor, or how many degrees you attain, or how good you are, or how hard you work. You have no chance of ever having a successful career in those evangelical seminaries, churches, and church associations controlled by oppressive cultures, not unless you aspire only to low-level staff positions. Dr. Strachan, a professor and theologian at Midwestern Baptist Theological Seminary in Kansas City, clearly explains the culture's position:

...God does not tell us to select leaders according to gifting and talent. The Lord working through the Spirit calls only godly men to provide spiritual leadership, shepherding, and teaching for the gathered assembly of God's people.[12]

Good News Note. The oppress and persecute women culture no longer controls all Christian churches, denominations and seminaries. This demeaning and destructive culture has been defeated in the United Methodist, United Presbyterian, Evangelical Lutheran Church of America, Anglican, United Church of Christ, and some other church denominations in America.

Bad News Note. The powerful male supremist oppress and persecute women culture, however, still has firm control of the Roman Catholic,

12 https://www.patheos.com/blogs/thoughtlife/2019/05/divine-order-in-a-chaotic-age-on-women-preaching

Southern Baptist, Lutheran Church-Missouri Synod, Evangelical Lutheran Synod, Presbyterian Church in America and some other fundamentalist churches with little (probably, no) hope of relief.

Rewards for Oppressing LGBTQs

The reward system described above for Christians who host oppress and persecute women cultures is duplicated by the oppress and persecute LGBTQs culture. The jobs and promotions go to those pastors and seminary faculty, administrators, and staff who strongly oppose the equal treatment of LGBTQs. The book and teaching literature contracts go to those who oppose. Donations from supporters go to those churches, seminaries, and denominations who aggressively support the oppression and persecution of LGBTQs. I have a friend who is an administrator at a Christian seminary that has policies prohibiting the hiring of gay faculty and staff. In this particular case, institutional administrators would love to remove those policies but have not done so because they know that they will lose significant financial support from their individual oppress and persecute LGBTQs donors. Because their annual donor revenue is critical to their budget, they feel that they cannot afford to remove those anti-LGBTQ policies. So, the policies stay in place because of the rewards.

Systemic Discrimination. If you have ever wondered what "systemic" discrimination looks like, simply review this chapter. You can see how thoroughly and effectively the oppress and persecute cultures have penetrated our Christian lives and organizations so that jobs and promotions are limited to those who support the oppress and persecute cultures. And those who object to the cultures' values do not get those jobs and promotions.

Please don't think for a moment that this is something that simply happened in the distant past. The accounts I give of today's ongoing treatment of women and LGBTQs by evangelical Christians are clear, chilling examples of how this mindset carries on today. The persecution itself has become an integral, "systemic" part of Christianity, perpetuating itself on to future generations, ensuring that the oppress and persecute cultures live on for years and decades to come...a dark, dark and cruel side of Christianity.

Chapter 12

Punishing Those Who Openly Object to the Oppression and Persecution

Perhaps the strongest tool in the oppress and persecute cultures' toolboxes, after the Bible, is the threat of punishment for those who openly object to the oppression and persecution of their victims. Get in the way of cultures' oppression and persecution of their victims, and you will pay a price…a price that few of us are willing to pay. And every oppress and persecute culture has used this tool.

Price for Not Persecuting Witches

The punishment of those who might have confronted the church's persecution of innocent people as witches during the European witch trials was made absolutely clear by Pope Innocent VIII's Directive. In essence, it said "don't get in the way of those who I am authorizing to find, convict and murder the witches among you." His Directive said of the church's agents:

….. permit them not to be molested or hindered in any manner whatsoever by any authority whatsoever in the matter of the aforesaid and of this present letter, threatening all oposers, hinderers, contradictors, and rebels, of whatever rank, state, decree, eminence, nobility, excellence, or condition they may be, and whatever privilege of exemption they may enjoy, with excommunication, suspension, interdict, and other still more terrible sentences, censures and penalties, as may be expedient, and this without appeal and with power after due process of law of aggravating and reaggravating these penalties, by our authority, as often as may be necessary, to this end calling in aid, if need be, of the secular arm.[1]

You may want to read the above excerpt again since it is a little difficult to understand, but the meaning is abundantly clear: Get in the way of our persecution of people who we accuse of being witches and you will

---

[11] https://www.sacred-texts.com/pag/twp/twp04.htm

be *"excommunicated, suspended, interdicted and given other more severe punishments including sentences, censures and penalties…all without appeal."*

In case you think that the above statement is just rhetoric, consider what happened to Friar Cornelius Loos in the 1580s. He lived in western Germany, a region where the witch hunt activities were described as:

From court to court throughout the towns and villages of all the diocese, scurried special accusers, inquisitors, notaries, jurors, judges, [and] constables, dragging to trial and torture human beings of both sexes and burning them in great numbers.[2]

In this cruel environment, Fr. Loos attempted to publish a manuscript entitled *De vera et falsa magia* (True and False Magic) that criticized witch hunters. When the authorities heard about his manuscript, Fr. Loos was imprisoned before the manuscript could be published. Under severe coercion, he recanted and was eventually released from prison. But the authorities did not trust him and kept him under constant surveillance, periodically imprisoning him, for the rest of his life.

You can be sure that word of Fr. Loos' treatment was discussed far and wide in those days, warning others who might object to the Christians' cruel persecution of witches. It was a concrete warning to all by the oppress and persecute culture of that time as to what could (in fact, most likely would) happen to anyone who opposed the murder of innocent people as witches.

So, what would you and I have done had we been a local church friar, priest, bishop, cardinal or other church official in those days? Sadly, we would probably have done exactly what many of those church officials did….start looking for innocent people who we could accuse, torture until they confessed, convict and execute for being witches. At the very least, we would have remained totally silent, voicing no objections, whatsoever, when others started persecuting innocent people. After all, killing a few innocent people is a small price (to us, not them) to keep our jobs and standing in the church.

---

[2] https://holyrosaryflint.com/these-three-priests-fought-against-witch-paranoia/#:~:text=At%20the%20forefront%20of%20combating%20this%20lethal%20paranoia,due%20to%20baseless%20accusations.%201.%20Fr.%20Cornelius%20Loos

And so, it was. The oppress and persecute witches culture's punishment was simply so strong that it kept good Christian people, people who I am sure were just like you and me, from voicing any objection to the murder of thousands of their fellow women and men over several hundred dark and cruel years under the Christian church.

Price for Opposing Slavery

The price for opposing antebellum slavery in the south was enormous. No one, especially white Christian pastors, in the South in the years leading up to the Civil War dared oppose slavery. The slave culture would have certainly caused them to lose their job, maybe to be beaten or even murdered. Even those far away who opposed slavery were condemned in no uncertain words. Christian George, in his March 1, 2017, article in *Christian Living* entitled "Why the American South Would Have Killed Charles Spurgeon" shows this clearly through the experience of one such brave Christian.

In the late 1850s, Charles Spurgeon was a young London, England, pastor, who was preaching and publishing strong abolitionist sermons. George explains how the white Christians in the South responded:

Anti-Spurgeon bonfires illuminated jail yards, plantations, bookstores, and courthouses throughout the Southern states. In Virginia, Mr. Humphrey H. Kuber, a Baptist preacher and "highly respectable citizen" of Matthews County, burned seven calf-skinned volumes of Spurgeon's sermons "on the head of a flour barrel." The arson was assisted by "many citizens of the highest standing." In North Carolina, Spurgeon's famous sermon "Turn or Burn" found a similar fate when a Mr. Punch "turned the second page and burned the whole." By 1860, slave-owning pastors were "foaming with rage because they [could not] lay hands on the youthful Spurgeon." His life was threatened, his books burned, his sermons censured, and below the Mason-Dixon Line, the media catalyzed character assassinations. In Florida, Spurgeon was a "beef-eating, puffed-up, vain, over-righteous pharisaical, English blab-mouth." In Virginia, he was a "fat, overgrown boy"; in Louisiana, a "hell-deserving Englishman"; and in South Carolina, a "vulgar young man" with "(soiled) sleek hair, prominent teeth, and a self-satisfied air." Georgians were encouraged to "pay no attention to him." North Carolinians "would like a good opportunity at this hypocritical preacher" and resented his "endish sentiments, against our Constitution and citizens." The Weekly Raleigh

Ken Boutwell

Register reported that anyone selling Spurgeon's sermons should be arrested and charged with "circulating incendiary publications."[3]

But, whenever possible, oppress and persecute cultures move beyond public social punishments for those opposing their oppression and persecution to institutionalize the punishment in laws that could be legally enforced by law enforcement agencies and courts. Accordingly, the oppress and persecute Blacks slave culture in the 1800s never hesitated to get federal, state and local laws passed that punished both Blacks and Whites who showed empathy for slaves.

For example, Alabama, Georgia, Louisiana, Mississippi, North and South Carolina, and Virginia all had laws prohibiting the teaching of slaves to read and write which would be punishable by fines, prison time and, in some cases, whippings.[4] The North Carolina Law passed in 1830-31 read:

Whereas the teaching of slaves to read and write, has a tendency to excite dissatisfaction in their minds, and to produce insurrection and rebellion, to the manifest injury of the citizens of this State:

Therefore,
Be it enacted by the General Assembly of the State of North Carolina, and it is hereby enacted by the authority of the same, That any free person, who shall hereafter teach, or attempt to teach, any slave within the State to read or write, the use of figures excepted, or shall give or sell to such slave or slaves any books or pamphlets, shall be liable to indictment in any court of record in this State having jurisdiction thereof, and upon conviction, shall, at the discretion of the court, if a white man or woman, be fined not less than one hundred dollars, nor more than two hundred dollars, or imprisoned; and if a free person of color, shall be fined, imprisoned, or whipped, at the discretion of the court, not exceeding thirty nine lashes, nor less than twenty lashes.

Of course, the punishment for helping a slave escape was far more severe. The Virginia law passed in 1856 reads:

---

3   https://www.thegospelcoalition.org/article/why-american-south-would-have-killed-charles-spurgeon/
4 https://en.wikipedia.org/wiki/Anti-literacy_laws_in_the_United_States

Any free person, who shall cause to be carried away, or be concerned in the escape of any slave, shall be confined in the penitentiary five to ten years; and, moreover, in lieu of damages forfeit to the owner double the value of the slave, pay reasonable expenses incurred in the attempt to regain the slave, and in the discretion of the jury be publicly whipped to such an extent and at such times as it may deem fit. No whipping shall exceed thirty-nine lashes for anybody in any one day. If the offender be in command or attached to a vessel, it shall be forfeited to the state. The section includes any master of a vessel, and any free person traveling by land.[5]

The 1850 Federal Fugitive Slave Law, among many things, provided punishments for anyone helping escaped slaves as follows:

Section 7

And be it further enacted, That any person who shall knowingly and willingly obstruct, hinder, or prevent such claimant, his agent or attorney, or any person or persons lawfully assisting him, her, or them, from arresting such a fugitive from service or labor, either with or without process as aforesaid, or shall rescue, or attempt to rescue, such fugitive from service or labor, from the custody of such claimant, his or her agent or attorney, or other person or persons lawfully assisting as aforesaid, when so arrested, pursuant to the authority herein given and declared; or shall aid, abet, or assist such person so owing service or labor as aforesaid, directly or indirectly, to escape from such claimant, his agent or attorney, or other person or persons legally authorized as aforesaid; or shall harbor or conceal such fugitive, so as to prevent the discovery and arrest of such person, after notice or knowledge of the fact that such person was a fugitive from service or labor as aforesaid, shall, for either of said offences, be subject to a fine not exceeding one thousand dollars, and imprisonment not exceeding six months, by indictment and conviction before the District Court of the United States for the district in which such offence may have been committed, or before the proper court of criminal jurisdiction, if committed within any one of the organized Territories of the United States; and shall moreover forfeit and pay, by way of civil damages to the party injured by such illegal conduct, the sum of one thousand dollars for each fugitive so lost as aforesaid, to be recovered by action of debt, in any of the District or Territorial Courts aforesaid, within whose jurisdiction the said offence may have been committed.[6]

[5] http://racetimeplace.com/ugrr/slavelawsofvirginiasince1705.htm
[6] http://www.compromise-of-1850.org/fugitive-slave-act-of-1850/

Most states also had their own laws that punished anyone helping a slave escape. Hence, the social and legal punishments for being anti-slavery in the South was simply too severe for anyone to object to slavery through words or action. The oppress and persecute Blacks culture had total control over the entire white population in the South. The people did exactly what that culture demanded and that was to support slavery from every white Christian pulpit, newspaper, legislature, court and law enforcement agency.

While these cruel slavery laws were passed by secular governments, we must remember that the majority of those writing the laws and voting to pass them were white male Christians. It was a sad and cold side of Christianity that Southern Christians willingly established and maintained. Jesus's command to "Do unto others as you would have them do unto you" was totally rejected.

Price for Treating Jews with Respect, Dignity and Equality

As documented in great detail by David Kertzer in his book *The Popes Against The Jews,* during the sixteenth through nineteenth centuries, the Catholic church made it crystal clear through mandates from popes, which were then enforced by cardinals and priests, that any Christians not oppressing and persecuting Jews would be punished by the Church. Those who spoke out in favor of social justice for Jews got few if any promotions within the church. Their careers were stymied for good.

The way that Jews were to be treated, along with what would happen to those Christians who did not adhere to church mandates, was clearly explained by Pope Pius VI in a papal order in 1775:

The Jew may not play, nor eat, nor drink, nor have any other familiarity or conversation with Christians, nor Christians with Jews, whether in buildings, houses, or vineyards, nor on the street, or in inns, taverns, stores, or elsewhere. And innkeepers, bartenders, and storekeepers shall not permit conversation between Christians and Jews, **under the penalty for Jews of ten scudi (Italian**

currency) and an indeterminate jail sentence, and Christian of ten scudi and other, corporal punishments.[7] *(Emphasis added)*

The Christian church (both Catholic and Protestant) was abundantly clear in the centuries leading up to the Holocaust that Jews were the lowest class of people, not for what they did, but simply for their heritage. As such, the European Christian oppress and persecute culture demanded that the Jews in their communities be held in walled-in ghettos of poverty and prevented from having any relationships with Christians. Any Christians violating these cruel cultural and legal mandates were fined and subjected to corporal punishment. I cannot even imagine a prohibition of my simply greeting someone and talking to them. But, that is the way that the oppress and persecute Jews culture of those centuries prevented Christians from obeying Jesus' mandate of "do unto others as we would have them do unto us." The culture easily over-ruled Jesus' command on how we should treat others by punishing those who did not adhere to the culture's commands.

The recrimination for those who helped Jews increased dramatically during the Holocaust years as illustrated by the following 1942 Warsaw poster (translated into English)[8]:

Announcement

Death Penalty for Aid to Jews who have left the Jewish residential areas without permission
Recently, many Jews have left their designated Jewish residential areas. For the time, they are in the Warsaw District.

I remind you that according to the Third Decree of the General Governor's concerning the residential restrictions in the General Government of 10/15/1941 (VBL; abbreviation for Verordnungsblatt Generalgouvernement, p. 595) not only Jews who have left their designated residential area will be punished with death, but the same penalty applies to anyone who knowingly provides refuge (a hiding place)

---

[7]   https://silo.pub/the-popes-against-the-jews-the-vaticans-role-in-the-rise-of-modern-anti-semitism.html

[8]   https://encyclopedia.ushmm.org/content/en/timeline-event/holocaust/1942-1945/german-poster-announces-death-penalty-for-aiding-jews

to such Jews. This includes not only the providing of a night's lodging and food, but also any other aid, such as transporting them in vehicles of any sort, through the purchase of Jewish valuables, etc.

I ask the population of the Warsaw Destrict to immediately report any Jew who resides outside of a Jewish residential area to the nearest police station or gendarmerie post.

Whoever provided or currently provides aid to a Jew will not be prosecuted if it is reported to the nearest police station by 4 pm on 9/9/42.

Likewise, those who deliver valuables acquired from a Jew to 20 Niska Street or the nearest police or gendarme post by 4 pm on 9/9/42 will not be prosecuted.

The SS- and Police Leader in the Warsaw District
Warsaw, September 5, 1942

Now, ask yourself what you would have done, had you been a Christian living in Warsaw in 1942. Would you have risked your life to save the life of a Jew? Some did, but most didn't. The punishment was simply too severe. I like to think that I would have helped the Jewish people, but I wonder. Would I have, when I have not even taken actions to actively protest the subordination of women and damnation of LGBTQs in my own time? What would you have done?

Price for Supporting Equality for Black People After the Civil War. There was no way that the dominant oppress and persecute Blacks culture was going to let freed slaves become equal to Whites in the former Confederate states after the war. The cruel white supremist culture monitored black people's actions, even their suspected actions, and used its special organization, the KKK, to deliver punishment to thousands of Blacks throughout the South as a warning to "stay in your place." Susan Bartoleth reports one such punishment, among thousands, in her book *They Called Themselves the K.K.K.*

The Klan also targeted black churches to prevent blacks from holding political meetings at night. On one moonlit night in Tuskegee, Alabama, Klansmen shot and killed three black men and wounded five or six others. The men, church stewards, were holding a late-night meeting to discuss the purchase of a church bell when the shots rang out and bullets sprayed their meeting room. The gunmen were never caught.[9]

And it wasn't just the black men and women who paid the price for opposing the dominant oppress and persecute Blacks culture. Any white person openly supporting equality was also quickly punished. In the same book, Bartoleth recounts the story of a white minister:

The Klan also targeted white ministers who didn't share their views on race. In Alabama, several Klansmen broke into Moses Sullivan's bedroom and at gunpoint forced the white minister outside, where they held a trial, accusing him of favoring racial equality. Finding him guilty, they beat him severely with hickory sticks. The final blow caught Sullivan above the forehead, breaking the bone. The beating was a warning, they told him. The next time, they promised, they would kill him. Sullivan and his family fled. It took him months to recover from the beating.[10]

To the pleasure of the oppress and persecute Blacks culture at that time, news of these "punishments" traveled fast among both black and white supporters of racial equality as a warning, causing many to give up all attempts to obtain equality for the recently freed slaves.

Price for Supporting Racial Equality and Integration During the Civil Rights Movement

Joseph Reiff, in his book *Born of Conviction: White Methodists and Mississippi's Closed Society*, documents what happened to the careers of 28 white Mississippi Methodist ministers who, in 1963, had the courage to write and sign a manifesto supporting racial integration.

After the manifesto was published in the *Mississippi Methodist Advocate* on January 2, 1963, the oppress and persecute culture demanded immediate punishment and, in some cases, continued that punishment for the entire careers of those pastors. Eighteen of the pastors were either fired by their congregations or resigned after seeing the "handwriting on the wall" and left the state. Most of the remaining ten spent their careers in small churches, never being advanced by the

---

9 Bartoleth, Susan, *They Called Themselves the K.K.K.*, Houghton Mifflin Harcourt Publishing Co. Copyright 2010, pg. 113
10 Ibid, pg. 114

Mississippi Methodist Conference to appointments in larger churches that paid higher salaries.

As was always the case, the message sent to other pastors in the South by the cruel culture during those years was "Want to keep your job? Then support our oppression and persecution of black people" or as a minimum "keep your mouth shut." Sadly, that is what most ministers in the South did during those years. And had I been a pastor during those years, I am now embarrassed to admit, that is almost certainly what I would have done. I would have chosen other "safe" sermon topics.

P.D. East, the editor and owner of a small-town newspaper in Petal, Mississippi learned the hard way that he would pay a huge personal price for speaking out in opposition to the oppression and persecution of his black neighbors and friends in the 1950s. As soon as he did so in a few editorials, his readers canceled their subscriptions and his advertisers dropped their ads, bankrupting the newspaper and leaving him in poverty.[11]

Unfortunately, as we have already seen, oppress and persecute cultures do not limit their punishments to social pressure or taking people's jobs and livelihood. As we have seen over and over, these cultures have no hesitancy in using violence. In the late 1950s, Rev. Germany, the father of a girl who I dated a few times in my teenage years was beaten unconscious because he supported racial integration and was founding a seminary that would accept both black and white students in Neshoba County, Mississippi. I, myself, was threatened with a switchblade knife by three white men, whom I had never before met, who said, "Anyone who will date one of them is no better than they are." (Fortunately, when threatened, I have the ability to run faster than lightning.)

But the beating of Rev. Germany during those years was not the only violence perpetrated by the oppress and persecute Blacks culture. You will recall that Medgar Evers, one of the leaders in the integration of public schools in Jackson, Mississippi, was murdered in the driveway

---

[11] East, P.D., The Magnolia Jungle, *Simon and Schuster, New York, 1960*). <pg. ##>

of his home. Three young Civil Rights workers were murdered in Neshoba County, Mississippi, and buried under a dam. Women and men protestors were publicly beaten during the Selma, Alabama, Civil Rights march, and Martin Luther King, Jr, was murdered while standing on the balcony of his hotel room.

As planned by the evil culture, all of this violence sent strong, clear messages to the pastors and leaders of white Christian Churches in the Southern states, and really to every one of us during those years, "There will be a price to pay, if you openly oppose our oppression and persecution of black people."

Now you may understand why so many white Christian pastors rejected social justice as being a part of salvation. To accept it and preach it could endanger not only one's job, but one's very life. The dark, cruel oppressive culture had almost total control over Southern white Christian ministers and their congregations, including me and my family, in those days.

Price for Not Keeping Women in Subordination

The pastor of my current Southern Baptist church is a nice man who embodies most of the self-acclaimed core Christian values of "love, justice, grace, worship, forgiveness, faith, repentance, hope, joy, humility, caring, compassion, kindness, generosity, empathy, hospitality, joy, and gratitude." I said "most" because, unfortunately, he lives and works in a local and national Southern Baptist male supremist culture that has robbed him of the values of justice, humility, compassion, and empathy by demanding his subordination of women.

What do you think would happen to him if he strongly supported the equal treatment of women in a sermon and then followed up with a proposal that our church have women deacons and be open to ordaining women pastors and hiring ordained women pastoral staff? You are right, again. The oppress and persecute women culture in our church would quickly demand punishment. He might be given a chance to repent and agree to never bring the subject up again. Failing that, he would most likely soon be looking for another job, like his predecessor.

But that is not all. His name would be "mud" among his male supremist Southern Baptist peers. He would be ostracized by them, would likely lose any memberships he might have in state and national Southern Baptist committees, would certainly not be appointed to any more association committees, and would never get a good recommendation for another Southern Baptist pastoral job. Even his chances of returning to his previous part-time faculty job at Liberty University would be gone. Basically, his livelihood would be gone. He would likely not be able to pay his home mortgage, buy groceries, maintain his health insurance, save for his children's college education, or support his young family in other ways. If he was lucky, he might find a job in another denomination, but he would have put himself and his family through a lot of trauma and upheaval.

News of these types of cultural punishments, when they happen, spread fast, especially in our electronic age. As throughout history, they serve as a warning to other white evangelical pastors, who might, deep down, want to treat women with respect, dignity, and equality. Accordingly, I am guessing that every male evangelical pastor fully understands the threat and, for this reason, never even considers supporting the equal treatment of women by the church. They all know that they must obey their culture. The punishment for not doing so is simply too severe. It is much, much easier to ignore the damage that this oppression does to the careers of women who feel called to serve as pastors. Besides, the Bible supports the subordination of women, and there are lots of other "safe" topics for sermons.

Price for Supporting Equality for LGBTQs

If you think the oppress and persecute culture's treatment of people who support equality of women is bad, what do you think would happen to my pastor if he advocated the full acceptance of LGBTQ members and staff? He might be given a decent severance package if he were dismissed for advocating the equal treatment of women. But if he preached a sermon advocating that our church become an LGBTQ open and affirming church, he would most likely have to clean out his office that afternoon and kiss any severance package goodbye. Our church's oppress and persecute LGBTQs culture would never, ever tolerate such belief and behavior and would tell him so in no uncertain terms on his way out the door.

So, if you are wondering if my pastor or any of our pastoral staff will ever advocate treating LGBTQ people with respect, dignity and equality, you can stop. They can't and won't. Our Southern Baptist church culture's punishment is simply too severe.

In fact, as discussed in the previous chapter, the culture does the exact opposite by rewarding those who take whatever steps are necessary to damn the equal treatment of women and members of our gay community. So, you now know why our pastoral staff led the initiative to ban the use of Smith and Helwys literature in our church studies...a literature that teaches that how we treat others matters. Such actions not only avoid all punishments but lead to great rewards within the Southern Baptist culture.

Other churches have become even more brutal in punishing those who support the equal treatment of LGBTQs. A mega church in Jacksonville, Florida required that its members sign the following pledge:

As a member of First Baptist Church, I believe that God creates people in his image as either male or female, and that this creation is a fixed matter of human biology, not individual choice, I believe marriage is instituted by God, not government, is between one man and one woman, and is the only contest for sexual desire and expression.[12]

Members of the church were told:

"Your signature and updated contact information on this document is required by March 19, 2023, and will ensure your membership at First Baptist Church continues without any interruption."

In other words, any member not signing the pledge was excommunicated from the church after March 19, 2023.

---

12   https://www.rollingstone.com/politics/politics-news/florida-megachurch-lgbtq-pledge-1234671423/

Chapter 13

Convincing the Majority to be Silent

You would think that we Christians. whose self-acclaimed core values are "love, justice, grace, worship, forgiveness, faith, repentance, hope, joy, humility, caring, compassion, kindness, generosity, empathy, hospitality, joy, and gratitude," would not be able to sit idly by while our brothers and sisters are being oppressed and persecuted and make no protests, whatsoever. Yet, that is exactly what our oppress and persecute cultures made most of our fellow ancestors do when Christians were accusing innocent women of being witches and burning them at the stake, confiscating the lands and homes of native Americans, holding millions of blacks in slavery, murdering millions of Jews, and keeping blacks in segregated poverty. And it is what our culture still makes us do today while our fellow Christians continue to persecute people of color, keep women in subordination, and damn our LGTBTQ brothers and sisters.

Why? Why turn a blind eye and move happily along, assuming no responsibility for helping the suffering victims? I have often wondered if God will ultimately hold us, especially we Christians, accountable for not at least saying something. Do we not have a personal responsibility to speak out when we see others being oppressed and persecuted?

Nobel laureate and Holocaust survivor Elie Wiesel clearly thought so and pledged:

"I swore never to be silent whenever and wherever human beings endure suffering and humiliation. We must take sides. Neutrality helps the oppressor, never the victim. Silence encourages the tormentor, never the tormented."[1]

---

[1] https://www.goodreads.com/author/quotes/1049.Elie_Wiesel

Dietrich Bonhoeffer, the German Christian leader who openly opposed the exile and persecution of Jews during the Holocaust, apparently had the same question. He concluded:

Silence in the face of evil is itself evil: God will not hold us guiltless. Not to speak is to speak. Not to act is to act.

Martin Luther King, Jr. asked himself that same question during the American Civil Rights movement and concluded that:

History will have to record that the greatest tragedy of this period of social transition was not the strident clamor of the bad people, but the appalling silence of the good people.[2]

You will recall, however, that Bonhoeffer was imprisoned and then executed by the Nazis and King was imprisoned 29 times and ultimately murdered by a white supremacist.

That might very well be the reason that so many of us good white Christians choose to see nothing, hear nothing, feel nothing, do nothing and say nothing. The oppress and persecute cultures' punishments, as we saw in the previous chapter, are simply too much for us to speak out.

But our silence is more complicated than that. Based on my experiences over the years, a multitude of reasons exist for our silence. In every one of our case studies of the oppressed and persecuted, there were those:

- Who remained quiet because they fully supported the oppression and persecution and, often, enjoyed the rewards for doing so.

- Who were bothered by the oppression and persecution but were unwilling to suffer the punishments for speaking out in opposition (the "go along to get along" group),

---

2   https://kinginstitute.stanford.edu/king-papers/documents/address-fourth-annual-institute-nonviolence-and-social-change-bethel-baptist

- Who simply did not care enough about the oppression of others to speak out. ("Let the victims fight their own battles. After all, I, myself, am not suffering.")

Silent Because We Agree

Sadly, there have been and continue to be silent Christians who are controlled by the oppressive cultures within which we find ourselves. During the European witch trials, there were silent Christians who believed with all of their heart and soul those Bible verses mandating that witches be executed. They did not see the witches as victims, but rather as evil cohorts of the devil who deserved to be hung or burned at the stake. That is what their culture, reinforced by messages from Catholic popes and protestant theologians, like Martin Luther and John Calvin, said and they believed. They had no empathy for the women and men as they were executed, sometimes in public celebrations. In fact, they felt that something good had been done. They did not speak out against the cruel, inhumane treatment of their fellow humans because, ultimately, they agreed with the executioners.

In the same way with Native Americans, there were millions of white Christians who fully believed that America was God's promised land for them to subdue, occupy, and own. Like the Canaanites in the Israelites' promised land, the Native Americans were simply obstacles to be conquered to fulfill God's promise. When they were murdered or marched on the Trail of Tears, these white people were totally silent in agreement.

Again, the same with black slavery. There were those white Christians who totally yielded to their culture's demand and believed with every fiber of their body that "Ham's curse" (Genesis 9:20-27) was a mandate from God commanding that black people be held in slavery. These Christians felt no empathy for those black mothers and fathers when their children were taken from their homes and sold to another white slave master. They had been convinced this was a predetermined, inherited fate ordained by God because their ancestor, Ham, saw his father naked and laughed. As mentioned earlier, that may seem silly to us today, but not to lots and lots of white Christians during the 400 years of black slavery in the southern states.

The same with the Holocaust. There were those German Christians and, later, Christians in other Nazi occupied nations, who believed deep within their souls those New Testament verses that said that Jews were evil. Those beliefs had been instilled in the European Christian oppressive culture for centuries going as far back as Martin Luther, whose book, *On the Jews and Their Lies*, damned the Jewish people. His very first advice in the book was:

First to set fire to their synagogues or schools and to bury and cover with dirt whatever will not burn, so that no man will ever again see a stone or cinder of them. This is to be done in honor of our Lord and of Christendom, so that God might see that we are Christians, and do not condone or knowingly tolerate such public lying, cursing, and blaspheming of his Son and of his Christians.

I have no doubt that Martin Luther and millions of other "good" European Christians who followed him for centuries leading up to the Holocaust were totally committed to the "authority of the Bible" and its classification of Jews as evil people (e.g., John 8:44). That is what their dark, cruel Christian supremist culture demanded and, as you might expect, these believing Christians voiced no objections when they saw their Jewish neighbors loaded onto trains bound for torture and execution in concentration camps.

The same today for the suppression of women. I have no doubt that there are hundreds of thousands of Christians who wholeheartedly believe their culture's demand that women be held in subordination. That is what the majority of the male members of my current Southern Baptist church believe. And that is what the nice man whom I met at my Epworth by the Sea retreat clearly believed. His church's oppress and persecute women culture demanded that he obey those biblical passages that say men must dominate the women in their families and churches, and he fully believed. So, you can be sure that he will never express any concern about their subordination. Neither will the male pastoral staff and lay members of my church

And again, it's the same today for LGBTQs. Evangelical churches throughout the world are filled with Christians whose culture demands that they deny all scientific and medical research, as well as personal testimonies of LGBTQ individuals, that, like all other natural born traits, sexual orientation is just that. Instead, their culture tells them to ignore the scientific and medical research and believe that one's sexual orientation is a choice and that choosing to be openly gay is a sin. The Bible says so and their culture tells them that they must obey the Bible's authority. Clearly, Satan will be building a snowman when these believers see anything wrong with the way that their church culture treats their LGBTQ brothers and sisters and speak out in opposition.

Silent Because We Fear the Punishment

Perhaps these are the good people to whom Bonhoeffer and King were referring...people like you and me who see the horrible oppression and persecution of these cultures' victims and agree that it is cruel, but still never say anything. Why? Because the costs of speaking out are simply higher than we want to pay.

As we saw in the previous chapter, in many cases over the centuries, the costs would almost certainly be social ostracization, but could be the loss of a job, or a burning of your home or a beating or death.

In the 1870s, the KKK undertook a campaign of burning homes and beating and lynching those blacks and whites supporting equal treatments of blacks in York County, South Carolina. When asked why he did not speak out in his sermons against all of the KKK terrorism in his community, Reverend Cooper, a York County pastor, responded:

I don't preach political sermons at all. I never conceived that I had any right to preach against raidings of that kind...I have no colored people belonging to my congregation at all. My idea is to preach Christ crucified, and I try to stick to my text.[3]

Although Rev. Cooper's reasons for his silence were not recorded, based on my own experiences during the 1960s Civil Rights era, I am sure that it had a lot to do with all of the violence and lynchings in his community. It is also highly likely that some of the KKK members were members of his church, maybe even on his board of trustees or deacons. Additionally, public KKK notices, like the following that was posted at a near-by store in Yorkville, as well as at other sites in the

---

[3] Bartoletti, Susan Campbell, *They Called Themselves the KKK*, pg. 119, Houghton Mifflin Harcourt Publishing company.

county, sent a strong message to all whites, including Reverend Cooper, to either join up or remain totally silent[4]:

Headquarters K.K.K.
January 22, 1871

Resolved, That in all cases of incendiarism, ten of the leading colored people and two white sympathizers shall be executed in that vicinity.

That if any armed bands of colored people are found hereafter picketing the roads, the officers of the company to which the pickets belong shall be executed.

That all persons reported as using incendiary language shall be tried by the high court of this order, and be punished at their discretion. *(Emphasis added)*

The different officers are charged with the execution of these resolutions.

By order of K.K.K.

And, so, the oppress and persecute Blacks culture had spoken. Reverend Cooper knew exactly what he had to do and not do, sadly, the same that you and I would probably have done…preach only Jesus crucified and remain totally silent about the frequent evil torture of his black brothers and sisters by his fellow white Christians. After all, his culture told him to ignore Jesus's statements about serving the least of these because he was "saved by the grace of God through faith alone, not by works." So, he could do absolutely nothing to help his black brothers and sisters who were being beaten and murdered and still be welcomed into heaven with open arms, and his parishioners could do the same.

I had far fewer reasons than Reverend Cooper but still remained silent, even after I came to see all types of oppression and persecution as cruel in the 1960s and '70s. As I grew into adulthood and moved away from my Mississippi hometown, giving my wife and me the opportunity to interact with people of other races, ethnicities, religions, and sexual orientations, we began to see these "others" not as people who were to be oppressed and persecuted, but people just like us.

---

[4] Ibid, pg. 117

They were good people who helped their fellowman. They laughed and cried, just like us. They had families who they loved, just like us. They wanted education and opportunities for rewarding careers, just like us. They wanted freedom from injustice, just like us. They wanted to be treated with respect, dignity and equality, just like us.

Our eyes were opened, and we came to see that the white supremacist culture that had dominated our youth was cruel and inhumane. I personally came to see the hypocrisy of selectively using the "authority of the Bible" to keep women in subordination and to oppress and persecute my black brothers and sisters while not applying that same "authority" to other biblical demands like killing people with other religions and all who work on Sundays...obviously, biblical mandates that our society no longer tolerates. My recognition of my own hypocrisy caused me to search for other criteria for choosing which biblical passages to obey. After lots of prayer and thought, I concluded that my criteria would be "Does this verse help or hurt another person?" If it helped, I would obey it. If it hurt, I would ignore it. That was the Jesus that I saw as I studied His life.

So, having taken this step, what did I start doing to speak out against the oppression of women, Blacks, Jews, Hispanics, Asians, LGBTQs and other oppress and persecute cultural victims? Again, you are right. Nothing. Absolutely nothing. I changed on the inside, but not on the outside. Why? Why did I choose to remain quiet while other more courageous white Christians were beginning to speak out? They participated in protest marches. They wrote letters to religious publications and to their state and federal governmental representatives. They spoke out in church meetings. Some moved their memberships to other, more open and loving churches. They did all of these things, and I did nothing, remaining silent.

Why?

The reason, of course, is that the white supremacist culture of my youth still had control of my actions. Although I no longer lived in my Mississippi home town, my family, my former white fellow church members and friends did. I knew that if word got back that I had participated in a Civil Rights freedom march or wrote a letter to a publication in support of racial integration, I would be rejected by my hometown family and friends. I knew because that is exactly what all of us thought about the "low life" Whites who teamed with black protestors when I lived there. My hometown family and friends would view me as a traitor to their oppress and persecute Blacks cultural values.

So, when Civil Rights leaders were murdered, when the four little girls were murdered in that church bombing, when the Selma Civil Rights marchers were beaten, I remained as quiet as a church mouse. I just could not bring myself to speak out in protest and, in not doing so, became a historical part of the "…the appalling silence of the good people" to which Martin Luther King Jr. referred. To my shame now, I let the oppress and persecute Blacks culture continue to control my voice and actions even though I had rejected its values. Rather than be subjected to social ostracization by my family and friends, I was perfectly willing to see my black brothers and sisters continue to be mercilessly oppressed and persecuted by a racially segregated and oppressive social, legal, and economic Jim Crow system.

Perhaps I am searching for an excuse for my lack of courage back in those days, but in many ways, both Reverend Cooper and I were also victims of the oppress and persecute Blacks cultures of our times. Rev. Cooper's only choice was to remain silent as the homes of his black brothers and sisters burned to the ground and they were, themselves, beaten and murdered…or risk suffering the same fate himself. So, he chose to be quiet. My costs of speaking out were miniscule in comparison to Rev. Cooper's potential costs. I only faced ostracization from my family and friends but was unwilling to run even that risk…a dark, dark time of my own Christianity. I sincerely hope that you would have spoken out.

Silent Because We Don't Care Enough About the Suffering of Those Who Are Oppressed and Persecuted

Then there are those of us who don't care enough to get involved. We have no feelings of empathy for the victims. The oppress and persecute cultures love us. I recall reading an Ann Landers letter many years ago in which she, facetiously, said that there were three categories of people: those who make things happen, those who watch things happen, and those who ask, "What happened?"

Ken Boutwell

I would add a fourth category, and that is those of us who refuse to acknowledge that anything is happening at all. We choose to not see the oppression and persecution around us because we, ourselves, are not suffering from it. Whether it was the witches being burned alive or the Jews being herded onto cattle trains headed for execution, or Blacks held in slavery or women held in submission or LGBTQs excommunicated, it is not our problem. It was (is) their problem and they need to do their own protesting.

Life is difficult for most of us. We have our own genuine problems like finding good jobs, keeping our family housed, fed, and clothed, handling our own health problems, participating in and supporting our own churches, paying for our own children's education, saving for our own retirement, and a host of other personal and family responsibilities. We simply don't have time to get involved, we tell ourselves.

I have to admit that at various times over the years I have also fallen into this category, and you may have too. The oppress and persecute cultures remove any guilt that we might feel by telling us that there is no way that we, personally, can make a difference. The culture says, "No one even knows who you are and those who do, don't care what you say, so keep quiet." And unfortunately, that is exactly what we do.

But neither you nor I are less qualified than Fannie Lou Hamer, a young black Mississippi sharecropper's wife with a sixth-grade education in the 1960s. You may very well have heard of her because she became one of the national leaders in the Civil Rights movement, making speeches all over the nation. She coined the phrase, "I am sick and tired of being sick and tired," which is now engraved on her tombstone. Surely if, at a time when Blacks were held in poverty and treated as the lowest of people, a young woman could speak out in the face of injustice, we can say something in our church or in our social group or to our pastor.

I am reminded at this point of the quote from Martin Niemoller, a German theologian and Lutheran pastor during the Holocaust:

First they came for the Socialists, and I did not speak out—
Because I was not a Socialist.

Then they came for the Trade Unionists, and I did not speak out—
Because I was not a Trade Unionist.
Then they came for the Jews, and I did not speak out—
Because I was not a Jew.
Then they came for me—and there was no one left to speak for me.[5]

---

5   https://encyclopedia.ushmm.org/content/en/article/martin-niemoeller-first-they-came-for-the-socialists

Chapter 14

Special Oppressive Organizations

Keeping us silent is not enough for these evil oppress and persecute cultures, however. They want us to commit even further to their cause by getting us to create and/or use special organizations dedicated to inflicting the oppression and persecution. These special organizations:

- Concentrate on harming the cultures' targeted victims.
- Aggressively recruit host members who can provide both the needed financial support and societal leadership to institutionalize their oppression and persecution in laws, news outlets, law enforcement agencies, court cases, church policies, creeds and beliefs, business operations, civic clubs, and other social organizations.
- Directly punish any who stand in their way.

Sadly, our history has too many of these specialized organizations for me to list them all. I will mention only four of the most prominent here, but you can find a long, heart-rendering list of those currently active at the web site of the Southern Poverty Center.

U.S. Army—Take the Land, Homes, and Lives of Native Americans

The more history I read about the oppression and persecution of Native Americans, the more I was struck by the cruel role that our U.S. Army played in removing them from their homes, marching them to barren lands, and mass murdering them when they protested. Unlike today, when our U.S. Army is prohibited from being involved in domestic activities, the armies of the 1700s and 1800s were the chief instruments in attacking Native American tribes. During this time of isolation and relatively slow communications, local army fort commanders were given broad authority to make decisions as to whom to attack, how to attack, when to attack, and when to negotiate peace agreements. This gave the oppress and persecute culture of that time the opportunity for extensive influence over the commanders and their troops. As I read accounts of their actions, it slowly and sadly dawned on me that our national army was the special organization that our oppress and persecute Native Americans culture used to implement its cruel policies, just as the oppress and persecute Jews culture later used the Nazi party. It was an army of primarily white men only, and since an estimated 75 to 80 percent of the U.S. white population in the 1700s professed to be Christians,[1] we must assume that a majority of those white soldiers were also Christians. And those percentages continued into the 1800s when Alexis de Tocqueville observed about the United States in 1830s that:

...there is no country in the world in which the Christian religion retains a greater influence over the souls of men.[2]

De Tocqueville, of course, was talking only about white Americans, not Black or Native Americans, who were considered to be "nobodies" in those days.

During these years, the United States government negotiated treaty after treaty after treaty with Native American tribes granting them ownership rights to parts of their original home lands. But the government exercised little control over white populations who systematically invaded those lands, especially when gold discoveries were made, but also to hunt game, build roads and establish white homesteads. Game animals (e.g., buffalo, elk, antelope and deer), the major sources of food for most Native Americans, were being rapidly depleted by white invaders. Protests to federal government officials by Native Americans, for the most part, fell on deaf ears forcing them to find their own ways of defending these invasions of their lands, including violence.

---

[1] https://www.loc.gov/exhibits/religion/rel02.html
[2] https://www.encyclopedia.com/history/news-wires-white-papers-and-books/1815-1850-religion-overview

A speech to a delegation from the federal government on November 9, 1887, by Bear Tooth, a Crow tribe chief, explains the plight of the Native Americans all over the country:

Fathers, fathers, fathers, hear me well. Call back your young men from the mountains of the bighorn sheep. They have run all over the country; they have destroyed the growing wood and the green grass; they have set fire to our lands. Fathers, your young men have devastated the country and killed my animals, the elk, the deer, the antelope, my buffalo. They do not kill them to eat them; they leave them to rot where they fall. Fathers, if I went into your country to kill your animals, what would you say? Should I not be wrong, and would you not make war on me?[3]

But the white oppress and persecute Native Americans culture of that time showed no empathy. Instead of helping the Native Americans protect the ownership of their granted lands, the U.S. Army was used to attack them time after time after time, sometimes in massacres. The desire to take the lands of the Native Americans was so embedded in the white culture that the lives of Native Americans had little to no value. Taking their lands, homes, and lives was part of white America's destiny believed to have been ordained by God, as noted by Denver Methodist minister, Reverend William Spencer in a September 25, 1864, letter:

For friends concerned about our safety, rest assured that we can defend ourselves against attack. There is one sentiment in regard to the disposition of the Indians; **let them be exterminated, men, women and children.** *They are regarded as a race accursed like the ancient Canaanites, devoted of the Almighty to utter destruction. I do not share these views, but my feelings have changed. The grace of God may be sufficient for them, but humanly speaking,* **there seems no better destiny ahead than to fade away before the white man.**[4] (Emphasis added)

Because of continued invasions by white miners, hunters, homesteaders, and military troops building forts and roads on lands

---

[3] Brown, Dee, *Bury My Heart at Wounded Knee*: an Indian History of the American West. New York: Holt, Rinehart & Winston, 1970, pg. 144

[4] Bob Scott, *Blood at Sand Creek: The Massacre Revisited*. Caldwell, Id.: Caxton Printers, 1994, pgs. 119-20

granted to the Natives through treaties, the Native Americans were forced into their last resort: war. As Red Cloud, a Cheyenne chief, explained:

The Great Father (federal government) sent his soldiers out here to spill blood. I did not first commence the spilling of blood.... If the Great Father kept white men out of my country, peace would last forever, but if they disturb me, there will be no peace.... The Great Spirit raised me in this land, and has raised you in another land. What I have said I mean. I mean to keep this land.[5]

And so, the die was cast. White invasions were not going to cease. The only alternative for the Native Americans was war, and the white army soldiers were given the mission, not of helping the Native Americans protect their lands, but of killing them to take their lands, homes, and sources of food. And that is just what happened.

Too many cases of this exist to describe them all, but I will share a few.

Sand Creek Massacre—The first is the Sand Creek massacre in Colorado, described in some detail by Dee Brown in his best-selling book *Bury My Heart at Wounded Knee*. The U.S. Army unit in Colorado was commanded by Colonel Chivington, a former Methodist minister who had been active in "organizing Sunday schools in the mining camps."[6] A Cheyenne tribe under the leadership of Black Kettle had negotiated an agreement with Major Wynkoop (under Colonel Chivington's command) giving the tribe the right to camp at Sand Creek and to send some of their hunters out to hunt buffalo for food. Additionally, the Major had provided the tribe with rations. With these two gestures, the tribe felt safe at its camp.

The Colonel was displeased with Major Wynkoop's friendly treatment of the Indians, however, and replaced him with Major Anthony. Even though Major Anthony had also given the tribe permission to camp at Sand Creek and for their hunters to hunt nearby for buffalo, he agreed with the Colonel that the tribe should be attacked. Some of the Major's lieutenants, however, disagreed. One of them even stated that "it

---

[5] Brown, Dee, *Bury My Heart at Wounded Knee: an Indian History of the American West*. New York: Holt, Rinehart & Winston, 1970. pg. 144
[6] Ibid, pg. 83

would be murder in every sense of the word." Colonel Chivington angrily responded, "Damn any man who sympathizes with Indians...I have come to kill Indians, and believe it is right and honorable to use any means under God's heaven to kill Indians."[7]

On November 28, 1864, the Colonel left Fort Lyon and headed for Sand Creek with a force of more than seven hundred men. Most of the young tribal men were away hunting buffalo, leaving about six hundred people in the camp, of which approximately two-thirds were women and children. So confident was Black Kettle and his people that they were, based on Major Anthony's word, safe they kept only one night watch to guard their ponies. The first warning of the tribe's approaching doom was the sound of hundreds of horse hooves hitting the ground.

Black Kettle rose quickly but was still confident of his people's safety and assured them that they were not being attacked. He came out of his tent and raised the American flag to show his confidence. Other tribal leaders, including White Antelope, moved rapidly toward the invading soldiers with white flags and other peaceful gestures. White Antelope was shouting "Stop! Stop!" in clear English, but to no avail. He was quickly shot and killed.[8]

I will let Robert Kent, who was, reluctantly, riding with Colonel Chivington tell you what happened:

I saw the American flag waving and heard Black Kettle tell the Indians to stand around the flag, and there they were huddled—men, women, and children. This was when we were within fifty yards of the Indians. I also saw a white flag raised. These flags were in so conspicuous a position that they must have been seen. When the troops fired, the Indians ran, some of the men into their lodges, probably to get their arms.... I think there were six hundred Indians in all. I think there were thirty-five braves and some old men, about sixty in all.... the rest of the men were away from camp, hunting....After the firing the warriors put the squaws and children together, and surrounded them to protect them. I saw five Squaws under a bank for shelter. When the troops came up to them, they ran out and showed their persons to let the soldiers know that they were squaws and begged for mercy, but the soldiers

---

[7] Ibid, pg. 86
[8] Ibid, pg. 89

shot them all. I saw one squaw lying on the bank whose leg had been broken by a shell; a soldier came up to her with a drawn saber; she raised her arm to protect herself, when he struck, breaking her arm; she rolled over and raised her other arm, when he struck, breaking it, and then left her without killing her. There seemed to be indiscriminate slaughter of men, women, and children. There were some thirty or forty squaws collected in a hole for protection; they sent out a little girl about six years with a white flag on a stick; she had not proceeded but a few steps when she was shot and killed. All of the squaws in that hole were afterwards killed, and four or five bucks outside. The squaws offered no resistance. Everyone I saw dead was scalped. I saw one squaw cut open with an unborn child, as I thought, lying by her side. Captain Soule afterwards told me that such was the fact. I saw a little girl about five years of age who had been hid in the sand; two soldiers discovered her, drew their pistols and shot her; and then pulled her out of the sand by the arm. I saw quite a number of infants in arms of killed with their mothers."[9]

According to Brown, Robert Trent's descriptions were confirmed by Lieutenant James Conner, who said:

In going over the battlefield the next day I did not see a body of a man, woman or child but was scalped, and in many instances their bodies were mutilated in the most horrible manner—men, women and children's privates cut out, &c(sic); I heard one man say that he had cut out a woman's private parts and had them for exhibition on a stick; I heard another man say that he had cut the fingers off an Indian to get the rings off the hand; according to the best of my knowledge and belief these atrocities that were committed were with the knowledge of J. M. Chivington, and I do not know of his taking any measures to prevent them; I heard of one instance of a child a few months old being thrown in the feedbox of a wagon, and after being carried some distance left on the ground to perish; I also heard of numerous instances in which men had cut out the private parts of females and stretched them over the saddle-bows and wore them over their hats while riding the ranks.[10]

You (or, at least, I) would think that Christian ministers of that time would have quickly condemned Colonel Chivington's cruel and inhumane treatment of the Indians at Sand Creek. But oppress and persecute cultures never, if they can stop it, let such condemnations occur. Instead, the cultures have their Christian hosts praise such

---

[9] Ibid, pg. 89-90
[10] Ibid, 90

"great" accomplishments. Denver's Methodist leaders, O. A. Willard, the District's presiding elder and George Richardson, pastor of the city's First Methodist Episcopal Church, issued the following joint statement praising Colonel Chivington accomplishments at Sand Creek:

As a military commander, we think his conduct has been worthy of equal commendation. To him, at the outset, Colorado owes deliverance from Texan invasion and internal strife. Through him the Indians have received at the battle of Sand Creek a chastisement, in the language of Acting Governor Elbert in his annual message, 'smiting and deserved.' For this act we are well aware he has received censure from malicious or ill-informed men but the people of Colorado who know the facts, fully justify his conduct and applaud the endurance, bravery, and self-denial of those who with him achieved so signal a success. We believe our only hope for safety as a Territory lies in the repetition of like battles with the same results. In the destruction of these Indians, the murdering and scalping of white men, women and children was by so much avenged. We are fully persuaded that the laws of war in this action were fully respected and only fear that similar occurrences are likely to be too unfrequent for an immediate and complete subjugation of the treacherous, blood-thirsty Red Men.[11]

What happened at Sand Creek was not just a spur of the moment set of bad judgements. It was the direct result of the oppress and persecute Native Americans culture that was firmly established in the U.S. Army in Denver and throughout the rest of the nation among almost all white people, including white Christians.

Once in a while, however, someone has the courage to stand up to these cruel cultures. Word about what happened at Sand Creek got back to federal officials in Washington, D.C., resulting in a congressional committee hearing. That Committee concluded that:

As to Colonel Chivington, your committee can hardly find fitting terms to describe his conduct. Wearing the uniform of the United States, which should be the emblem of justice and humanity; holding the important position of commander of a military

---

[11] Christopher Rein, "'Our First Duty Was to God and Our Next to Our Country'" Religion, Violence, and the Sand Creek Massacre" in *Great Plains Quarterly*, Vol. 34, No. 3 (Summer 2014), pg. 228-29

district, and therefore having the honor of the government to that extent in his keeping, he deliberately planned and executed a foul and dastardly massacre which would have disgraced the verist (sic) savage among those who were the victims of his cruelty. ... Whatever may have been his motive, it is to be hoped that the authority of this government will never again be disgraced by acts such as he and those acting with him have been guilty of committing. ... the truth is that he surprised and murdered, in cold blood, the unsuspecting men, women, and children on Sand creek, who had every reason to believe they were under the protection of the United States authorities, and then returned to Denver and boasted of the brave deed he and the men under his command had performed.[12]

In spite of the congressional criticism, however, I could find no record that Colonel Chivington was ever disciplined for his cruel and murderous behavior.

I mentioned earlier, that based on our history, these oppress and persecute cultures have no conscience when it comes to right and wrong. After reading about Sand Creek and the following story, I am now convinced that neither do they have any human decency, whatsoever.

Invitation to Talk Peace. In 1862, after several years of warring with the Apache Indians to seize their homes in the Southwest, including their lands and sources of food, the Army sent word to Chief Red Sleeves, inviting him to come under a temporary truce to discuss a peace treaty. Because of the constant battling and deteriorating condition of his people, the Chief reluctantly agreed. When he approached the Army camp, he searched for and found the high-flying white truce flag promising his safety. It was all a lie, however. Immediately upon entering the camp he was captured, and General West immediately told his guards "I want him dead or alive tomorrow morning, do you understand, *I want him dead.*" That night, the guards murdered him, scalped him, cut off his head, threw his body in the ditch and boiled the flesh off his head to produce a naked skull that could be sold to phrenologists back east.[13]

---

[12] Report of the Joint Committee on the Conduct of the War at the Second Session Thirty-Eighth Congress (Washington, D.C.: Government Printing Office, 1865), pg. v

[13] Brown, Dee, *Bury My Heart at Wounded Knee: an Indian History of the American West.* New York: Holt, Rinehart & Winston, 1970. pgs. 198-99

Wounded Knee Massacre. On December 29, 1890, the U.S. Army captured approximately 350 (120 men and 230 women and children) Sioux Indians and marched them to Wounded Creek in South Dakota. Once camp had been set up, the army demanded that all Indian weapons be surrendered, and the Indians complied. After the completion of a final weapons inspection, a scuffle broke out between an Indian warrior and a soldier, causing the other soldiers to start shooting at the unarmed Indians. At least 150 Indians were killed, of which about half were women and children. The wounded Indians were taken into a white church. It was four days after Christmas and a church banner above the pulpit read "PEACE ON EARTH, GOOD WILL TO MEN."[14]

And how did the white Christian ministers react to the Wounded Knee massacre? *The Word Carrier*, a monthly white Christian publication of the Dakota Indian mission in Santee, Nebraska, published in its January 1891 issue:

Taking it in its bearings on the whole condition of things among the rebellious Titon Sioux it was a blessing. It was needful that these people should feel in some sharp terrible way the just consequences of their actions, and be held in wholesome fear from further folly. … It was better that two hundred should die than that a nation should perish.[15]

Trail of Tears. In 1890, U.S. Cavalry veteran, John G. Burnett, wrote a letter to his grandchildren recounting his 1838-39 experience in marching the Cherokee Indians on their trail of tears to their reservation destination west of the Mississippi river. Mr. Burnett was eighteen years old at the time of his participation in the march. He wrote:

The removal of the Cherokee Indians from their lifelong homes in the year of 1838 found me a young man in the prime of my life and a private soldier in the American Army. Being acquainted with many of the Indians and able to fluently speak their language, I was sent as an interpreter into the Smokey Mountain Country in May

---

[14] Ibid, pgs. 439-445.
[15] Rani-Henrik Andersson, *The Lakota Ghost Dance of 1890* (Lincoln, Neb.: University of Nebraska Press, 2008, pg. 190

1838 and witnessed the execution of the most brutal order in the of History American Warfare. I saw the helpless Cherokees arrested and dragged from their homes, and driven at the bayonet point into the stockades. And in the chill of a drizzling rain on an October morning I saw them loaded like cattle or sheep into six hundred and forty-five wagons and started toward the west.

One can never forget the sadness and solemnity of that morning. Chief John Ross led in a prayer and when the bugle sounded and the wagons started rolling many of the children rose on their feet and waved their little hands good-by to their mountain homes, knowing they were leaving them forever. Many of these helpless people did not have blankets and many of them had been driven from home barefooted...

The long painful journey to the west ended March 26th, 1839, with four thousand silent graves reaching from the foothills of the Smokey Mountains to what is known as Indian territory in the West. And covetousness on the part of the white race was the cause of all that the Cherokees had to suffer...

The doom of the Cherokees Was sealed, Washington, D.C. had decreed that they must be driven West, and their lands given to the white nan, and May 1838 an Army of four thousand regulars, and three thousand volunteer soldiers under the command of General Winfield Scott, marched into the Indian country and wrote blackest chapter on the pages of American History...

Murder is murder and somebody must answer, somebody must explain the streams of blood that flowed in the Indian country in the summer of 1838. Somebody must explain the four thousand silent graves that mark the trail of the Cherokees to their exile. I wish I could forget it all, but the picture of six-hundred and forty-five wagons lumbering over the frozen ground with their Cargo of suffering humanity still lingers in my memory.
Let the Historians of a future day tell the sad story with its sighs, its tears and dying groans. Let the great Judge of all the earth weigh our actions and reward us according to our work.

Children—Thus ends my promised birthday story
This December the 11th, 1890[16]

---

[16] Ehle, John. Trail of Tears: *the Rise and Fall of the Cherokee Nation.* New York: Doubleday, 1988, pg. 394

The above accounts are, as you surely know, only a few of the U.S. Army's many absolutely cruel historical treatments of Native Americans. It was an army that, along with the nation's white civilian population, was controlled by an oppress and persecute Native Americans culture that believed that America had been given to white people by God to conquer and occupy. The culture required that white Christians oppress and persecute Native Americans and, oh, how well our ancestors obeyed that culture!

There may be no clearer way to sum up the culture's mission than an exchange from 1867-1868 when Comanche Chief Tosawi said in broken English, "Tosawi, good Indian," and General Sheridan gave his now immortal reply, "The only good Indians I ever saw were dead." To our shame, those cruel words carry on now in the expression, "The only good Indian is a dead Indian."[17]...A dark and cruel time in our Christian history.

Ku Klux Klan—White Supremacists

After the American Civil War ended, white people in the defeated Confederate states faced the possibility that the federal government's reconstruction programs would elevate the freed slaves to equal status. Blacks were beginning to vote, own property and businesses, occupy law enforcement positions, be appointed to judgeships, and even be elected to state and local governmental positions. If this continued, whites could find Blacks sitting beside them in their white churches, restaurants, and waiting rooms. They might even find black people using the same restrooms, drinking from the same water fountains, swimming in the same swimming pools, and staying in the same hotels. Something had to be done. The white oppress and persecute Blacks culture could lose everything it had accomplished with slavery, and it was not about to let that happen. The war between the armies had been lost, but the Southern oppress and persecute Blacks culture had not been defeated and was not about to let white Christians start treating the recently freed slaves with Christian love, respect, dignity and equality.

---

[17] Brown, Dee, *Bury My Heart at Wounded Knee*: an Indian History of the American West. New York: Holt, Rinehart & Winston, 1970. Pgs. 170-72

Hence, immediately after the Confederacy surrendered, the oppress and persecute Blacks culture demanded that every white Christian church, social group, family and state and local government in the South do everything they could to keep their black brothers and sisters suppressed. But even that was not enough. This evil culture could take no chances that the federal reconstruction programs might elevate black people to a status equal to that of white people. Every effort had to be made to keep Blacks in submission, and groups of host white Christians quickly responded.

The war ended on May 9, 1865 and by January, 1866, only months later, white Christians in Pulaski, Tennessee, had founded the first Ku Klux Klan for the sole purpose of preventing black people from gaining any legal, political or economic power or social standing. By 1870, just five years after the war ended, loosely affiliated Ku Klux Klan dens and other similar organizations had spread to all of the former Confederate states. Initially pitched as secret Christian social organizations, white southern cultural pressures quickly caused the Klan dens to evolve into terrorist organizations dedicated solely to terrorizing black people as well as any whites who supported blacks.

Donning their white robes and hoods, they rode their horses through black neighborhoods during the dark hours of night as a warning to not seek equality. Because oppressive cultures have no conscience of right or wrong, these rides soon deteriorated into breaking into black homes and pulling family members from their beds, then into beatings and lynchings and burning the homes. During the brief time period between 1865 and 1869, hundreds of acts of violence were carried out against both blacks and those whites who supported them by Klan dens in every Southern state. A combined 136 people were lynched in the states of Arkansas, Kentucky, Tennessee, South Carolina, and Georgia.[18]

For almost five years, the KKK terrorized blacks and their white supporters with utter impunity. State and local white law enforcement officers were either members of the Klan or fearful for their own lives if they challenged the KKK's violence. However, three things

---

[18] http://www.fofweb.com/Electronic_Images/Maps/AHOL-AUSH-KKK.pdf

happened in the early 1870s to significantly reduce Klan memberships and activities:

- The oppress and persecute Blacks culture, with the help and support of Klan dens, had for the most part, re-established white dominance of economic, political, religious, justice, and social organizations and activities so that the need for the Klan's terrorism had diminished.

- Congress passed the Klan Act in 1871 which allowed the federal government to arrest and convict Klan members for violence.

- After years of terrorism without consequences, word spread quickly when Klan members in South Carolina were arrested by federal agents, convicted, and given prison sentences. Members could no longer beat, burn, and murder people with impunity. They could be arrested, convicted, and imprisoned.

The result was that the KKK lost members, and many of their affiliate organizations were disbanded during the 1870s. But cultural pressures to oppress and persecute people never fully die, and the KKK, serving as the oppressive culture's special organization, remained alive in the background until it found new supporting hosts in 1915.

The revival of the KKK is documented in great detail by Linda Gordon in her book, *The Second Coming of the KKK*. Based on Gordon's extensive research, the "new" KKK had its start when William Simmons (a preacher who had lost his job with the Methodist Episcopal Church because of "inefficiency") led a group of his friends and two elderly men who had been members of the original Klan to the top of Stone Mountain, Georgia, where they burned a cross and inaugurated the rebirth of the Ku Klux Klan with fifteen charter members. (This was the first reported time that the Klan used the burning cross that would become its terrifying trademark in the ensuing years. Most people assume that Simmons got the idea from the movie, *The Birth of a Nation*, which showed the burning cross as an emblem in its portrayal of the KKK as a kind, benevolent organization that saved innocent Southern white women from the sexual assaults of overly aggressive savage black men.)

Interestingly, Simmons established the revised Ku Klux Klan as a for-profit company owned by him, alone, and he pitched it as a moral, Christian organization dedicated to protecting "true" Americans who were defined as white Anglo-Saxon Protestant Christians. He was a very polished speaker with the ability to engender and exploit fear in his audiences, playing off growing anxiety that the American way of life (for white Protestant Christians) was being destroyed by not only blacks, but also by Catholics, Jews, and immigrants (primarily Chinese, Japanese, and Mexicans).

Simmons' Klan grew slowly for several years but took off when he contracted with Elizabeth Tyler and Edward Clark to help promote the organization. Tyler and Clark established a nation-wide pyramid-type sales program where each sales person and their managers up the line got a percentage of both the initiation fee and the annual membership dues paid by members. Their national sales program found fertile ground. A white Protestant Christian supremacy oppress and persecute culture had been growing for years across most of the nation leading up to the 1920s. This cruel culture of denigrating, excluding, persecuting, and even murdering Blacks, Catholics, Jews, Chinese, Japanese and Mexicans had a firm grip on the host white Protestant Christians in large parts of our country. Those host Christians were ready and waiting for an opportunity to unleash their persecution and oppression.

In 1885, white coal miners in Rock Springs, Wyoming, rioted against their fellow Chinese miners and their families. Before the riot was over, 700 to 900 Chinese men, women and children had been murdered or chased out of town into freezing nighttime temperatures with none of their possessions and their homes burned, with not a single home left standing.[19]

In 1905, a mob of white men in Harrison, Arkansas, stormed the local jail and captured two black men accused of breaking into a white man's

---

[19] Loewen, James. W. *Sundown Towns: A Hidden Dimension of American Racism.* New York, NY: The New Press, 2018, pg. 50

home. They took the two men to the country where they beat them and told them to leave the town. The mob, then with guns and clubs, went through the black community capturing both men and women, beating some, throwing some into a nearby creek, burning several homes and warning all to leave. Many did leave, some without taking any of their possessions with them.[20]

In 1907, the whites in Bellingham, Washington drove out its entire Hindu population of 200 to 300. The white county sheriff stood silently by while the white mob did the cruel deed.[21]

In 1908, Terry County, Texas, advertised itself with the message "leave the niggers, chiggers, and gravediggers behind you."[22]

In 1910, Oklahoma amended its constitution with a "grandfather clause" that established literacy requirements to keep African Americans from voting. Whites were exempt from the requirement if their ancestors could vote in 1861.[23]

In 1912, the Forest Home Cemetery near Chicago adopted a resolution that from that point on the remains of white persons only could be buried in the cemetery, except for those colored people already owning lots.[24]

White supremacy's subordination of Blacks even reached the White House in the 1913–1920 period when President Woodrow Wilson racially segregated federal government workers. He either fired black employees and replaced them with white workers or forced black employees to remain in back rooms or behind screens. Prior to his election, the U.S. Navy had been integrated, but Wilson ordered it segregated and limited black Navy men to serving as cooks, firemen and dishwashers at sea.[25]

---

[20] Ibid, pg. 37
[21] Ibid, pg. 76
[22] Ibid, pg. 46
[23] Ibid, pg. 83
[24] Ibid, pg. 124
[25] Ibid, pg. 40

In the early 1920s and continuing for many years, the residents of Dearborn, Michigan, took pride in saying "The sun never set on a Negro in Dearborn."[26]

From 1890 to 1930, white-only towns, like Dearborn, arose all over the nation. Many of the towns had signs on the roads leading into their communities that said "Nigger, Don't Let the Sun Go Down on You in ____." Residents of Anna, Illinois even claimed, after they ran all Blacks out after a nearby lynching in 1909, that the name of their town stood for "Ain't No Niggers Allowed."[27]

Hundreds of other examples could be given, but the above are enough to show the receptive attitude of the national white Protestant Christian culture. They were ready and more than willing in the 1915 to 1925 time period to pay big bucks to become part of an organized movement to oppress and persecute Blacks, Catholics, Jews, Asians, and Mexicans. Simmons, Tyler, and Clark, through their "new" white Protestant Christian KKK, were more than happy to provide that opportunity. Their pyramid-type sales program combined with an aggressive national fear-based advertising and marketing program quickly grew the new Klan's national membership to somewhere between three and five million by the early 1920s. Oregon and Indiana became the two largest membership states. Needless to say, Simmons, Tyler, and Clark became wealthy, all based on selling the oppression and persecution of others to white Protestant Christian supremacists. It doesn't get much better than that for an oppress and persecute culture.

Although Simmons, Tyler, and Clark presented the new Klan as an upright, moral, Christian organization, its impact on our nation may have been even more devastating than the original Klan's terrorism because it permanently engraved its white supremacy into the "DNA" of white Protestant Christians all over the nation for decades to come. Sadly, it could be so even to the day that you are reading these words, no matter when that is.

---

[26] Ibid, pg. 116
[27] Ibid, pg. 3

Membership. According to Gordon, the new Klan penetrated almost every segment of the white Protestant Christian society 1915 to 1925. Members included governmental officials, business owners, attorneys, farmers, automobile dealers, engineers, chemists, physicians, pharmacists, dentists, accountants, schoolteachers, artists, and veterinarians.[28] The new Klan's emphasis on law and order brought in many Police chiefs and Sheriffs, who often brought their subordinates along with them.[29]

Now, may I remind you that the sole purpose of the Klan was to enforce white Protestant Christian supremacy by oppressing and persecuting other groups who were different in some way. Even given the core values of Christians, I was surprised, but probably should not have been, to learn that an estimated 40,000 white Christian ministers were Klan members…40,000 white Christian ministers willing to pay their own hard-earned dollars to be members of an organization dedicated solely to oppressing and persecuting their brothers and sisters of different races, heritage, and religions!

I wonder if I had lived back then and had surveyed those Klan minister members about their core Christian values, if they would have responded as my friends recently did with "love, justice, grace, worship, forgiveness, faith, repentance, hope, joy, humility, caring, compassion, kindness, generosity, empathy,, hospitality, joy, and gratitude?" Or would they have responded with "oppression, subordination, racial segregation, persecution, condemnation, torture, execution, exile and lynching?"…things to which the Klan, of which they were members, was utterly committed.

But the participation and support of Christian ministers went far beyond the 40,000 who joined as members. Gordon's research found that 26 of the 39 travelling Klan speakers (called Klokards) were white Protestant ministers …67% of the traveling KKK oppress and persecute culture motivation speakers were Christian ministers![30] Their

---

[28] Gordon, Linda. The Second Coming of the KKK. New York City, NY: W. W. Norton & Company, 2017, pg. 184
[29] Ibid, pg. 186
[30] Ibid, pg. 89

dark and cruel culture called on them to oppress and persecute, and they willingly took the lead.

Political Power. Oppressive cultures crave political power because that is their avenue to institutionalizing their oppression and persecution. Once their goals are institutionalized, they can remain in power for decades or even centuries. That is just the gift that the KKK gave to the oppress and persecute Blacks culture in the 1920s.

By the early 1920s, the Klan had become the dominant political force in many states far beyond the South, including Oregon, Colorado, Oklahoma, Indiana, and Maine.[31] Klan leaders boasted that 26 governors and 62 percent of the U.S. congress were Klan members. That may have been an exaggeration, but Gordon's research found that the numbers were at least 11 governors, 12 U.S senators and 75 congressmen. A majority of the U.S. House representatives from Texas, Colorado and Indiana were Klan members.[32] But it was not just the high-level governmental positions that the Klans controlled, they also controlled many city, county and school board positions. The mayors of Dallas, Fort Worth, Portland, Oregon, Portland, Maine, and all except one city in Colorado were all Klan members.[33] With these federal, state, and local governmental controls came the ability to institutionalize the powers of oppress and persecute Blacks cultures from slavery times all over the nation, ensuring that their cruelty would endure far into future.

- State legislation established what was taught (including daily reading of the Protestant Bible) and what was not taught in the schools, thereby passing the white Protestant Christian oppressive cultural beliefs and values on to future generations.[34]

- Through its members who were Christian ministers, politicians, editors of local newspapers, and those publications specifically

---

[31] Loewen, James. W. *Sundown Towns: A Hidden Dimension of American Racism*. New York, NY: The New Press, 2018, pg. 41
[32] Gordon, Linda. *The Second Coming of the KKK*. New York City, NY: W. W. Norton & Company, 2017, pgs. 164-65
[33] Ibid, pgs. 164-170
[34] Ibid, pg. 156

produced by the Klan, the Klan was able cement the oppress and persecute cultural "beliefs, knowledge, norms, and values" and "correct way to perceive, feel, think, and act" into the minds and hearts of white Protestant Christians all over the nation during the decade of the 1920s. Language ridiculing Blacks, Jews, Chinese and Mexicans were openly and proudly used.

In a 1922 speech in the Oakland Auditorium, a Klan speaker supporting gubernatorial candidate Richardson announced, "the election of Richardson is imperative if we are to remove the Jews, Catholics, and Negroes from public life in California." Richardson won the election by a landslide.[35]

- The October 29, 1923, the Seattle Klan newspaper, *The Watcher on the Tower,* declared: "We believe in the supremacy of the white race, and that it is just and right the younger brothers should be taught to respect those lines of birth which the Creator in His superior wisdom has drawn."[36]

- Led by Klan members, Congress passed legislation prohibiting the immigration of all Asian people. Klan members in the U.S House of Representatives also blocked the passage of anti-lynching legislation.[37]

- Klan-promoted eugenics laws that provided for the sterilization of "defective stock," usually defined as the poor and people of color, were adopted by thirty states.[38]

- Perhaps the most devastating long-term impact of the "new" Klan, however, was its cementing the feeling in white Protestant Christians that "black lives don't matter," whether the murder be a lynching or gun shots or riots or burning homes.

Loewen recounts the story of what happen in Ocoee, Florida, (west of Orlando) in 1920. Mose Norman, a black man, tried to vote but was

---

[35] Ibid, pg. 166
[36] Ibid, pg. 40
[37] Ibid, pg. 195
[38] Ibid, pgs. 194-95

turned away. He made the sad "mistake" of returning with a shotgun, insisting that he be allowed to vote. Instead of being allowed to vote, he was beaten. Colonel Salisbury then organized a lynch mob to punish Norman and one of his black friends, Julius Perry, who had also tried to vote. By nightfall, over 250 Klansmen plus other white men gathered in the town and attacked its black neighborhoods. More than 300 African Americans fled for their lives. Many were burned in their homes or shot as they tried to flee. Twenty-five homes, two churches, and a masonic lodge were burned with the number murdered being between 8 and 60. Julius Perry's body was found hanging from a light pole the next morning.[39]

Not only did black lives not matter to the evil oppressive culture of those years, black individuals themselves did not matter and could be denigrated, humiliated, and beaten at the drop of a hat. P.D. East, in his autobiography, *Magnolia Jungle*, tells of the time in about 1936 when he, as a young student, was traveling with his Mississippi middle school principal, who was also the basketball coach, to play a neighboring school's team. The principal's car tire was running low on air, so they stopped at a service station to have the tire looked at. They stopped in front of a gas pump, and a young black man came out asking if they wanted some gas. (Unlike today, gas stations attendants actually pumped the gas for customers those days.) The principal said no, he wanted someone to look at his car tire. The young man responded with something like, "Okay, I can look at it in a minute. Would you mind pulling up a bit so as to not block the gas pump?" According to East, the principal went into a rage. Grabbing an iron tire tool, he jumped out of the car screaming "No ___damn nigger tells me what to do." He hit the young man's head, splitting it open and knocking him to the ground, unconscious. East goes on to say that the incident was ignored by the local police, but word about what happened went out into the community, and the principal became a hero among his white peers.[40]

Loss of Power. After firmly establishing the oppression and persecution of particularly African Americans, but Jews and Mexicans

---

[39] Loewen, James. W. *Sundown Towns: A Hidden Dimension of American Racism.* New York, NY: The New Press, 2018, pg. 170
[40] East, P.D. The Magnolia Jungle: The Life, Times and Education of a Southern Editor. Literary Licensing, LLC, 2011. pg. 32

also, as a part of the values of our nation's dominant white society, the "new" Ku Klux Klan began to lose its power in the late 1920s. The loss was not due to a loss of faith in the Klan's goals of oppression and persecution, but rather the public exposure of the Klan's own wide-spread internal corruption. In Oregon, Klan leader and dentist Wilson was convicted of murder after raping his secretary and killing her by trying to perform an abortion.[41] Philip Fox, the editor of a Klan newsletter was sentenced to life in prison after murdering his rival.[42] Klan member Indiana Governor Ed Jackson was indicted for bribery, and a major Indiana Klan bank was indicted for embezzlement and grand larceny.[43] In Louisiana in 1922, the FBI found that the Klan had not only been intercepting the governor's mail and wiretapping his phone calls but had tortured and murdered two of his allies. Klan-supporting juries refused to convict them.[44] Indiana Grand Dragon Stephenson was convicted of kidnapping, raping and murdering his secretary in 1925.[45] Early leaders of the "new" Klan, Elizabeth Tyler and Edward Clark, had already been arrested for possessing whiskey (while strongly professing support for Prohibition) and having an illicit sexual affair while married to their respective spouses.[46] As Klan membership and associated revenues began to decline, Klan Klaverns (local chapters) were unable to pay their local bills, further damaging the organization's reputation, and the membership decline became a downhill spiral.

By 1927, the Klan's national membership had declined from several million to only about 350,000,[47] and by 1930 it was only about 30,000,[48] but the damage to our nation had already been done. The evil and inhumane white supremacist culture had become the dominant culture in our nation. Its cruel "beliefs, knowledge, norms, and values" and "correct way to perceive, feel, think, and act," which were dedicated to the oppression and persecution African Americans, Jews, Asians, and

---

[41] Gordon, Linda. *The Second Coming of the KKK*. New York City, NY: W. W. Norton & Company, 2017, pgs. 192
[42] Ibid, pg. 193
[43] Ibid
[44] Ibid, pg. 192
[45] Ibid, pg. 193
[46] Ibid, pg. 114
[47] Ibid, pg. 191
[48] Branan, Karen. *The Family Tree*, Atria Books, 2016, pg. 204

Mexicans, had been firmly embedded in society. They permeated our state and local laws and ordinances, our white church policies and creeds, our law enforcement and criminal justice system, our schools, colleges, universities, and Christian seminaries, our political parties, voting laws and systems, our financial systems, businesses, even deed restrictions regarding who can live where.

However, perhaps most importantly of all, the culture was now embedded and entwined in the minds, hearts and souls of white Protestant Christians all over America. The institutionalization of these cruel, oppressive KKK values had become so wide spread that they became the "norm"…the way that things are supposed to be. By the 1930s, we white Christians no longer recognized what we were doing to our fellow humans so that when they protested, we called them "criminals, thugs, communists, and sons-of-bitches."

The powerful influence of the KKK of the 1920s so thoroughly embedded the white supremacist cultural beliefs and subsequent behavior in our nation's institutions and cultural behavior that our society could kill unarmed George Floyd, Breonna Taylor, and Rayshard Brooks in 2020, almost a hundred years later. And sadly, those cruel beliefs and values show few signs of abating.

But even though the Klan's membership had declined dramatically, and it had lost almost all of its once dominating political power by the 1930s, the oppress and persecute Blacks culture was not about to let it die. There was still too much cultural hate that had to be dispensed. Between 1930 and 1965, the Tuskegee Institute reports that 183 people were lynched in the nation; all except 14 were black. How was this possible? While the Klan lost its national organizational structure after the 1930s, local, independent klaverns were popping up all over the place, often in competition with each other for the membership fees.

Michael Newton reports in his thoroughly researched book, *The Invisible Empire: The Ku Klux Klan in Florida,* that Klan chapters, mostly independent, remained active in Florida in the 1930s. They were responsible for 14 lynchings between 1931 and 1941 with all except one being black.[49] Even though the Klan had lost most of its political power, it continued to speak out in elections. Franklin Roosevelt's appointment of a Catholic campaign manager and his later appointment of two Jews to cabinet positions was just too much for the Klan. In their newspapers, they called his "New Deal" a "Jew deal" and published a cartoon showing Roosevelt saying to his wife "You kiss the niggers and I'll kiss the Jews and we'll stay in the White House as long as we choose."[50]

The Florida Klans continued their violence into the 1950s with crimes like the beating and shooting of a black janitor at a white Orlando elementary school because they heard a rumor that he had entered the girls' bathroom unescorted. A month later, the janitor's brother-in-law was dragged from his home, beaten, and then shot to death.

The same crimes continued in Mississippi where the list of Klan murders included NAACP activists Reverend George Lee (1955), Medgar Evers (1963), Louis Allen (1964), and Vernon Dahmer (1966). Mississippi Klansman Sam Bowers boasted after he was indicted for murdering Mr. Dahmer, "A jury would not dare convict a white man for killing a nigger in Mississippi." He was not convicted.[51]

The same KKK campaign of beatings and murder were occurring in Louisiana and Alabama during the 1960s in response to the Civil Rights protests led by Martin Luther King.[52] The dynamite that killed the four little girls in the 1963 Birmingham church bombing was planted by white Birmingham Klan members.

And what were our Christian churches in the South saying about all of this during the almost 100 years of KKK violence? With a few notable exceptions, we were either granting our full support or voicing no opposition whatsoever. Remember that in the 1920s, the Klan had over 40,000 white evangelical Christian minister members. The oppress and persecute Blacks culture had total control over us. Instead

---

[49] Newton, Michael. *The Invisible Empire: The Ku Klux Klan in Florida*, pg. 75
[50] Ibid, pg. 77
[51] https://segregationinamerica.eji.org/report/massive-resistance.html
[52] Nelson, Stanley. *Devils Walking: Klan Murders Along the Mississippi in the 1960s*. Louisiana State University Press, 2016

of speaking out as Jesus did about those who were oppressed and persecuted during His human time with us, we were preaching that we are "saved by the grace of God through our faith, alone, not by works." It didn't matter how we treated Blacks, Jews, Mexicans, and Asians. All that mattered was whether we, ourselves, got to heaven. Apparently, our support for the hell on earth for others that our cruel culture and its special KKK organization created with our help was just fine. It had nothing to do with our salvation. A cruel, dark, dark time in our Christian history,

Nazi Party—German Supremacists

It may be wrong to claim that the Nazi party was created solely for the purpose of oppressing and persecuting Jews. A host of additional factors played a role, including resentment from the WW I treaties which conceded pre-war German territory to other nations, subsequent high rates of unemployment, Hitler's demagogical personality and leadership, as well as other factors contributed to the success of this evil movement in Germany in the 1930s. Under Hitler's leadership, the majority of Germany's Christian population quickly bought into the goal of creating a superior race of people by removing all non-German people through exportation and outright executions, and by eliminating all physically and mentally handicapped through eugenics. This was exactly what the oppress and persecute Jews culture was looking for, and it quickly adopted the Nazi movement as its special organization to oppress and persecute Jews.

This evil culture had been a parasitic part of Christianity in Europe for centuries, waning sometimes and then rising again to take the homes, businesses, and lives of thousands of Jews. The following are simply a sample of examples of Jewish persecution from 1200 to 1800 CE.[53] As heart wrenching as they are, they will give you clear sense for the ways that European Christians viewed and treated Jews in the centuries leading up to the Holocaust.

- 1261: Duke Henry III of Brabant, Belgium, stated in his will that "Jews...must be expelled from Brabant and totally

---

[53] http://www.religioustoleration.org > jud_pers3

annihilated so that not a single one remains, except those who are willing to trade, like all other tradesmen, without money-lending and usury."

- 1267: The Synod of Vienna ordered Jews to wear horned hats. Thomas Aquinas (renowned Italian philosopher and theologian) said that Jews should live in perpetual servitude.

- 1290: Jews are exiled from England. About 16,000 left the country.

- 1298: Jews were persecuted in Austria, Bavaria, and Franconia. 140 Jewish communities were destroyed; more than 100,000 Jews were killed over a 6-month period.

- 1306: 100,000 Jews are exiled from France. They left with only the clothes on their backs and food for only one day.

- 1320: 40,000 French shepherds went to Palestine on the Shepherd Crusade. On the way, 140 Jewish communities were destroyed.

- 1321: In Guienne, France, Jews were accused of having incited criminals to poison wells. 5,000 Jews were burned alive at the stake.

- 1338: The councilors of Freiburg banned the performance of anti-Jewish scenes from the town's passion play because of the lethal bloody reactions against Jews which the performances.

- 1391: Jewish persecutions begin in Seville and in 70 other Jewish communities throughout Spain.

- 1394: Jews were exiled, for the second time, from France.

- 1431: The Council of Basel "forbade Jews to go to universities, prohibited them from acting as agents in the conclusion of contracts between Christians, and required that they attend church sermons."

- 1434: "Jewish men in Augsburg had to sew yellow buttons to their clothes. Across Europe, Jews were forced to wear a long undergarment, an overcoat with a yellow patch, bells, and tall pointed yellow hats with a large button on them."

- 1453: The Franciscan monk, Capistrano, persuaded the King of Poland to terminate all Jewish civil rights.

- 1478: Spanish Jews had been heavily persecuted from the 14th century. Many had converted to Christianity. The Spanish Inquisition was set up by the Church in order to detect insincere conversions. Laws were passed that prohibited the descendants of Jews or Muslims from attending universities, joining religious orders, holding public office, or entering any of a long list of professions.

- 1492: Jews were given the choice of being baptized as Christians or being banished from Spain. 300,000 left Spain penniless. Many migrated to Turkey where they found tolerance among the Muslims. Others converted to Christianity but often continued to practice Judaism in secret.

- 1497: Jews were banished from Portugal. 20,000 left the country rather than be baptized as Christians.

- 1543: Martin Luther wrote his book *Jews and Their Lies* which condemned Jews and recommended that they be expelled and that their synagogues and schools be burned.

- 1555: The Roman Catholic Papal bull "Cum nimis absurdum" required Jews to wear badges and live in ghettos. They were not allowed to own property outside the ghetto. Living conditions were dreadful: over 3,000 people were forced to live on about 8 acres of land. Women had to wear a yellow veil or scarf; men had to wear a piece of yellow cloth on their hat.

- 1582: Jews were expelled from Holland.

- 1648-9: Chmielnicki Bogdan led an uprising against Polish rule in the Ukraine. The secondary goal of Bogdan and his followers was to exterminate all Jews in the country. The massacre began with the slaughter of about 6,000 Jews in Nemirov. Other major mass murders occurred in Tulchin, Polonnoye, Volhynia, Bar, Lvov, etc. Jewish records estimate that a total of 100,000 Jews were murdered, and 300 communities destroyed.

- 1744. Archduchess of Austria Maria Theresa ordered that "... no Jew is to be tolerated in our inherited duchy of Bohemia" by the end of Feb. 1745. In December 1748 she reversed her position on the condition that Jews pay for readmission every ten years. This extortion was known as malke-geld (queen's money). In 1752 she introduced the law limiting each Jewish family to one son.[54]

- 1871: Pope Pius IX calls Jews "dogs" in a speech to a women's group.[55]

- 1917-1921: after the Russian Revolution, more than 500 Jewish communities in the Ukraine were wiped out in pogroms. About 60,000 Jewish men, women and children were murdered.[56]

- 1935: The Nazis reprinted Martin Luther's book *Jews and Their Lies.*[57]

As you can see, by the time the Nazi Party came into power in the 1930s, the oppress and persecute Jews culture had maintained control over Germany's (and other European) Protestant and Catholic Christians for centuries. It was only a small step for this well-

---

[54] Timeline of antisemitism - Wikipedia
[55] Wills, Garry. "The Popes Against the Jews: Before the Holocaust," *New York Times*, September 23, 2001
[56] www.adl.org > assets > pdf > education-outreach
[57] Ibid

established culture to use this opportunity to accomplish its goal of mass execution of the Jews, whereas it had previously only been able to do that on a smaller scale (e.g., killing a few hundred Jews here and a few thousand there every few years).

The setting was perfect, and the oppress and persecute Jews culture took full advantage of it. The Protestant and Catholic Christians (with a few notable courageous exceptions) who put Hitler and his Nazi party in power and kept them in power were ready and eager to carry out the demands of their oppress and persecute Jews culture.

As described by Peter Hayes in his extremely well written book "Why? Explaining the Holocaust," the Nazis first tested the German people to see how much oppression and persecution of Jews they would accept. On pages 77 and 78, Hayes describes the cultural environment leading up to the Holocaust:

The year 1934 brought a legislative lull, as the Third Reich decreed only one major antisemitic measure, a law that increased the government's ability to deport people it denaturalized. Then, in 1935, the regime closed the ranks of the German military to Jews, forbade them to display the German flag on national holidays, and completed the agenda laid down before 1933 by stripping Jews of German citizenship and reducing them to resident "subjects" of Germany, banning new intermarriages and all extramarital sexual relations between Jews and non-Jews, … and dismissing the last Jews from civil service. Nineteen thirty-six saw another lull, as the regime downplayed its antisemitism in the run-up to the summer Olympics in Berlin, lest other nations decline to participate, and little happened at the national level in 1937, either, aside from a prohibition on granting doctoral degrees to Jews.

The staccato pattern of increasing persecution at the national level from 1933 to 1937 belied, however, a continuous "squeezing" of Jews by Nazi activists at the local or street level, usually out of ear-or eyeshot of foreign reporters. Even in big cities, but especially in small towns, pressure was brought to bear on Jews' jobs and businesses in a host of ways. While the brown-shirted storm of the SA (the Nazi Party's paramilitary wing) threatened or inflicted harm on Jew's property or children, Nazi officeholders canceled contracts or refused to entertain bids from firms owned or led by Jews, welfare agencies prohibited the use of payments or vouchers at Jewish-owned shops, local leaders forbade their employees to buy at such establishments or to patronize Jewish professionals and publicly posted lists and/or pictures of people who did so, Jews' businesses became identifiable by the absence of "German firm" … window signs that now proliferated among competitors, municipal councils banned Jews from having stands at public market halls or using public swimming pools, local and regional savings banks and credit unions stopped making loans to Jews or their businesses, branches of the Nazi labor union…insisted on dismissals of mangers, tax authorities seized ledger books and charged Jews with tax evasion or illegal transfers of money abroad, and in many places, Nazi stalwarts intimidated non-Jewish shopkeepers, especially sellers of foodstuffs, into refusing to accept Jewish customers, thus forcing them either to move or shop far from home where they would not be recognized. All the while, the Nazi-controlled press kept up a barrage of allegations regarding supposed Jewish criminality and deceitfulness.[58]

Across the country, in 1933, clubs, singing groups, bowling leagues, and similar organizations began restricting membership to so-called Aryans and thus inflicting on Jews… "social death." Jews found themselves increasingly abandoned and alone.

The Nazi party got its answer, the German non-Jewish Christian population was ready and willing to not only accept, but to also help impose cruel and inhuman treatments on Jews. The hate Jews culture that had been promoted by Catholic and Protestant Christians for centuries was firmly in control of the German non-Jewish population. With this assurance, the Nazi party moved ahead to develop and implement plans to murder over six million Jews beginning with mass killings in 1941 and continuing until the Nazis were defeated by the Allies in 1945. During the period between 1941 and early 1943, Jews were being killed at the rate of 225,000 per month. At its peak between 1942 and 1943, the Jewish murders were approximately 325,000 per month or over 10,000 per day.[59]

And who was ordering and executing these murders? The tragic answer is German Christians. As mentioned, earlier in Chapter 5, 54 percent of the German population in 1939 were Protestant Christians, 40 percent Catholic Christians and 6 percent, other. It was primarily members of Germany's 94 percent Christian population who were ordering and executing the Jews.

---

[58] Hayes, Peter, *Why? Explaining the Holocaust*, pgs. 77-78
[59] Ibid, pg. 115.

There were, of course, a few hundred, maybe a few thousand, courageous Christians who risked their own lives to save the lives of their Jewish friends and neighbors, but the vast majority of the nation's Christians were fully on board with the mass murders or cared so little that they said nothing. The oppress and persecute Jews culture's special organization, the Nazi party, had done its job. It was a horribly dark, cold, and cruel side of Christianity that the world should have never seen and, hopefully, will never see again.

White Citizen's Council—White Supremacists

In spite of all of its southern white Christian support, Jim Crow laws, and KKK terrorism, the oppress and persecute Blacks culture was slowly losing the battle in the 1950s to keep African Americans oppressed in an inferior, subordinated, and segregated sector of American society and economy. Again, like the Israelites in Egypt, African Americans continued to protest their own persecution and on Monday, May 17, 1954, won a U.S Supreme Court decision (*Brown vs Board of Education*) to give black students access to the same higher quality schools in which white students were enrolled. The future looked bad for the oppress and persecute Blacks culture. It had to become much more aggressive or find itself, someday, perhaps in the near future, being forced by federal laws to treat their black neighbors with respect, dignity and equality…maybe even let them attend our white churches…something that the culture and its host white Christians simply could not tolerate.

By then, the KKK had lost its national organizational structure and deteriorated into highly splintered groups. The local chapters were competing with each other and had little political influence (except in some local governments) as well a growing reputation of being a bunch of white criminal thugs. The oppress and persecute Blacks culture had to find a stronger, more upscale and effective special organization dedicated to maintaining white supremacy in the southern states and, hopefully, the nation as a whole.

The culture did not have to wait long. In fact, only weeks after the Supreme Court decision, elite white Mississippi political, religious and business leaders responded to their culture's call.

231

John Bell Williams, a Mississippi congressional representative, branded the day of the Supreme Court opinion as "Black Monday."

Tom P. Brady, a Yale graduate and Mississippi Circuit Court judge, delivered a speech which he then converted into a book entitled *Black Monday Segregation or Amalgamation...America Has Its Choice.* Brady went after racial integration with everything he had. Black people were savages. Racial integration was being promoted by socialists and communists. It would lead to the black men raping white women. It would result in the amalgamation of the white race. White people had to organize and do everything they could to protect the purity of their race.

He began his book by saying that it was "dedicated to those Americans who firmly believe socialism and communism are lethal 'messes of porridge' for which our sacred birthright shall not be sold." He then proceeded to write:

'Black Monday' is the name coined by Representative John Bell Williams of Mississippi to designate Monday, May 17th, 1954, a date long to be remembered throughout this nation. This is the date upon which the Supreme Court of the United States handed down its socialistic decision in the Segregation cases on appeal from the States of Kansas, South Carolina, Virginia and Delaware. 'Black Monday' is indeed symbolic of the date. Black denoting darkness and terror. Black signifying the absence of light and wisdom. Black embodying grief, destruction and death. Should Representative Williams accomplish nothing more during his membership in Congress he has more than justified his years in office by the creating of this epithet, the originating of this watchword, the shouting of this battle cry. Black Monday ranks in importance with July 4th, 1776, the date upon which our Declaration of Independence was signed. May 17th, 1954, is the date upon which the declaration of socialistic doctrine was officially proclaimed throughout this nation. It was on Black Monday that the judicial branch of our government usurped the sacred privilege and right of the respective states of this union to educate their youth. This usurpation constitutes the greatest travesty of the American Constitution and jurisprudence in the history of this nation.[60]

---

[60] http://www.hcaauctions.com/%e2%80%9cBlack-Monday%e2%80%9d-Pro-Segregation-Propaganda-LOT27950.aspx

Brady minced no words in his Black Monday book about how he and the white supremacist culture of that time felt about black people. On page 12, he opined:

*You can dress a **chimpanzee**, housebreak him, and teach him to use a knife and fork, but it will take countless generations of evolutionary development, if ever, before you can convince him that a caterpillar or a cockroach is not a delicacy. Likewise the social, political, economical, and religious preferences of the negro remain close to the **caterpillar** and the **cockroach**. This is not stated to ridicule or abuse the negro. There is nothing fundamentally wrong with the caterpillar or the cockroach. It is merely a matter of taste. A cockroach or caterpillar remains proper food for a chimpanzee.*

Robert B. "Tut" Patterson, a former Mississippi State College football star, World War II veteran, and manager of a large delta plantation near Indianola, Mississippi, was inspired by Brady's words. He called for a meeting of concerned citizens on July 11, 1954, at the Indianola town hall, just two months after the Supreme Court decision. The meeting was attended by the community's white leaders (no black leaders were invited), including Indianola's mayor. It concluded with a commitment to create the Citizens Council (the official name) with membership restricted to whites and dedicated totally to maintaining a segregated society with an emphasis on keeping blacks from voting and black children out of white schools.

Off and Running The oppress and persecute Blacks culture was excited and determined. It had its new special organization and was on a roll! Within just a few months, membership in the Council had spread to twenty-two Mississippi counties. The Citizens' Councils of Mississippi, headquartered in Greenwood, was created to support the rapidly growing number of local councils. Patterson was chosen to serve as its executive secretary, the only salaried administrator.

One year later, 250 independent White Citizens' Councils had been established in other southern states with an estimated membership of 60,000. A year later in 1956, White Councils were operating in 30 states, and by 1957 national membership had reached an estimated 250,000. Membership was made up of leading white civic, business, religious, law enforcement, judicial, and political leaders which included mayors, sheriffs, police chiefs, governors and U.S. senators and representatives.

The rapid national growth resulted in the creation of the Association of Citizens' Councils of America to provide the needed coordination and support. Patterson was selected as its salaried leader.[61]

White leaders all over the South responded to their culture's call. Mississippi U. S. Senator James O. Eastland and Representative John Bell Williams, South Carolina U. S. Senator J. Strom Thurmond and Representative L. Mendel, and Georgia Governor Marvin Griffin agreed to serve on the Advisory Council to the Association of Citizens' Councils of America.

Senator Eastland declared in a speech:

On May 17, 1954, the Constitution of the United States was destroyed because of the Supreme Court's decision. You are not obliged to obey the decisions of any court which are plainly fraudulent [and based on] sociological considerations.[62]

Reverend Guy T. Gillespie, a theologian and president emeritus of Mississippi's Belhaven College responded quickly, delivering a speech entitled *A Christian View on Segregation* to the Synod of Mississippi of the Presbyterian Church in the U.S. on November 4, 1954. His audience, of course, consisted only of white church members. The oppress and persecute culture of that time would have never let a black person attend unless they happen to be cleaning the bathrooms or emptying the trash cans.

Reverend Gillespie used the biblical texts about the "curse of Ham" and the "tower of Babel" to establish, beyond any doubt, that God intentionally created separate races and absolutely forbade racial amalgamation. He then went on to blame Communists for forcing racial integration on the nation.

---

[61] https://calendar.eji.org/racial-injustice/jul/11
[62] Williams, Juan, *Eyes on the Prize: America's Civil Rights Years, 1954–1965*, Viking Penguin, January 1, 1987, p. 38.

Here, therefore, is the crux of this whole problem of racial relations. Whether we face it in America or in the world at large. It is essentially a choice between the Angelo-Saxon ideal of racial integrity maintained by a consistent application of the principle of segregation, and the communist goal of amalgamation, implemented by the wiping out of all distinctions and the fostering of the intimate contact between the races in all the relations of life.

…if we believe that the welfare and happiness of both races would be promoted by intermarriage and the development of a hybrid race, then all we need to do is to let down the bars of segregation in the homes, the schools, the churches and in all areas of community life and let nature take its course.[63]

The White Citizens Council loved his speech and had it printed in a pamphlet and widely distributed.

Dr. George Cheek, minister of the Selma, Alabama, Avenue Presbyterian Church declared that *"God was the first segregator"* and used scriptures from Genesis to describe how God had used three men to establish three different racial groups: Shem was sent to Asia to establish the Semitic race, Jacob was used to establish the Caucasian race who settled in Europe and Ham was used to establish the Canaanites and Negro groups who were sent to Africa.[64]

Bull Conner, perhaps most notably remembered for ordering the beating of the Selma, Alabama, bridge protestors, declared in a 1956 speech to the Central Park Citizens' Council in Birmingham, "If you don't register and vote [the NAACP is] going to outvote you." On another occasion he boasted, "All you gotta do is to tell them you're going to bring the dogs. Look at 'em run. Bring the dogs anyway, captain."

Alabama Dallas County State **Senator Walter C. Givhan** told a Council meeting that the NAACP hoped "to open the bedroom door of our white women to the Negro."

---

[63] https://archive.org/stream/1954Gillespie/1954_gillespie_djvu.txt
[64] [Birmingham 105-299, #39 which is *Tuscaloosa AL News*, 5/6/56, p1]

As you might expect, **Robert "Tut" Patterson**, the head of the Association of Citizens' Councils of America, often wrote and spoke promoting the Councils' oppression and persecution of black people. For example, he wrote in 1956:

Integration represents darkness, regimentation, totalitarianism, communism and destruction. Segregation represents the freedom to choose one's associates, Americanism, State sovereignty and the survival of the white race. These two ideologies are now engaged in mortal conflict and only one can survive.[65]

Mississippi **Judge Tom P. Brady** also continued to make the speaking rounds. In an October 28, 1954, speech, Brady re-enforced the oppress and persecute Blacks cultural belief that black people were inferior. He proclaimed that:

1620—that is when the seed was planted on the shores of the Atlantic at Jamestown. That seed has now grown into a tree and is bearing fruit today. That is the trouble which faces us now. Of course, they were considered just a little better than a good saddle horse—we know it—a little under, perhaps, a good hunting dog. Three were savages, the Congo flossed deep in their brains. They had no such thing as a code of ethics or morals. They were abysmal savages. Just a few months before, they had sharpened their teeth with rocks so that they could easily tear human flesh; they were cannibals.[66]

Mississippi **Governor Ross Barnett** (and Sunday School teacher at First Baptist Church, Jackson, Mississippi) declared that:

There is no case in history where the Caucasian race has survived social integration. We will not drink from that cup of genocide.[67]

As a side note, Governor Barnett appointed Judge Brady to the Mississippi Supreme Court, thereby handsomely rewarding him for his relentless attacks on black people. Such appointments were just one of the many ways that oppress and persecute cultures get

---

[65]   https://www.splcenter.org/fighting-hate/intelligence-report/1999/racist-council-conservative-citizens-finds-home-mainstream-politics
[66] https://archive.org/stream/1954Brady/1954_brady_djvu.txt
[67] Dupont, Carolyn Renee, *Mississippi Praying*. New York University Press, Copyrighted 213, pg. 115

institutionalized. You can be almost certain that there was no equal justice for Blacks where Brady was the judge.

South Carolina **Governor Olin D. Johnson** proudly boasted, "I don't run from niggers. But I run them from me."[68]

Relentlessly bombarding white communities with fear. The supportive words of political, religious, and business leaders set the stage from which the White Citizens Councils bombarded southern white communities with messages of fear and hate day after day, week after week and month after month.

In Evelyn Kerns's honor thesis[69], she documents that during the 1950s and 1960s the Councils:

- Established a logo showing the American and Confederate flags with crossing staffs. The logo clearly "shouted" to both whites and blacks that "We strongly endorse and will enforce the racial ideals of the Confederate culture." The logos were printed in color on signs similar to civic club signs and posted in many communities.
- Placed ads and had numerous supporting articles published in state and local newspapers such as the *Jackson Daily News*, *Meridian Star*, and the *Lexington Advertiser*
- Produced their own radio program that was carried on 50 stations across the southern states
- Hosted their own television program, carried on 12 stations in Georgia, Tennessee, Mississippi, Louisiana, Texas, and Virginia
- Posted over 200 billboard signs with messages of fear and condemnation of racial equality, often portraying Martin Luther King and the NAACP as communists
- Published textbooks for children's schools
- Printed and distributed pamphlets, posters, and brochures

---

[68] https://www.jstor.org/stable/resrep30692.7
[69] Kerns, Evelyn. Arguments Against Amalgamation: The Citizens Council Battles Integration by Controlling the Narrative." Eastern Kentucky University: December 2017

- Provided a steady supply of speakers for local Council meetings
- Produced its own monthly newspaper, *The Citizens Council,* with an estimated circulation of about 50,000 white citizens, especially in the South, were constantly bombarded with messages that:

  ✓ Blacks were naturally inferior people with limited abilities,
  ✓ Black men were over sexed and desired white women,
  ✓ Racial segregation was not only ordained by God but mandated by the Bible and God,
  ✓ Racial integration would lead to interracial marriages and the amalgamation of the Angelo-Saxon race,
  ✓ The racial integration movement, including the NAACP, was being financed and promoted by Communists.

This was the cultural environment in which I grew up. I remember as a child hearing Mississippi Governor Bilbo speak from the city hall steps of my hometown of Newton. The part that has stuck with me all these many years is when he shouted, *"I have nothing against colored people."* And then he looked above the white people gathered closest to him to glare directly at the black people in the back and declared with a superior smirk on his face, *"In fact, I love you. I love you so much that I want to send every one of you back to Africa."*

That was what our white oppress and persecute Blacks culture wanted from Governor Bilbo and what he proudly delivered with no consideration, whatever, for the feelings of the black people in attendance. They couldn't vote, so they did not matter. In fact, as Judge Brady would say a few years later, they were not even worth as much as "a good hunting dog." Even as a child, I remember feeling terrible for the black people as our white audience laughed and clapped and the humiliated black people in the back began to ease away. I don't recall whether my parents voted for Bilbo or not, but I am guessing that they did.

Actions did the horrors. Words set the stage and provided the motivation. But the actions of the Citizens Councils and their members carried out atrocity after atrocity to make sure that the southern oppress and persecute Blacks culture's demands were obeyed.

- Through its political powers, the Councils got over 400 state laws passed to protect racial segregation. These laws included laws like Mississippi's Freedom of Choice law that allowed parents to choose the school for their children which enabled white parents to move their children to schools with mostly other white children. Also, they helped enact Arkansas's law that enabled the governor to close public schools and South Carolina's prohibition against state government employment of members of NAACP, including employees of public black colleges.

- The Council published manuals on how to create private white K-12 schools, and then aggressively promoted the establishment of such schools by local communities. And the local communities did just that with white-only private schools springing up all over the South. Almost every community or county founded at least one such school with the larger communities having more. My own home county in Mississippi established one that was an immediate success, and although it is now slightly integrated, the school is still going strong in 2023. My wife's aunt was the principal at a newly started school in a neighboring county. There is one such school less than a mile from my current home in Tallahassee, Florida. Although that school is now somewhat integrated, the institution itself is still going strong. Sadly, these schools, including the one near my current home, often had the word "Christian" in their name. The message, while veiled in "nice" language, clearly communicates to all that their founding rationale of racial segregation was the Christian thing to do.

- Governor Faubus, a White Citizens Council member, called in the state National Guard to block the integration of Little Rock Central High School in 1957, and then closed all of Little Rock's public high schools for the entire 1958-59 school year rather than allow the integration of the schools.

- Although portraying themselves as "nonviolent," the Councils frequently used intimidation and retaliation to punish blacks who joined the NAACP, who participated in black voter registration drives and who signed petitions seeking school integration. Names of the "offending" blacks were published either in ads placed in local newspapers or in the local White Citizens Council's newspaper. Employers were called. Suppliers to black businesses were called. Banks were called. Law enforcement officials were notified. In other words, community-wide efforts were made by the Councils to let all white people know who the black "troublemakers" were. The results were devastating for those blacks seeking to throw off the white culture's oppressive bonds of segregation. Hundreds of "offending" blacks were fired from their jobs or evicted from their sharecropping farms. They had their home mortgages and business loans called due, lost the suppliers for their retail and construction businesses. They were even refused services by white-owned businesses, including gas stations, and harassed by white law enforcement officers on "trumped up" charges. And it worked, just as the white culture wanted and the White Councils had planned.

In October 1955, 53 black residents of Yazoo County, Mississippi, signed a desegregation petition launched by the NAACP. The local White Citizens Council published their names in a newspaper ad, and they quickly faced widespread harassment, lost their jobs, and had their bank accounts cancelled. A few weeks later, all 53 signers withdrew their names and the Yazoo County NAACP was disbanded. The following year, 17 black parents in Elloree, South Carolina, signed a pro-integration petition. Within two weeks, all had lost their jobs or been evicted from their share cropping farms. Fourteen of the seventeen withdrew their names from the petition.[70]

White Citizen Council members and supporters showed up in droves when black students, with the backing of court orders, attempted to

---

[70] https://segregationinamerica.eji.org/report/massive-resistance.html

enroll in white public schools. The white oppress and persecute Blacks culture was being threatened and had to be protected.

In Little Rock, Arkansas, the integration of Central High School in September 1957 was aggressively opposed by both The Capital Citizens Council and the Mother's League of Central High School which mounted both legal challenges and anti-integration media campaigns. The legal challenges failed, but the media campaigns had the white community up in arms. On the first day when the "Little Rock 9" black students arrived for the start of the new school year, so did hundreds of white parents and their supporters. The whites showed up with their Confederate flag and signs like "Race Mixing is Communism," "Go Back to Africa Negroes," and "Stop the Race Mixing March of the Anti-Christ." White people shouted racial slurs and spat on the young black students as they walked toward the school doors while chanting "two, four, six, eight. We ain't gonna integrate." Once the black students were inside the school, a white mother was overheard shouting out to her white children who were already in the building, "Come out! Don't stay in there with those niggers."

The power of Little Rock's white oppress and persecute Blacks culture was on full display that day. When asked about what happened at the school, the editor of the *Arkansas Gazette* responded, "I'll give it to you in one sentence. The police have been routed, the mob is in the streets, and we're close to a reign of terror." That is what oppress and persecute cultures do to otherwise "good" Christian people…make us trample Jesus' admonition to "do unto others as you would have them do unto you" into the mud under our feet like his words were no more than garbage.[71]

As horrifying as the desegregation conflicts at Little Rock's Central High School were, it was far worse in Birmingham, Alabama, that same year when Reverend Fred Shuttlesworth led an initiative to desegregate the Birmingham public schools. While the Birmingham Citizens Council created the fear-based environment necessary, it was the local KKK that responded with its customary acts of terror.

---

[71] http://www.watson.org/~lisa/blackhistory/school-integration/lilrock/9enter.html

Ken Boutwell

In her dissertation, *To Give Racism the Face of the Ignorant: Race, Class, and White Manhood in Birmingham, Alabama, 1937-1970*, Heather Bryson describes what happened:

In the summer of 1957, Shuttlesworth announced that his children would attend the all-white Phillips High School during the upcoming school year. On September 2, one week before the first day of school, six officers of the East Lake Klan in Birmingham met to decide who would be the Captain of the Lair, second only to the Exalted Cyclops. Five of the officers listened as Bart Floyd made his pitch for Captain. Sitting in their lair, a small, cement building with kerosene lamps, dirt floors and windows with blackout curtains, Floyd told the others that he was ready —to prove himself worth by getting—nigger blood on his hands. Rather than taking him at his word, the six jumped into two cars and went hunting for a victim as well as for Floyd's credentials as captain. After stopping at a drugstore for razor blades and a bottle of turpentine, the six headed to Zion City, a poor, black neighborhood to select a —Negro to scare the hell out of. When they came upon an African American couple talking outside of a home, a few of the Klan members jumped out of their car and grabbed the thin man (Edward Aaron) and forced him in the backseat of the car and drove back to the lair. On the way, Floyd pistol-whipped the man, upon arrival at their small lair, told him to —make like a dog and clutched him by his neck as he forced him to crawl into the dark room.

Once the kerosene lamps were lit, the Klansmen put on their hoods and stood over their victim. Exalted Cyclops Pritchett told the man to give Reverend Shuttlesworth a message. —I want you to tell him to stop sending nigger children and white children to school together or we're gonna do to him like we're fixing to do to you. ...The men knocked their victim to the ground and pinned him to the dirt while Floyd knelt down and sliced off the man's scrotum. ....Just before cutting him, the six Klansmen shouted questions at Aaron: —You think you're as good as I am? You think any nigger is as good as a white man? You think nigger kids should go to school with white kids? ...Floyd then poured turpentine on the wound to intensify the pain of the mutilation. ...The Klansmen gathered up their victim and threw him into the trunk of one of the cars and drove him to Tarrant-Huffman highway where they left him for dead.

...In September of 1957, despite the Klan's warning... On the morning of September 9, Christian Movement vice-president Reverend J.S. Pfifer drove Reverend Shuttlesworth, his wife, their two daughters, Pat and Frederika, and two other young African American men to all-white Phillips High School. When they pulled up to the school, they saw TV crews, about twenty white men, and a few

police officers. Shuttlesworth stepped out of the car and was immediately attacked. In the following moments, the white men assaulted Shuttlesworth with brass knuckles, wooden clubs and chains. Most of the skin was scraped off of his face and ears. He heard men yell, —Let's kill him and women cheer, —Kill the m_____ f____g nigger and it will all be over. Let's end it today. They opened the door and lashed Reverend Pfifer with a chain and then reached into the car and stabbed Mrs. Shuttlesworth in the hip. After a few minutes, patrol cars and motor scooters arrived on the scene and Reverend Pfifer was able to drive through the crowd to escape the mob.[72]

I hope that you don't mind if we stop here for a moment and, once again, ask that critical question: what would we have done had we been one of the white governmental officials or civic leaders or church leaders during the time immediately after Reverend Shuttlesworth's beating while attempting to enroll his children in the school? What would you have done? What would I have done?

Looking back now, almost 65 years later, you would think that common decency, human compassion, and empathy would have led the Birmingham white leaders to not only cry out in anguish but take immediate action to condemn those who committed such horrible acts. You would want to believe that all white Christian people in the Community would do so. But they couldn't because their white oppress and persecute culture would not let them. They would never be able look their fellow white friends and family members in the eyes if they expressed even a hint of compassion for Reverend Shuttlesworth, his wife, and their children.

I am sure that you would not only have stood up for Reverend Shuttlesworth and his wife, but would have volunteered to accompany them the next day when they tried again. Sadly, however, that is not what I, as a young teenager, my family, and my fellow Christians did in our nearby Mississippi hometown. We heard and read the news about what was happening in Birmingham and held exactly the same opinions as the white leaders of Birmingham did, as described by Ms. Bryson in her dissertation:

---

[72] Bryson, Heather. *To Give Racism the Face of the Ignorant: Race, Class, and White Manhood in Birmingham, Alabama, 1937-1970.* <pages?>

The responses of local city officials and the newspapers to these acts of horrific violence made it clear that the whites in Birmingham would stand united when faced with integration. Shuttlesworth was branded —a troublemaker who —has courted this violence. In a typed statement to the city regarding Shuttlesworth's attempt, Mayor James Morgan clarified the stand of the city government: —Negro agitators sought to create a condition of general disturbance at Phillips High School . . . the good citizens stood up and the guilty were punished — there is one thing that I am certain of — the good citizens of Birmingham do not want rabble rousers of either race to disturb the peaceful conditions of the city . . . each race has its time honored traditions and except for the few occasions on the part of the hot heads and rabble rousers nothing has occurred to unduly disturb our happy existence in this beautiful valley.[73]

Oppressive cultures require hosts to survive and thrive, and it was the White Citizens Councils, with some help from local KKKs who served as those hosts throughout the latter half of the 1950s and most of the 1960s. While the Councils continued to portray themselves as upright citizens trying to protect their "way of life," their constant messages of fear and intimidation encouraged violence on the part of extremists and enforced silence through intimidation among others. Byron De La Beckwith, a White Citizens Council member, murdered Medgar Evers who was leading the efforts to integrate Jackson, Mississippi's schools. Three Civil Rights workers were murdered in Philadelphia, Mississippi. The four young girls were murdered in the Birmingham church bombing.

But it wasn't just the White Citizens Councils that kept the oppress and persecute Blacks culture alive and active. It was also the white leadership in the community at large (civic, church, business, governmental, law enforcement, legal system, and others) who joined in to create the environment where the Councils could flourish. It was also me, my family and my fellow church members. It was every one of us Southern white people who were controlled by an evil culture that we, in turn, fed and practically worshiped every day.

I remember a visit to one of my relatives during those years. I asked to use his telephone (no cell phones in those days), and he suggested that I use the one in his bedroom. As I was talking on the phone, I noticed

---

[73] Ibid

a stack of White Citizens Council pamphlets and brochures on his nightstand, including Judge Brady's *Black Monday* book. After completing my call and returning to the living room to join other family members, I commented on his stack of reading material and asked where he got them. He said from the pastor of his church. That is all that we need to know about how his pastor and his fellow church members thought black people should be treated. All of those who were beaten and murdered were communist-backed agitators who got what they deserved for disturbing our peaceful way of life....and it was all blessed by God...a sad and dark, dark side of Christianity!

Council on Biblical Manhood and Womanhood (CBMW)—Male Supremacists

By the 1980s, women had made slow but significant progress in achieving equality in the secular world:[74]

- **1920**: Over the objection of lots of male evangelical Christians, women won the constitutional right to vote.[75]

- **1963**: Congress passed the Equal Pay Act, prohibiting sex-based wage discrimination between men and women performing the same job in the same workplace.

- **1964**: The national Civil Rights Act was passed and included Title VII that prohibited employment discrimination based on race, religion, national origin, or sex.

- **1966**: The National Organization for Women (NOW) was formed for the purpose of promoting "feminist ideals, lead societal change, eliminate discrimination, and achieve and protect the equal rights of all women and girls in all aspects of social, political, and economic life."

---

[74] https://www.history.com/topics/womens-history/womens-history-us-timeline
[75] Partridge, Brittany M., *Georgia Women and Their Struggle for the Vote*, University of Georgia Honors Thesis, 2014

- **1972**: Title IX of the Education Amendments became federal law with the requirement that "No person in the United States shall, on the basis of sex, be excluded from participation in, be denied the benefits of, or be subjected to discrimination under any education program or activity receiving Federal financial assistance."

- **1973**: The U.S. Supreme Court ruled that the Constitution protects a woman's legal right to an abortion.

- **1981:** Sandra Day O'Connor became the first woman to serve on the U.S. Supreme Court.

- **1983**: Sally Ride became the first American woman to fly in space.

- **1984**: Geraldine Ferraro became the first woman to be the vice president nominee by a major party.

It was happening everywhere, it seemed. Women were progressing toward equality. And it was even happening in the Christian oppress and persecute women culture. In 1970, the Lutheran Church in America ordained Rev. Elizabeth Platz—a woman! The Methodist church had been ordaining women since the late 1800s, but in 1980, it did the unthinkable: Rev. Marjorie Mathews was elected to a bishop position, giving her authority over male ministers.[76]

Something had to be done. The Christian oppress and persecute women culture was already losing its dominance over the secular oppression of women, and now it was in danger of losing male domination of women within its own host churches as well. And even worse, men were in danger of having to compete with women for pastoral and seminary faculty jobs. The outlook was bleak for the Christian oppress and persecute women culture. Special efforts were needed if the culture was to survive.

76

https://en.wikipedia.org/wiki/Ordination_of_women_in_Protestant_denominations#Methodist

So, the culture did what it had to do. It reached out to its evangelical male hosts, asking them to create a special organization that could continue the oppression and persecution of women. And that is just what happened when a group of oppress and persecute women cultural hosts established the Council on Biblical Manhood and Womanhood (CBMW) in 1987 with only one purpose in mind: keep women in submissive roles in the homes, in the churches, and, as a side benefit, in the business and political worlds.

CBMW's web site clearly explains the need for the national organization:

At this time many evangelicals were beginning to experiment with an ideology that would later become known as evangelical feminism. This was a significant departure from what the church had practiced from its beginning regarding the role of men and women in the home and local church. The effects of this departure have not been benign. **As evangelical feminism continues to spread, the evangelical community needs to be aware that this debate reaches ultimately to the heart of the gospel.** *(emphasis added).*[77]

Following the historical pattern of justifying the oppression and persecution of oppress and persecute cultural victims, CBMW's web site goes on to show the devastating things that will happen if women are treated equal to men[78]:

1. The authority of Scripture is at stake.
The Bible clearly teaches that men and women are equal in value and dignity and have distinct and complementary roles in the home and the church. If churches disregard these teachings and accommodate to the culture, then the members of those churches and subsequent generations will be less likely to submit to God's word in other difficult matters as well.

2. The health of the home is at stake.
If families do not structure their homes properly, in disobedience to the teachings of Ephesians 5, 1 Peter 3, and Colossians 3, then they will not have the proper foundation from which to withstand the temptations of the devil and the various onslaughts of the world. This hinders the sanctification of married couples and also

---

[77] https://cbmw.org/about/mission-vision/
[78] Ibid

introduces confusion about basic parenting issues such as raising masculine sons and feminine daughters.

3. The health of the church is at stake.

Just like the home, if the church disobeys the teachings of 1 Timothy 2, 1 Corinthians 11 and disregards the structure that God put into place for the community of faith from the beginning, then the church will be weakened. If the church is weakened in its convictions, it will be less effective in accomplishing its mission.

4. Our worship is at stake.

Increasingly, members of the evangelical community, in the name of gender equality, are advocating calling God "mother" as often as we call him "father." God has named himself and for us to make changes to his self-revelation not only undermines the written Word, but also undermines God's authority in our lives.

5. Bible translations are at stake.

There are many who are currently advocating for Bible translations that would essentially be "gender-neutral." These translations, in hundreds of places, remove the words he, him, his, brother, father, son, and man. Our concern is that in the name of gender equality, the Bible is undermined and the very words of God end up being revised.

6. The advance of the gospel is at stake.

Ephesians 5 calls husbands and wives to relate to one another as a picture of Christ and the church. The picture involves the humble, sacrificial leadership of the husband and the joyful, intelligent submission to that leadership by the wife. Husbands and wives who model this improperly portray a distorted and false picture of Jesus Christ, the Head and Savior of his bride, the church. Deviation from biblical teaching on manhood and womanhood hinders the advance of the gospel.

Just like the KKK and the White Citizens Councils, the CBMW has worked hard and been highly successful since its founding in 1987. As reported on its web site[79]:

The organization (CBMW) built steam for several years, running an ad in Christianity Today that drew a huge response. It was clear that CBMW

---

[79] Ibid

represented the concerns of a large, and to that point relatively quiet, constituency. During this period, Grudem and Piper (two of the founders) worked on assembling and editing essays for a project released by Crossway in 1991 entitled Recovering Biblical Manhood and Womanhood: A Response to Evangelical Feminism. Now known as RBMW (or, among younger complementarians, the "blue book"), the text was named "Book of the Year" by Christianity Today in 1992. It signaled that complementarianism rested upon extensive scholarship and featured an impressive array of essays on exegetical, theological, and applicatory topics. Later in the 1990s CBMW engaged several issues related to "gender neutral" Bible translation, contending for the importance of fidelity to the original text.

CBMW has played a formative role in helping numerous denominations and organizations promote gospel-driven gender roles, including the Southern Baptist Convention and the Presbyterian Church of America. Under the leadership of leaders like Randy Stinson, Bruce Ware, and J. Ligon Duncan, CBMW increased its influence in the first decade of the 21st century, holding several major conferences on gender roles, launching CBMW.org, and publishing the Journal for Biblical Manhood & Womanhood. JBMW has been published in journal form since 1994 and has fostered critical academic discussion of crucial exegetical, theological, and pastoral issues. In 2019, the journal underwent restructuring and is now published under the new masthead, Eikon: A Journal for Biblical Anthropology.

Today, many evangelical groups are convictionally complementarian. The contemporary surge of interest in the gospel and the greatness of God has coincided with widespread adoption of complementarianism, with many prominent churches, seminaries, authors, and para-church organizations joyfully celebrating God's good design for manhood and womanhood, home and church.

CBMW is in its fourth decade of operation. But in the thirty years since the drafting of the Danvers Statement (you can find the statement in Chapter 5 of this book) *challenges to the Bible's teaching have not abated. In fact, the challenges have only increased and broadened. Western culture has embarked upon a total revision of sexual and gender norms. It has evicted the male-female complement from the definition of marriage. Indeed, with the transgender challenge, it has thrown into question the meaning of the sexual binary that God has encoded into every cell in our bodies.*

As a result, churches find themselves facing questions about manhood and womanhood that were barely imagined when the Danvers Statement was written. Under the leadership of Dr. Denny Burk, CBMW focuses its resources and conferences on addressing this full range of challenges to what scripture teaches about manhood and womanhood.

The challenges are ongoing and so must be CBMW's work.

In keeping with its own belief that women must be held in submission, CBMW's name, itself, lists "Manhood" first and "Womanhood" last. Its governing board consists of only males. It does have token women representation on its non-governing council, with six of its thirty council members being women, at my last review.

CBMW Expands its Victim List. There is something attractive to oppress and persecute cultures about extending their cruel treatments to other victims. So, it is not uncommon for an oppressive organization to add even more victims to its original target. We saw this earlier when the KKK added Jews, Catholics, and immigrants to its victims list in the 1920s. CBMW is no exception.

As mentioned earlier, over the last several decades, the LGBTQ community was making major progress in achieving equal treatment under local and state laws around the nation, culminating in a U.S. Supreme Court ruling in 2015 allowing same-sex marriages. A majority of the nation's people, especially young people, readily endorsed this equal treatment of their gay brothers and sisters with the result that the Christian oppress and persecute gays culture suddenly found itself losing power. Again, something had to be done. It needed a special organization to promote its damnation of and discrimination against LGBTQs. CBMW readily accepted the responsibility as described below on its web site:

In 2017, CBMW convened a meeting of over 80 evangelical leaders in Nashville, Tennessee, to draft a consensus document on biblical sexuality. This document came to be known as the Nashville Statement. Since its release, the Nashville Statement or its language has been commended or adopted by denominational organizations like the PCA and the SBC, as well as incorporated into the governing documents of several evangelical schools, including Cedarville University, Union University, SBTS, and MBTS.[80]

---

[80] https://cbmw.org/about/history/

The Nashville Statement contained the following 14 articles that both justified the oppression and persecution of LGBTQs and demands that Christians treat them accordingly[81]:

Article 1

WE AFFIRM that God has designed marriage to be a covenantal, sexual, procreative, lifelong union of one man and one woman, as husband and wife, and is meant to signify the covenant love between Christ and his bride the church.

WE DENY that God has designed marriage to be a homosexual, polygamous, or polyamorous relationship. We also deny that marriage is a mere human contract rather than a covenant made before God.

Article 2

WE AFFIRM that God's revealed will for all people is chastity outside of marriage and fidelity within marriage.

WE DENY that any affections, desires, or commitments ever justify sexual intercourse before or outside marriage; nor do they justify any form of sexual immorality.

Article 3

WE AFFIRM that God created Adam and Eve, the first human beings, in his own image, equal before God as persons, and distinct as male and female.

WE DENY that the divinely ordained differences between male and female render them unequal in dignity or worth.

Article 4

WE AFFIRM that divinely ordained differences between male and female reflect God's original creation design and are meant for human good and human flourishing.

WE DENY that such differences are a result of the Fall or are a tragedy to be overcome.

---

[81] https://www.desiringgod.org/articles/precious-clarity-on-human-sexuality

Article 5

WE AFFIRM *that the differences between male and female reproductive structures are integral to God's design for self-conception as male or female.*
WE DENY *that physical anomalies or psychological conditions nullify the God-appointed link between biological sex and self-conception as male or female.*

Article 6

WE AFFIRM *that those born with a physical disorder of sex development are created in the image of God and have dignity and worth equal to all other image-bearers. They are acknowledged by our Lord Jesus in his words about "eunuchs who were born that way from their mother's womb." With all others they are welcome as faithful followers of Jesus Christ and should embrace their biological sex insofar as it may be known.*

WE DENY *that ambiguities related to a person's biological sex render one incapable of living a fruitful life in joyful obedience to Christ.*

Article 7

WE AFFIRM *that self-conception as male or female should be defined by God's holy purposes in creation and redemption as revealed in Scripture.*

WE DENY *that adopting a homosexual or transgender self-conception is consistent with God's holy purposes in creation and redemption.*

Article 8

WE AFFIRM *that people who experience sexual attraction for the same sex may live a rich and fruitful life pleasing to God through faith in Jesus Christ, as they, like all Christians, walk in purity of life.*

WE DENY *that sexual attraction for the same sex is part of the natural goodness of God's original creation, or that it puts a person outside the hope of the gospel.*

Article 9

WE AFFIRM *that sin distorts sexual desires by directing them away from the marriage covenant and toward sexual immorality— a distortion that includes both heterosexual and homosexual immorality.*

WE DENY *that an enduring pattern of desire for sexual immorality justifies sexually immoral behavior.*

Article 10

WE AFFIRM *that it is sinful to approve of homosexual immorality or transgenderism and that such approval constitutes an essential departure from Christian faithfulness and witness.*

WE DENY *that the approval of homosexual immorality or transgenderism is a matter of moral indifference about which otherwise faithful Christians should agree to disagree.*

Article 11

WE AFFIRM *our duty to speak the truth in love at all times, including when we speak to or about one another as male or female.*

WE DENY *any obligation to speak in such ways that dishonor God's design of his image bearers as male and female*

.

Article 12

WE AFFIRM *that the grace of God in Christ gives both merciful pardon and transforming power, and that this pardon and power enable a follower of Jesus to put to death sinful desires and to walk in a manner worthy of the Lord.*

WE DENY *that the grace of God in Christ is insufficient to forgive all sexual sins and to give power for holiness to every believer who feels drawn into sexual sin.*

Article 13

WE AFFIRM *that the grace of God in Christ enables sinners to forsake transgender self-conceptions and by divine forbearance to accept the God-ordained link between one's biological sex and one's self-conception as male or female.*

WE DENY *that the grace of God in Christ sanctions self-conceptions that are at odds with God's revealed will.*

Article 14

WE AFFIRM *that Christ Jesus has come into the world to save sinners and that through Christ's death and resurrection forgiveness of sins and eternal life are available to every person who repents of sin and trusts in Christ alone as Savior, Lord, and supreme treasure.*

WE DENY *that the Lord's arm is too short to save or that any sinner is beyond his reach.*

In other words, same sex marriage is a major sin and one can easily cancel the "sinful" love they have for their same-sex partner by accepting God's grace that "...*gives both merciful pardon and transforming power, and that this pardon and power enable a follower of Jesus to put to death sinful desires and to walk in a manner worthy of the Lord.*"

Active Promotion of its Oppression and Persecution. CBMW works hard to serve its oppress and persecute cultures:

- to help spread its messages, it has a full-time staff.
- Publishes a semi-annual journal in which Christian theologians, ministers, editors and other writers publish their justifications for the oppression of women and LGBTQs and explain their claims that treating these victims with respect, dignity and equality will harm our churches, us as individuals, our families and our children and will, ultimately, destroy our Christian faith.
- Maintains a library filled with books, articles and papers that provide supporting teaching and learning materials that will help local pastors and church leaders learn how to more effectively oppress and persecute women and LGBTQs.
- Publishes blogs designed to support the CBWM's mission of oppressing and persecuting women and LGBTQs.
- Holds periodic seminars

Summary

As I believe you can see from the multitude of examples in this chapter, the parasitic oppress and persecute cultures attached to the Christian church have not been content with simply influencing host Christians to adopt their beliefs and ideals. While passive support of the persecution and oppression of others is damaging enough, these cultures want and demand action from us so that we work to achieve their goals.

To achieve these goals, these cultures have created structures to organize, equip, and encourage dominant Christian groups to not simply believe, but to act. These organizations make it easy for supporting Christians to move from thought to word and then deed in the pursuit of persecution and oppression. The special organizations described in this chapter, as well as many other oppressive special organizations, have served throughout history to promote and spread fear, hate, and condemnation within our communities, churches, families, and nations to ensure their own survival and perpetuation. Such a sad, sad, dark and cruel side of Christianity.

Chapter 15

Are These Really Christians?

As you read about these special organizations dedicated to suppressing and persecuting targeted cultural victims, including mass murders, you, like me, may be wondering if those who perpetuated the suffering really were (are) Christians.

In fact, as we look at the full history of Christian persecutions, we have to wonder if those who murdered innocent women as witches, those who held Blacks in slavery, those who slaughtered the unarmed Native Americans, and those who joined the KKK and lynched and burned the homes of African Americans were really Christians? And what about those who participated in the murder of millions Jews, those who passed and enforced Jim Crow laws that kept Black Americans in poverty and prevented them from voting? And to this very day, what do we think of those who aggressively promote the suppression of women and the damnation of our homosexual friends and family? Are they really Christians?

It would be easy to say, historically speaking, that they were not really Christians. We can believe that they would not be Christians today because they betray everything that Jesus stood for in His human time with us. In fact, we Christians have a long history of saying that any other "Christian" not agreeing with our personal beliefs are not really Christians. But would that be an accurate conclusion?

My Webster dictionary says that a Christian is "a person who believes in Christ and follows His teachings; person belonging to the religion of Christ." That definition, however, begs the question as whether a person is really a Christian or is just saying that they are.

Since only each individual knows what she or he, within their own mind and soul, really believes, I finally concluded that I am in no position to judge and, hence, must accept what each individual says. If they say that they are a Christian, then they are, indeed, a Christian.

With that acceptance, however, must also come the acceptance that all of these historical evil deeds were done by Christians and all of the evil suppressions and persecutions today are being done by Christians. We cannot run from that fact.

If a priest said that he was a Christian and then lights the fire that burns an innocent woman accused of being a witch at the stake, it was a Christian who murdered the woman. If a man, who beats a black slave mother until she can no longer hold onto her young daughter who is then sold as a slave said that he is a Christian, then it was a Christian who beat the mother. If a Nazi soldier who shot a Jew in the back of the head and then pushed his dead body into the Rhine River, said that he was a Christian, then it was a Christian who murdered the Jew. I and my family were sure that we were Christians in the 1950s and '60s when we approved of Jim Crow racial segregation laws and customs. That meant that we were Christians oppressing and persecuting African Americans.

And today, if you are a member of a Christian church and denomination which refuses to treat women equally, then you are a Christian oppressing and persecuting women.

This is the dark side of Christianity controlled by evil oppress and persecute cultures, and we must recognize and decide whether we want to perpetuate or reject these cultures. It is a decision that each of us must make, either implicitly or explicitly. And if we choose to ignore the decision, we are really making the decision to perpetuate them.

As has been credited to Edmund Burke by some authors, "The only thing necessary for the triumph of evil is for good men to do nothing." If you and I continue to support oppressive Christian cultures with our membership, our donations, our silence and our lack of opposition, we are Christians keeping this dark and cruel side of Christianity alive and well.

Chapter 16

Sincerity of Beliefs

I want to pause for a moment to make it clear that, just as I accept that every person who calls themselves a Christian is, indeed, a Christian, I also accept the sincerity of their beliefs.

I readily accept the sincerity of the beliefs of my fellow Christians who joined and supported organizations like the KKK, the Nazi party, the White Citizens Council (WCC) and the Council of Biblical Manhood and Womanhood (CBMW) and other similar oppressive organizations. I do not question that the 40,000 white Christian ministers who joined the KKK in the 1920s sincerely believed that God wanted them to be part of oppressing and persecuting blacks, Catholics, Jews, and immigrants.

I do not question the sincerity of the beliefs of the thousands of white Christian members of the White Citizens Councils in the 1950s and 1960s. I don't think for a moment they could have done those horrible things to our black brothers and sisters during those years if they had not believed that they were doing God's will.

I do not question the sincerity of the beliefs of the members of the Council on Biblical Manhood and Womanhood (CBMW) and those Christian colleges, seminaries and churches who have adopted their policies that oppress women. I don't think they could preach those sermons or write and enact those oppressive church policies if they did not sincerely believe that God demands that women be held in submission.

Neither do I question the sincerity of the beliefs of those European Christians in the Middle Ages who executed innocent women as witches. I don't think that any good Christian could stack the wood to burn a fellow human being alive unless they believed with all their heart that they were doing what God asked of them.

Neither do I question the sincerity of those Southern white men who bought and sold black slaves as if they were cattle, thinking nothing of tearing a child from her or his clinging parents at a slave auction. I don't think that any good Christian could do that unless they believed deep down in their soul that what they were doing was ordained by God.

Neither do I question the beliefs of those Christians who dogmatically oppose gay marriages. Good Christians wouldn't condemn another person for wanting to marry the person they love unless they think that they are following God's commandments. And I don't even question the sincerity of the pastoral staff in my church who are banning literature that teaches social justice as part of the Christian gospel. Surely, no pastor could declare to his congregation that it does not matter how we treat other people if he did not sincerely believe that social justice has no role in church responsibilities.

I don't question the sincerity of any of these beliefs because, except for the strongest among us, we believe what our cultures tell us to believe. That is what we have done historically and what we do today. I know because I've been there. That is exactly what I did in my youth when it came to the oppression and persecution of African Americans. I, my family, and our fellow church members believed with every fiber in our bodies that we were doing exactly what the Bible told us to do. The social pressure of the oppress and persecute Blacks culture in which we lived did that to us: made us passionately believe that denigrating, subordinating, rejecting, beating and even condoning the murder (by others) of black "troublemakers" was exactly what God, through His Bible, required of us to keep our white race pure and to protect our nation from the evils of communism. That was the kind of god (please notice that I did not capitalize this god) that our culture forced us to worship.

Please remember, however, that the definitions of "oppression" and "persecution" do not have attached footnotes that say that oppression and persecution are not truly oppression and persecution if we sincerely believe, deep within our souls, that what we are doing is mandated by God. We oppressors and persecutors do not get to determine if oppression and persecution is occurring. The victims get to make that decision.

So, regardless of all of the justifications that these cruel parasitic cultures make us believe, oppression and persecution is still oppression and persecution. Whether it is my belief or your belief or someone else's belief that another person should be lynched or executed in a gas chamber or held as a slave or kept out of my church with shotguns or prevented from holding a pastoral position because they are a woman or excommunicated because they are gay does not make it right. No matter how sincere our beliefs or how many Bible verses we quote, the victims are still suffering at our hands. I, of course, cannot speak for God, but I must wonder if Bonhoeffer may not be right: *God will not hold us guiltless.*

Chapter 17

Friendship is a Tool to Keep Cultures Alive and Well

The oppress and persecute cultures are clever and cunning in terms of the tools that they effectively use to keep their cultural values instilled in us host Christians. We have already seen how these cultures use the Bible, the justifications written by theologians, editors and ministers, and rewards and punishments to get us to do their bidding. But these cultures can and do use simple things like our friendships to stay alive and well.

My wife and I helped maintain an oppress and persecute women and LGBTQs culture in our Tallahassee Baptist church for years because we had dear friends in that culture. The church was a major part of our social life, and over the years we had built deep friendships with other church members. We knew that if we left the church, we would likely lose many of those friendships.

So, what did we do? We played like our views that women and LGBTQs should be treated with respect and equality was simply a "difference in beliefs" from our fellow church members...differences like people may have over whether the biblical creation story is literal or figurative. The result was that we continued to attend church services, serve on church committees, participate in church projects, donate funds...**all of which not only kept an oppress and persecute women and LGBTQs culture alive and well in our church but enabled it to strengthen its hold over our church.** As that hold grew, the culture was able to replace most of the pastoral staff with men dedicated to suppressing women and gay people, ban all Sunday morning Bible study literature that taught that social justice was a part of being a Christian, and sever all relations with an outside association that supported the equal treatment of women and LGBTQs. **And it was our membership, participation, and donations that**

supported and enabled this, all because we did not want to lose our friends,

After my wife's death, I could no longer tolerate my church's oppression and persecution and found another church with a loving culture where I fit. However, I still have friends who remain members of my former church because they "don't want to lose their friends," although I know they share my values about how other people should be treated. The church's oppress and persecute culture still uses its "friendship" tool to keep their membership and support and, thus, perpetuate its dark and cruel activities.

Chapter 18

Oppress and Persecute is Hidden Behind a Façade of Worshiping, Praying and Doing Good Things

Finally, the oppress and persecute cultures that have attached themselves to us and our Christian institutions need us Christians to regularly attend and worship in our churches. They need us to regularly sing hymns, pray, have Bible study, preach and listen to sermons and do good things for others. They need us to do all these things because they produces two wonderful results for these cruel parasitic cultures:

1. They make us think that we are fully serving the God that we worship, that we have a special relationship with Him and, because of that relationship, we are authorized to speak for Him. We come to believe that everything that we say and do, including the oppression and persecution of others, is mandated by God. If others disagree, they not are not only wrong, but are sinners catering to Satan's wishes.

2. They produce a loving Christian façade behind which these cultures can conceal their oppression and persecution of their victims.

Were you to walk into one of our church services, you would think "These are some of the most wonderful, God-worshipping people in the world! Just listen to the words of their songs, the words of their prayers, their Scripture readings, and their sermons. Every word portrays a kind, loving, and dedicated commitment to serving a God of love." That is what these evil cultures want you to believe.

However, as I experienced in my youth, my church's commitment to keeping black people out of our church and in maintaining a segregated and oppressive Jim Crow society and economy would have been hidden from your view if you had attended one of our church services. Hidden during the slavery years would have been their Christian approval of slavery. Hidden during the Holocaust would have been their hatred, persecution and murder of Jews. Even today, many evangelical churches don't overtly show their commitment to suppressing women and damning LGBTQs. You don't see those women prevented from preaching or serving on governing boards or teaching mixed gender Bible studies. You don't see the lesbian couple with their adopted children and other LGBTQ Christians who were asked to leave the church last year. You don't see the literature that was banned from the church last year because it taught that women and gay people should be treated equally to all other people by the church. You only see and hear our façade of how we are committed to serving Jesus, our Lord and Savior. You don't see the cruel, rotten treatment of other people hidden behind the façade.

If we go to the web sites of Christian groups controlled by oppress and persecute cultures, we see the same facades of love, worship and service, we do not see the behind the scene agenda of oppression and persecution. The websites of the Catholic church and the Southern Baptist Convention portray churches of love, devotion, and service to God and to our fellow human beings. Hidden behind this façade is a full commitment to a culture of oppressing women and condemning LGBTQs. Similarly, a visit to the Global Methodist church's web site makes one think that it is an association of the most caring and loving Christians in the world. Hidden behind this façade is the association's total adherence to an oppress and persecute LGBTQs culture.

As mentioned earlier, this façade of love, service, and worship was actively in place within the church my wife and I served most of our lives and felt good about doing so. We regularly attended church services where we worshiped God through song and Bible study. We carefully listened to the sermons and joined in praying for our fellow Christians. We took food to those in our congregation who were sick. We served on church committees, participated in church service projects, and periodically taught Bible study classes.

In addition to our church, I served on the local boards of the Boy Scouts, Community Foundation, and United Way. My wife and I faithfully contributed to local charities like the United Way, the Red

Cross and the Second Harvest food bank. We donated to and personally served food at our local homeless shelter. In doing all of these "good things," we felt that we were genuinely serving the God who we worshiped, while, in obedience to our church culture, continuing to support (via our membership, complicit silence, and donations) our church's oppression of women and condemnation of our gay brothers and sisters, sons and daughters, and friends.

Like my wife and I, as well as millions of other Christians, I am sure that you, too, have faithfully attended church services, worshipped God, sang hymns, prayed, and done many good things for others. Hopefully, you have done better than we did in rejecting the control of the oppress and persecute cultures so that your love, worship and service is not a façade, but rather genuine.

Looking back at our history, I am also sure that Pope Innocent VIII who issued the official document sanctioning the execution of witches in 1464, worshiped God, sang hymns, prayed for his fellow Christians, and did many good things for other people.

I am sure that Kramer and Sprenger, the theologians who wrote the book, **Malleus Maleficarum** (the Hammer of Witches), that served as the guide and basis for arresting over 100,000 innocent people as witches and led to the execution of over 60,000, also worshiped God, prayed a lot, joyfully sang hymns, and did lots of good things for their communities.

I am sure that Pope Nicholas V, who issued his papal bull Dum Diversas in 1452 that became known as the Doctrine of Discovery and later provided Christian approval for taking the lands and homes of millions of Native Americans, regularly attended church service, worshiped God, prayed for his fellow man, and did many good things in his community.

I am sure that Reverend Martin Luther, who wrote the book *On the Jews and Their Lies* that recommended burning all Jewish synagogues and schools, and John Calvin, who strongly advocated that the minister who theologically disagreed with him be put to death for "heresy," also worshiped God, sang hymns, prayed for others, and did many good things in their churches and communities.

I am sure that Reverends Benjamin Palmer from New Orleans and Ebenezer W. Warren from Macon, Georgia, both men who preached sermons purporting that slavery was endorsed by God and was good for black people and also Robert Breckinridge and Henry Ruffner who wrote the papers advocating and articulating those beliefs, worshiped God, joyfully sang hymns, prayed for their fellow man, and did lots of good things in their communities.

I am sure that William Simmons, Elizabeth Tyler, and Edward Clark, all who led the resurgence of the KU Klux Klan in the 1920s, made many good contributions to their communities, as did the over 40,000 evangelical Christian ministers who joined the Klan.

I am sure that Reverends Guy T. Gillespie, George Cheek, and Bob Jones, all pastors who preached well-known sermons supporting racial segregation and Jim Crow laws that oppressed black people in the 1950s, spent a lot of their time worshiping God, praying for others, studying the Bible, and doing good things for other people.

I am sure that Judge Brady and Tut Patterson, who led the founding of the White Citizens Councils that fought black voter registration and racial integration in 22 states in the 1950s and '60s, did some really nice things in their communities.

I am sure that Dr. Strachan, Rev. Pat Robertson, and all the board members of the Council on Biblical Manhood and Womanhood who have spoken out so strongly in support of the church's suppression of women, have worshiped God, prayed for others, and done some wonderful things in their communities.

I am sure that Franklin Graham, Ronnie Floyd, Mike Huckabee, and Dr. James V. Heidinger II, all who have ridiculed and condemned LGBTQs, worship God, sing hymns, pray for others, and do many very good things for other people.

All of these people over the years, including me and, I am sure, you, have worshiped, sang loving hymns, studied the Bible, prayed and done good things for other people. **But while worshiping, singing, praying, listening to or even preaching loving sermons, and doing good things are wonderful, they are simply a cruel façade**

if, behind those things, we oppress and persecute our fellow humans.

It was no consolation to an elderly woman accused of being a witch when she was being led to the gallows that her executors worshiped God, studied the Bible, sang beautiful hymns, prayed, and did good deeds in their communities. She would still soon be murdered.

It was no comfort whatsoever to the Native Americans being driven from their homes and lands that those taking their lands and homes worshiped God, sang hymns of love and grace, prayed beautiful prayers of worship, and did many good things in their communities. Their ancestral homes and lands (and often lives) were still being taken from them by white Christians.

It was no relief to the antebellum slaves that their white Christian owners worshiped God, sang hymns, preached messages of love, prayed for their fellow man, and did some really nice and kind things for their white friends and neighbors. They were still enslaved with no hope of freedom.

It was absolutely no consolation to the Jews who were being loaded onto train cars headed for their execution that those loading them were Christians who worshiped God, sang hymns of love, preached sermons of salvation and service, prayed beautiful prayers, and did good things for other Christians. They would still soon be shot in the head or gassed to death and their bodies burned or thrown into rivers and mass graves.

It did not help African Americans held in an oppressive Jim Crow segregated society and economy one iota that those white Christians establishing and enforcing those laws and social practices also worshiped God, preached biblical sermons, sang hymns of love and praise, prayed, and did some really nice things for their fellow white supremacists. The African Americans were still victims of suppression and persecution that humiliated them and kept them in poverty with little to no hope of escape.

It is no consolation at all to women who are being prevented from successful careers in their churches that those male supremacist

Christians who establish and enforce those oppressive polices worship God, preach sermons of love and service, sing beautiful hymns, pray prayers of love, and do some really nice things for other people. The women are still being denied equality within their churches, no matter how talented they are or how hard they work.

Neither is it any consolation to our LGBTQ family members and friends that the Christians who ridicule them and kick them out of their churches also worship God, sing beautiful songs of love and devotion, pray prayers of love and forgiveness, and do some really good things in their communities. They are still being belittled, ridiculed, denied fellowship, and kicked out of the churches.

Worshiping, singing hymns, praying, preaching, teaching, studying the Bible and doing good deeds simply do not offset our cruelty in building and keeping these evil parasitic oppress and persecute cultures alive and well. Victims are still suffering, and we are still enabling, enforcing, and sustaining a dark and cruel Christianity behind a façade of love and devotion to God.

Chapter 19

The Lives of Oppress and Persecute Cultures are Eternal

I wish that I could tell you that the title of this chapter is a false statement, or at least an exaggeration, and I hope and pray that the day will come when that is the case. But I think that William Faulkner was correct when he said, **"The past is never dead. It's not even past."**

If we examine the history of human relations and look around us today, oppress and persecute cultures have never been defeated. Sometimes their control over their hosts wane or their methods of oppression and persecution change, but they are always out there, like the cruel parasites they are, waiting to attach themselves to the next receptive host, no matter whether that host be a loving Christian or a hate-filled extremist.

Execution of Witches in Our Modern Times

You would think that, as humans with the ability to learn and reason, we would see the sins of our past and not continue them, but oppressive cultures will never let that happen. As horrible and utterly nonsensical the oppress and persecute witches culture was during the European witch trials, it still has hosts in our modern times who accuse innocent people (mostly women, but increasingly children) of being witches, then torturing and murdering them. Thousands of innocent people are still being persecuted as witches in places like India, New Guinea, Saudi Arabia, and throughout Africa today. Although I could find no accurate count of the number of accused "witches" killed through "legal" and illegal executions, the data suggests several thousand per year over the past few decades.[1]

---

[1] https://www.nytimes.com/2014/07/05/opinion/the-persecution-of-witches-21st-century-style.html

We are tempted to attribute these horrible actions to local "pagan" religions, and there is almost certainly some of that because oppressive cultures will attach themselves to every willing host. But in Nigeria, the Liberty Foundation Gospel Ministries (an evangelical Christian organization), based in Calabar, has been identified as "causing widespread harassment, torture and violent deaths of children accused of witchcraft."[2]

Antisemitism Still Strong in the Twenty-First Century

In spite of the multitude of museums throughout Europe, Israel, and the United States, the hundreds of books, and thousands of news and magazine articles, as well as numerous movies and television programs that vividly portray the inhumane suffering of Jews during the Holocaust, our world is still filled with antisemitic hatred.

In October 2018, eleven Jewish people were killed and six others wounded by an antisemitic terrorist at the Tree of Life synagogue in Pittsburg. Also, in 2019, a California man set fire to one synagogue and then moved to a second synagogue where he murdered one Jewish worshiper and wounded three others.

The Anti-Defamation League reported a total of 2,024 antisemitic acts in the United States in 2020, which is an average of almost six per day. These consisted of 1,242 harassments of Jewish people, 751 vandalisms where Jewish property was damaged, and 31 personal assaults.[3] Germany reported 2,051 antisemitic crimes in 2020, an increase of 15.7 percent over 2019.[4]

And what are we Christians saying about Jews? You are right.

Too many of us continue to strongly support the oppress and persecute Jews culture by claiming, loudly in some cases, that all Jews are going to hell when they die because they have not become

---

[2] https://en.wikipedia.org/wiki/Helen_UkpabioActs
[3] https://www.adl.org/resources/press-release/us-antisemitic-incidents-remained-historic-high-2020
[4] https://www.timesofisrael.com/germany-says-far-right-attacks-on-the-rise-antisemitic-crimes-up-15-in-2020/

Christians. That allegation will never change within some Christian groups. The oppress and persecute Jews culture has such a strong hold on so many host Christians that, sadly, it will be alive and well another thousand years from now.

Black Slavery Continued for Over a Half Century After the End of the Civil War

You would have thought that a civil war that killed more than 600,000 young men—young men who only got to live once—would have defeated the oppress and persecute Blacks culture in the Southern states. But that was not the case at all. The Confederate army was defeated, but black slavery continued in the Southern states, just in a different form.

In *Slavery by Another Name*, one of the most thoroughly researched and documented books I have ever read, Douglas A. Blackmon, documents how the dominant white culture in the Southern states continued the terrible legacy of slavery. Following the Civil War, the culture corrupted the state criminal justice systems to keep thousands of Blacks, mostly young men, in slavery for another fifty plus years. White business owners and managers would inform local white law enforcement officers which young black man they wanted. The officers would then arrest the young man on trumped up charges, sometimes as trivial as vagrancy. Conviction by a corrupt court system occurred quickly, often the following week.

A company was eagerly awaiting the trial outcome and would pay the court and law enforcement agencies their "administrative" costs and then agree to keep the new convict in their private prison for the duration of the internment. The "prison" was the company's plantation or mine, sawmill, or other business where the new convict, along with other similarly "convicted" convicts, worked for the duration of their sentences. The company "prisons" were seldom monitored (not that it would have done any good) by local, state, or federal officials. Blackmon documented case after case after case of beatings, starvation, and even murder of the prisoners at the hands of the private companies' white guards.

Sometimes, as in the case of the young man in the Valdosta, Georgia, story at the end of Chapter 1 of this book, a falsely arrested young black man would fight back against his cruel treatment with devastating results. Now that you know about this system, you may want to go back and reread the section entitled, "It is in the year of our Lord, 2020" at the end of Chapter 1. This knowledge makes the story even more devastating.

The Oppress and Persecute Blacks Culture Became Even More Cruel and Inhumane After the Civil War

Blackmon's research did not primarily address the role of churches during this time period, but rather the role of law enforcement, the courts, and supporting local and state laws; however, all these were established and enforced by white Christians. Blackmon does, though, document one case with church involvement in Pine Apple, Alabama, where a young white man, Pig Melton, was wounded while gambling with a group that included some black men. According to Blackmon's research, there was no evidence to support the arrest of Arthur Stuart, a young black man who happened to be found walking in another part of town. Arthur was 31 years old and lived near the edge of town with his wife, two-year-old son, and infant daughter.

The Melton family vowed that a lesson must be taught. According to Blackmon's documentation (pages 259-260):

Late on Christmas night, (1903) after the day's church services in praise of the birth of Jesus, family dinners, and carols had been finished, a small group of white men led by fifty-one-year-old Evander M. Melton assembled at the center of Pine Apple. At 4 A.M., the mob easily broke into the jail—the constable was assisting them—and beat Stuart senseless in his cell. In short order, the men doused his body with kerosene and set it on fire.[5]

The Civil War had been over almost 40 years, and yet the oppress and persecute Blacks culture was still alive and well among white Christians in Pine Apple, Alabama. It had, in no way, been defeated by the war. And, as illustrated yet again by this historical account, these cruel

---

[5] Blackmon, Douglas. *Slavery by Another Name.* New York City: Doubleday, 2008, pgs. 259-60

cultures have no decency or compassion or even the basic conscience to know right or wrong. They will use any means they can marshal to make their victims suffer, going so far as murder, as long as their hosts are willing to follow the cultures' cruel demands and peer pressure. And sadly, that is what this dark side of Christianity did that night in 1903 and has done over and over and over again, again and again, and still does today.

But the corruption of the criminal justice system was only a small part of the new ways that the cruel culture was finding to get its white Christian hosts to oppress and persecute black victims in the Southern states. Following the Civil War, Jim Crow laws and social customs were specifically designed to tell all people of color that they and their children were inferior people.

- Black children were sent to intentionally inferior schools.
- Black people had to ride in the back of busses, wait in inferior black-only waiting rooms, use black-only bathrooms, eat in black-only restaurants or separate black-only rooms of white restaurants with back entrances, swim in black-only swimming pools, be members of black-only sports teams who played only other black teams, be members of black-only churches, and stay in the black-only wings of hospitals.
- When entering and leaving buildings, black people always had to let the white person go first.
- Black people could not try on clothes and hats at clothing stores.
- When necessary to contact a white person in their home, black people had to go to the back door, never the front door. Even in the coldest of weather, the black person had to stay outside to have conversation with the white person.
- Black people, of course, could never have a meal with a white person in their home, at a restaurant, or anywhere else and vice versa.
- Black people were denied the right to vote and could never be elected to a publicly held office.
- Black people were denied high-paying professional jobs.

- Black people had to treat all white people with respect and dignity, saying "yes, ma'am" and "no, ma'am" to white women and "yes, sir" and "no, sir" to white men.
- White people could and did denigrate black people at will, frequently calling them "boys" and "niggers." Few black people were ever referred to as "sir" or "ma'am" by white people.

The oppress and persecute Blacks culture will never give up. When one way of oppressing and persecuting Blacks is lost, it will always find other ways. As I write these words in 2023, white Christians in seventeen U.S. states are passing laws to suppress black voters, and these politicians (almost all white Christians) have the full and enthusiastic support, including large financial donations, of a large majority of the U.S. white evangelical Christian population.

The Devil will be Shoveling Snow When the Christian Oppress and Persecute Women Cultures Dies

Let's start with the good. As mentioned in previous chapters, significant progress toward equality for women has been made in the last hundred years in both the secular sector and in most mainline Christian church denominations. A hundred years ago, women could not even vote in most American states. Fifty years ago, women were limited to support jobs, like secretaries, clerks, receptionists, waitresses, stewardesses, and nurses. Today, (2022) the Vice President of the United States is a woman. Today, women hold public offices, serve as dentists, doctors, accountants, CEOs of large companies, airplane pilots, and in lots of other professional positions. Today, women are serving as pastors of Methodist, Episcopal, American Baptist, Evangelical Lutheran, Presbyterian Church (U.S.A.), United Church of Christ, Unitarian, Disciples of Christ, Assemblies of God, and Christian Science churches.

Clearly, the oppress and persecute women culture is losing its ability to suppress women, at least in the United States. But it will never, ever die, and today it has a strong stranglehold on the Catholic, Southern Baptist, and independent evangelical churches. The Catholic church's position is as clear as the blue mountain sky in Montana: Women in priesthood is not open to discussion. It is reserved for men alone. Women are not welcome. The Southern Baptist Faith and Message Statement declares in Article VI, *"While both men and women are gifted for service in the church, the office of pastor is limited to men as qualified by Scripture."*

In 2019, some members of the Southern Baptist Convention scared the daylights out of its oppress and persecute women culture, especially the Conventions' male supremacist hosts. Beth Moore, a highly respected Christian leader and speaker, was being invited to speak at some of the local Southern Baptist churches. That was bad enough, but when she was criticized by committed male supremacist Baptist preachers, some other Southern Baptist male leaders defended her. This was incredibly threatening for SBC's oppress and persecute women culture. It had to start taking actions to maintain its suppression of women and that is just what it did in October 2019, at Grace Life Church of the Shoals (Alabama), a Southern Baptist church.

Rev. Jeff Noblit, the church's pastor, announced that the church was canceling its membership in the Southern Baptist Convention. The reason: The SBC seemed to be getting soft on letting women preach. In other words, the SBC seemed to be leaning (not actually doing it, but just leaning) towards stopping the oppression of women, something that the oppress and persecute women culture in his church simply could not tolerate. Rev Noblit explained:

The straw broke the camel's back for me, and a few logs have been thrown on that camel also. One of those is the rise and the embracing and the affirming of Beth Moore's ministry. Beth Moore is a charismatic, gifted communicator who's drifted toward considering herself a preacher. She does a lot of internet things where she kind of gets in the face of those of us who are conservative in our doctrine, saying 'I'm preaching at so-and-so church this Sunday morning,' kind of like 'nah-nah-nah boo-boo, what are you going to do about it?' This is a serious issue. Southern Baptists from all ages have held that the scriptures are unequivocally clear here, that women do not hold the office of preaching or pastoring the church. Women do not exercise authority by preaching the word in the congregational meetings of the church. Now we have key, prominent Southern Baptist leaders who are accommodating and blessing this. You want me to tell you why? Because she has a million followers online. She has a huge influence. And the great idol of Southern Baptist life is pragmatism — it's working, it brings in the money, so hands off. We died to that idol a long time ago. [6]

Grace Life Church's actions and Rev. Noblit's message accomplished four major things for the oppress and persecute women culture:

1. Rev. Noblit reaffirmed the culture's reasons for suppressing women: "The scriptures are unequivocally clear here, that women do not hold the office of preaching or pastoring the church. Women do not exercise authority by preaching the word in the congregational meetings of the church."

2. Rev. Noblit and his church sent a strong message to those who might oppose oppress and persecute women cultures by ridiculing them: "She (Beth Moore) does a lot of internet things where she kind of gets in the face of those of us who are conservative in our doctrine, saying 'I'm preaching at so-and-so church this Sunday morning,' kind of like 'nah-nah-nah boo-boo, what are you going to do about it?'"

3. The church's action sent an even stronger message to the Southern Baptist Convention which has lost approximately two million members over the last decade: "Let women preach and you will lose even more members and their dollars!"

   The church's action's and Rev. Noblit's message states unequivocally that the oppress and persecute women culture will live forever at Grace Life...or, at least as long as Rev. Noblit is their pastor.

But what happens when an SBC church does oppose the Convention's oppress and persecute women culture? The First Baptist Church of Jefferson City, Tennessee, found out when they called Rev. Ellen Di Giosia, a highly respected and experienced minister, to be their senior pastor. There was no way that the Tennessee Baptist Convention's oppress women culture could let this stand. If it failed to punish Rev. Di Giosa and First Baptist, then other member churches might start

---

[6]   https://disrn.com/news/large-alabama-church-leaving-sbc-over-beth-moore-support-straw-broke-the-camels-back

calling women pastors and the culture would lose its power. So, again, the culture did what it had to do. It had its Tennessee Baptist Convention host expel First Baptist from the Convention. Dr. Dandy Davis, the male Executive Director of the Tennessee Baptist Mission Board, explained why:

I hope that the message it sends is that we're going to be committed to scripture. In spite of the way others may interpret this action, it is very important that we have some anchors and a belief system that is tied to the scripture.[7]

In other words, the oppress and persecute women culture clearly told the Tennessee Baptist Convention that suppressing women is a requirement to be a Christian, and that requirement will continue as long as possible, hopefully, in the culture's mind, forever.

The Christian Oppress and Persecute LGBTQs Culture Thrives in Our Churches

Again, let's start with the good news. A 2019 PEW survey found that approximately sixty percent of the U.S. population supports same sex marriages. That percentage is up from approximately 48 percent in 2010. Among mainline Protestant Christians, 66 percent support same sex marriages and 61 percent of Catholics are supportive.[8]

Further, although mostly small in size, a significant number of Protestant Christian denominations have had the courage to totally reject the oppress and persecute LGBTQs culture. They now openly and proudly affirm and accept their fellow LGBTQ members with the same respect and love that they have for their heterosexual members. They are all "just members." These denominations include, but not limited to[9]:

---

[7] https://patch.com/tennessee/brentwood-tn/tennessee-baptist-convention-expels-church-female-pastor
[8] https://www.pewforum.org/fact-sheet/changing-attitudes-on-gay-marriage
[9] https://en.wikipedia.org/wiki/List_of_Christian_denominations_affirming_LGBT_people

Anglican

- Episcopal Church (United States)
  Evangelical Anglican Church in America Baptist
- Alliance of Baptists
- Association of Welcoming and Affirming Baptists
- Cooperative Baptist Fellowship (Each congregation determines its own position)

Catholic

- American National Catholic Church
- Ecumenical Catholic Church
- Ecumenical Catholic Communion
- Evangelical Catholic Church
- Old Catholic Church
- Traditionalist Mexican American Catholic Church

Pentecostal

- Affirming Pentecostal Church International
- Global Alliance of Affirming Apostolic Pentecostals
- Gay Apostolic Pentecostals
- Christian Church (Disciples of Christ)

Presbyterian

- The Presbyterian Church (USA Reformed)
- Reformed Church in America (Gay pastors may serve congregations if they were ordained in another denomination; some member churches allow gay marriage)
- Presbyterian Church (USA)
- United Church of Christ Lutheran
- The Evangelical Lutheran Church in America

But, true to the title of this chapter, the oppress and persecute LGBTQs culture is still thriving in the larger Christian denominations that include, but not limited to[10]:

---

[10]

https://en.wikipedia.org/wiki/List_of_Christian_denominational_positions_on_homosexuality#Baptist

- The Seventh-day Adventist Church
- The Anglican Church in North America
- Assemblies of God
- Southern Baptist Convention
- The Canadian and American Reformed Churches
- The Christian Reformed Church in North America
- The Eastern Orthodox Church
- Jehovah's Witnesses
- The Church of Jesus Christ of Latter-day Saints
- The Lutheran Church–Missouri Synod
- Global Methodist Church
- The Church of God (Cleveland, Tennessee)
- Presbyterian Church in America,
- The Evangelical Presbyterian Church
- The Roman Catholic Church

Christian denominations controlled by this evil culture have no hesitation in taking drastic actions to oppress and persecute their LGBTQ victims. Any local churches accepting LGBTQ members are quickly punished, as illustrated by the Southern Baptist Convention's 2021 expelling of St. Matthews Baptist Church in Louisville, Kentucky, and Towne View Baptist Church, in Kennesaw, Georgia.[11]

As I write these words in 2023, the United Methodist Church (UMC) is in the process of splitting because some member churches are openly accepting gay members and ministers. The Church's oppress and persecute LGBTQ culture, which controls a large number of local UMC churches, is forcing the split. Just as the oppress and persecute Blacks cultures in the mid-1800s caused the national Baptist and Methodist associations to split so that the oppress and persecute Blacks culture could hold on to its control of the Southern churches, today's oppress and persecute LGBTQs culture readily endorses the UMC split so that it can continue to control as many local churches as possible.

---

[11] https://abcnews.go.com/US/wireStory/southern-baptists-oust-churches-lgbtq-inclusion-76072901

Just recently, a large Tallahassee Methodist church, controlled by its own oppress and persecute LGBTQs culture, announced that it was leaving the United Methodist national organization. As these cultures always do, the church hid its oppression of gay people behind a façade of Christian love as it announced to local news reporters, "As we always have done so, we will continue to reach out to all people with God's love."[12] Obviously, their oppressive culture celebrated with glee. It had guaranteed its survival through one more local church.

It is my own sad personal experience to know that this cruel culture is still alive and well in my Tallahassee Southern Baptist church as evidenced by the pastoral staff banning literature that supports treating our LGBTQ brothers and sisters with respect, dignity, and equality, and also to damn other denominations (e.g., United Church of Christ) who openly affirm LGBTQs, calling them non-Christians.

Summary

So, what does all of this mean for us today? We can fervently hope that progress is being made, but even the oppress and persecute cultures that have died within America have still found ways to survive somewhere else in the world. The oppress and persecute "witches" culture moved on and spread from Europe and North America to the rest of the world. Even when wars are fought for the rights of black citizens, oppression and prejudice still burst forth with violence today. The persecution and oppression of our Jewish brothers and sisters has continued unrelenting for thousands of years, and the hatred thrives even today. So, I don't know about you, but I am sadly convinced that hundreds of years from now, oppressive cultures will still be alive and well in a large number of Christian churches, so long as "good" Christians are willing to serve as the hosts of these terrible parasitic cultures...a dark and cruel side of Christianity that refuses to go away.

---

[12] Burlene, Jeff. "Killearn UMC splits Over Gay Marriage, Clergy," *Tallahassee Democrat*, September 14, 2022, page 1.

Chapter 20

So, Are We (You and Me) Really Responsible?

So, what about you and me? Are we really responsible for the pain that victims of these oppress and persecute cultures have suffered century after century after century, and that they still suffer today? When I talk to my white family and friends about all the oppression and persecution of people of color, women, and LGBTQs that continue today, we all (well, most of us) claim that it is not us. We tell ourselves and each other that we treat other people with respect and dignity; we believe in equality. We are not the ones shooting unarmed black people. We're not the ones passing state laws that suppress black and other minority voters. We are not the ones establishing the policies that keep women suppressed, and we're not the ones voting to expel LGBTQ people from our churches. We see and hear the news about other people doing these horrible things, but it is not us doing it, we claim.

But way back in the crevices of our minds, back where we don't want to go, we sometimes wonder, "Do I have some responsibility here?"

Maybe Charles Morgan, a young white Birmingham attorney, has our answer. In 1963, he threw away his prepared speech for a downtown Birmingham business club and wrote the following at the last moment after the four little girls were killed in the Birmingham church bombing:

Four little girls were killed in Birmingham yesterday.

A mad, remorseful worried community asks, "Who did it? Who threw that bomb? Was it a Negro or a white?" The answer should be, "We all did it." Every last one of us is condemned for that crime and the bombing before it and a decade ago. We all did it.

A short time later, white policemen kill a Negro and wounded another. A few hours later, two young men on a motorcycle shoot and kill a Negro child. Fires break out, and, in Montgomery, white youths assault Negroes.

And all across Alabama, an angry, guilty people cry out their mocking shouts of indignity and say they wonder "Why?" "Who?" Everyone then "deplores" the "dastardly" act.

But you know the "who" of "Who did it" is really rather simple. The "who" is every little individual who talks about the "niggers" and spreads the seeds of his hate to his neighbor and his son. The jokester, the crude oaf whose racial jokes rock the party with laughter.

The "who" is every governor who ever shouted for lawlessness and became a law violator.

It is every senator and every representative who in the halls of Congress stands and with mock humility tells the world that things back home aren't really like they are.

It is courts that move ever so slowly, and newspapers that timorously defend the law.

It is all the Christians and all their ministers who spoke too late in anguished cries against violence. It is the coward in each of us who clucks admonitions.

We have 10 years of lawless preachments, 10 years of criticism of law, of courts, of our fellow man, a decade of telling school children the opposite of what the civics books say.

We are a mass of intolerance and bigotry and stand indicted before our young. We are cursed by the failure of each of us to accept responsibility, by our defense of an already dead institution.

Yesterday while Birmingham, which prides itself on the number of its churches, was attending worship services, a bomb went off and an all-white police force moved into action, a police force which has been praised by city officials and others at least once a day for a month or so. A police force which has solved no bombings. A police force which many Negroes feel is perpetrating the very evils we decry. . . .

Birmingham is the only city in America where the police chief and the sheriff in the school crisis had to call our local ministers together to tell them to do their duty. The ministers of Birmingham who have done so little for Christianity call for prayer at high noon in a city of lawlessness, and in the same breath, speak of our city's "image." . . .

Those four little Negro girls were human beings. They have their 14 years in a leaderless city; a city where no one accepts responsibility; where everybody wants to blame somebody else. A city with a reward fund which grew like Topsy as a sort of sacrificial offering, a balm for the conscience of the "good people". . . .

Birmingham is a city ... where four little Negro girls can be born into a second-class school system, live a segregated life, ghettoed into their own little neighborhoods, restricted to Negro churches, destined to ride in Negro ambulances, to Negro wards of hospitals or to a Negro cemetery. Local papers, on their front and editorial pages, call for order and then exclude their names from obituary columns.

And, who is really guilty? Each of us. Each citizen who has not consciously attempted to bring about peaceful compliance with the decisions of the Supreme Court of the United States, every citizen and every school board member and schoolteacher and principal and businessman and judge and lawyer who has corrupted the minds of our youth; every person in this community who has in any way contributed during the past several years to the popularity of hatred, is at least as guilty, or more so, than the demented fool who threw that bomb...[1]

We were responsible. I see it now and have for years, but during the 1950s and 1960s we white people in the South, or at least my family, friends, fellow church members and governmental leaders, did not see it this way. So, a few white people did bad things to black people, but we did not do them. It was not our fault. Besides none of these bombings and beatings and murders would be happening if the "troublemakers" would just stop their protests and let us get back to our normal, everyday lives where everyone, both Blacks and Whites, stayed in our place and obeyed our state and local racial deprivation and segregation laws, ordinances and social customs. It was their fault, not ours. They were responsible, not us.

But I am sure that you join me now in recognizing that Charles Morgan was right. All of us white people were responsible for the murder of

---

[1] https://www.theatlantic.com/national/archive/2013/09/the-speech-that-shocked-birmingham-the-day-after-the-church-bombing/279565/

those four little girls in 1963. We were responsible because, as discussed in Chapter 2, we supplied the brains, the voices, the resources, and the social pressures that kept the oppress and persecute Blacks culture alive and well. And, in turn, that evil culture led to those four little girls and many more Blacks being murdered during the Civil Rights protests. We white people kept the evil culture alive by:

- Condemning the Civil Rights protestors instead of joining with them.
- Being members of white churches that not only prohibited the membership of our black brothers and sisters, but even their visitations.
- Contributing money to our white-only churches that was used to pay the salaries of pastors and theologians to preach sermons, write books and articles, and publish church literature that justified racial suppression and segregation.
- Teaching our children that black people were inferior and had to be treated that way.
- Rewarding those white politicians who wrote oppressive Jim Crow laws and ordinances, including black voter suppression laws, with our votes and financial contributions.
- Supporting school boards that funded white schools at levels twice that of black schools.
- Maintaining the idea that black people were inferior by telling jokes that belittled them.
- Criticizing, condemning, and ostracizing fellow white people who supported equality for people of color.
- Perpetuating social customs that humiliated black people. (For example, the black maid who helped my mother once a week in our home was never allowed to eat lunch with our family.)
- Serving on juries that refused to convict white people for the cruel treatment, including murder, of black people.
- Never, ever speaking out in favor of respect, dignity, and equality for black people.

Every one of these acts and many, many more kept the cruel oppress and persecute Blacks culture alive and well. In turn, that culture, through its social and legal control, kept us white people perpetuating those same cruel acts over and over and over. And the really sad fact is that we never saw or recognized the damage that we were doing to our black brothers and sisters. We had no empathy for them when they cried out for equal treatment—not preferred treatment, just equal treatment—including the right to not die in a church bombing. In fact, we loved our dominant white culture so much that we went to great lengths trying to keep this dark and cruel side of our white Christianity alive forever.

We are still responsible today. I was shocked, although I shouldn't have been, when a woman minister and friend recently recounted her experience at one of our Tallahassee Christian churches. She had been invited to speak to a group at the church but was hesitant to accept the invitation because the male pastor had a reputation for being strongly opposed to women preachers. After some persuasion from the group leader, however, she reluctantly accepted since she would not be preaching, just speaking at a weekday luncheon. According to the program, the male pastor was to introduce her for the speech. Out of courtesy, my friend arrived at the meeting in advance to greet the pastor whom she already knew. But that never happened. The pastor came in at the last moment, walked past her without bothering to speak or even look at her, and went directly to the speaker's rostrum. He gave her a two-minute or less introduction and immediately left the room, still refusing to speak to or look at her. Apparently, there was no way that his oppress and persecute women culture would allow him to treat my friend with respect, dignity, and equality by warmly welcoming her to his church and staying for a few moments to hear her talk. At the very least, he could have apologized for having to leave early. The ostracization was so obvious that several of the women in the audience apologized to my friend after the program.

This, of course, was nothing near the murder of the four little Birmingham girls, but it was the intentional humiliation and oppression of a woman by a Christian man. So, who was responsible for that humiliation and oppression? Was only the male supremacist pastor responsible, just like it was only the white supremacist criminals who planted the bomb that killed the little girls? I think that Charles Morgan would say again: it is all of us. It is every member of the male pastor's church. It is me; it is you; it is our friends, and it is our friends'

friends. It is all of us who keep this male supremacist culture alive and strong, and it is this culture that caused the male pastor to be so condescending and rude.

We keep this male supremacist culture alive by:

- Pretending as if the oppression of women is just a difference in religious beliefs, not the cruel suppression of women that it really is.
- Refusing to confront the perpetrators of these acts of oppression.
- Implying our full support of this oppression by being members of churches that host and keep oppress and persecute women cultures alive and well.
- Contributing money to these types of churches that not only pay the salaries of the male supremacist pastors and staff but also financially support the church's regional and national associations and seminaries that, in turn, write the books, articles, blogs, and materials that teach the suppression of women.

We are still responsible. A few years ago, I took some vegetables from my garden to some friends. When they came to the door, I could tell that they had been crying. They insisted that I come inside and visit with them. I already knew that my friends and their son's family were extremely active in their church. My friends taught Sunday school classes and were active leaders in the church's weekly manna program for hungry families by sorting, packaging, and delivering food every week. Their son was also a leader who, just a few weeks earlier, had taken several days off from work to voluntarily help clean and relandscape the church's grounds after the construction of a new sanctuary. Their grandson was a highly respected youth leader and a member of the church's praise band.

Immediately upon sitting down, my friends began their devastating story. Someone had just told their pastor that their grandson was gay, and the pastor had called their grandson into his office to tell him that he was being immediately removed from all of his roles at the church, including his membership in the praise band. The pastor told their grandson that he could still come to church services as long as he told no one about his sexual orientation, but that was all. Their grandson was crushed.

As my friends relayed the story, they began to cry again, and I found myself crying with them.

So, who did this cruel and devastating deed to my friends' grandson? I think again that Charles Morgan would say: "We all did it." It was not just the pastor. It was all of us who have kept a Christian oppress and persecute LGBTQs culture alive and well in our own churches, our church associations, and our communities. Sure, the pastor was the one who personally delivered the cruel words, just as the KKK members planted the bomb that killed the little girls. But the pastor would not have been so cruel and inhumane without the support of an oppress and persecute LGBTQs culture that my friends and their fellow church members had kept alive and well through their silence, their memberships, and church donations.

I know that this is coincidental, but just as I finished writing the previous paragraph, I received an email from the pastor of my Southern Baptist church that included a recommended list of concerns for which to pray. Included in the list were:

Pray that the lies of homosexuality will be broken off this nation. Pray for people to see truth on this issue and people to be set (free) from the lifestyle of bondage.

Pray for those in Hollywood to stop promoting the homosexual lifestyles and stop producing degrading films and television shows.

So, who is responsible for these prayer requests? You may think, "Well, it was your pastor who sent them. He is responsible." But it is really me and all of the other members of my church who are responsible. We are the ones who keep the oppress and persecute LGBTQs culture alive and well in our church, and it is this culture that compelled our pastor to include these two requests. He simply did what was demanded by our church culture, just as the oppress and persecute Blacks culture of my youth demanded that our deacons stand in the doors of our church with shotguns to keep potential black visitors out.

I am the one of the ones who have remained silent when church staff and fellow church members ridiculed and condemned LGBTQs in conversations and class discussions. It has been me who has made donations that, along with the donations of others, enabled the church to hire anti-gay staff, buy anti-gay literature, teach anti-gay lessons, and adopt anti-gay policies.

These oppress and persecute cultures are so adept at using us to support their cruel oppression and persecution of their targeted victims that we often don't even know we are being used. But, if you and I are members of one of these churches or other organizations that is dominated by an oppress and persecute culture, we are responsible for all that the organization and its members do. We cannot run from that responsibility as long as we are members.

Chapter 21

Going Beyond Religious Institutions to Obtain Political Power.

As we have discussed in previous chapters, whenever possible throughout history, oppress and persecute cultures have extended their power beyond control of Christian churches to gain control of local, state, and national political organizations and governments as well. When this has happened, thousands have suffered and died, sometime hundreds of thousands, and sometimes even millions.

We saw this when the oppress and persecute Blacks culture went beyond its control of the Christian church in the Southern states in the 1850s to gain control of the Democrat party in the Southern state which in turn gained control of the state governments in the South, leading them to form the Confederate States and secede from the United States. The result was the death of over 600,000 young men in the Civil War.

We saw it again when the oppress and persecute Jews culture went beyond its control of the European Catholic and Protestant Christians to take control of the German Nazi party in the 1930s and '40s. The result was the murder by the Nazis of over six million Jews and five to thirteen million non-Jews, including those who dared support the Jews.

We saw it in the late 1800s and into the 1900s when the oppress and persecute Blacks culture went beyond its control of white Christians and their churches to gain control of many local and state American governments and become a major force in the U.S. House of Representatives. Through the KKK, first in the 1880s and again in 1920s and '30s, and then through the White Citizens Council in the 1960s and '70s, this cruel culture-controlled society incited the lynching of 4,733 individuals as well as the murder of others with guns and bombs, almost all of whom were people of color.

We saw it immediately after the Civil War when the oppress and persecute Blacks culture in the previous Confederate states continued its control of the Democrat parties in the Southern states which established numerous state and local Jim Crow laws, keeping black citizens in segregated and impoverished societies and economies. This evil culture dominated the Democrat parties in the Southern states until the latter 1960s.

When I was a youth during those years in Mississippi, a member of the Republican party in my state was scarcer than "hen's teeth." No self-respecting adult in my community would have ever admitted to voting for a "left wing liberal" Republican in those days. After all, it was the Republicans who led the reconstruction of the former Confederate states after the Civil War and had had the audacity to let former black slaves vote, leading to some black people actually holding elected offices. It was the Democrat party that came to the culture's rescue when it gained control of southern state and local governments in the early 1900s and rid the polls of black voters. In the adult conversations that I heard, as a youth in the 1940s and 50s, we were proud that our voters had kicked the Republican party liberals out of our Southern states because the party was still letting black people vote in the northern states where it had political control. Our Mississippi culture was not about to let its voters vote for these flaming liberal republicans and none who I knew did (or, at least, admitted to doing so).

That all changed in the late 1960s, however, when President Johnson signed the 1964 federal civil rights act giving black citizens equal rights to whites. Legend has it that Johnson, a Democrat, said to an aide when he signed the federal legislation, "I think we just delivered the South to the Republican Party for a long time to come." Whether the legend is true or not, that is exactly what happened. National Republican leaders recognized the opportunity and immediately accepted the long-time Democrat oppress and persecute culture hosts into their party where the culture has remained for the past sixty plus years. It is the exact same Southern oppress and persecute Blacks culture, just now strongly attached to the Southern Republican state parties instead of its long-time favorite, the Southern state Democrat parties.

In the 2020s, the setting was almost perfect for the oppress and persecute cultures to go beyond controlling just the Republican party in the Southern states to make a run at capturing the entire national Republican party. As documented so well by Robert P. Jones in his book *The End of White Christian American,* after almost 250 years, white evangelical Christians are in danger of losing their political hold on governments in the United States. Jones's data shows that the percentage of U.S voters who are white Christians has declined from 73 percent in 1993 to a projected 48 percent in 2024.[1]

For the first time in American history, white Christians will no longer compose a majority of the American voters, if all eligible people are allowed to vote. The result has created absolute fear among the white evangelical Christian hosts of the oppress and persecute cultures. The cultures realize that they are in danger of losing the political power that has enabled them to maintain, for centuries, local, state, and national laws and customs that oppress and persecute women, Jews, LGBTQs, and non-white populations, first through the Democrat party and now through the Republican party in some states. The result is that the Republican party in many states, in the late 1990s and early 2000s, has come under the control of a white Christian oppress and persecute culture desperate to hold onto its historical political power with approximately 80 percent of white evangelical Christians voting Republican. No culture in our world's history has ever voluntarily given up its political power, and the white evangelical Christian oppress and persecute cultures are not about to be the first to do so.

Something had to be done while the culture still has a strong enough Christian voter power base to enact local, state, and national election laws to keep them in power. This means that the culture has to:

- Consolidate its control of white Christian voters to make sure that they always vote Republican. It has to convince white Christians that the Democrat party is out to destroy both their Christian political power base and, in fact, Christianity, itself by promoting the following alleged acts:

    ✓ Allowing more immigrants to enter the nation and become Democrat voters;

---

[1] Jones, Robert J., *The End of White Christian America,* Simon and Schuster Paperbacks, 2016, pg. 106.

- ✓ Recognizing the equal rights of women, LGBTQs, and transgender individuals;
- ✓ Registering non-white as well as non-Christian (including Muslim) voters;
- ✓ Enabling non-white voters to both register to vote and actually vote with the same ease as white voters are able to register and vote;
- ✓ Enabling Jews to gain more economic, social, and political power;
- ✓ Rigging elections so that Democrat candidates more often get elected;
- ✓ Allowing public schools to teach history lessons showing the evil imposed on women, Jews, Muslims, Native Americans, Blacks, and LGBTQs by white Christians; and
- ✓ Prohibiting the public funding of religious schools where white Christians can teach both their own versions of history and their own oppress and persecute culture values.

- Because white Christian voters will represent less than half of the total voters in the future, the culture is trying to force its Republican party to find ways other than a majority of votes to maintain political power. In other words, it is seeking election laws that allow only the votes of white Christians to determine who controls local, state and federal governments. Fortunately for the oppress and persecute cultures, this is not the first time they have faced this problem. They had the same problem after the Civil War when the threat of thousands of new black voters existed. The oppress and persecute Blacks culture of that day quickly solved the problem by having its Democrat party representatives rig the voter systems to prevent former black slaves and their decedents from voting for decades. And what an outstanding job the party did! Even as late as 1940, only three percent of eligible black voters were registered to vote in the Southern states.[2] The culture simply had to now repeat this exact same strategy in the 2020s and is attempting to do so by:

- ✓ Gerrymandering voter districts to prevent people of color and their white supporters from being the majority in as many voting districts in the United States as possible;
- ✓ Making it difficult for people of color to vote, including complicated requirements to obtain voter ID cards and inconvenient locations of voter registration offices;
- ✓ Preventing former convicts (the vast majority of whom are non-white) from voting;
- ✓ Establishing voting hours that are inconvenient (e.g., during weekday working hours only) for people of color;
- ✓ Reducing the number of polling locations in non-white neighborhoods to produce long voter lines and wait times;
- ✓ Preventing mail-in and early voting which, historically has been used most often by people of color and their white supporters;
- ✓ Allowing willing white Christian oppress and persecute culture hosts to volunteer as armed guards at voting polls to intimidate voters of color;
- ✓ Trying to establish election committees controlled by white Christian voters that have the legal authority to overrule election outcomes that the culture does not like;
- ✓ Filling court judgeships with white Christians who have strong records of supporting oppress and persecute culture values;

Through the examples above, as well as many other similar actions at the local, state, and national levels, the oppress and persecute cultures are getting closer and closer to achieving their goal of holding on to their political power beyond the time when white evangelical Christians will no longer comprise a majority of the nation's potential voters.

---

[2] https://checkyourfact.com/2018/06/06/fact-check-right-to-vote/

The big question, as I write these words, is whether the other members of the Republican party will be able to eject the oppress and persecute cultures from their party. Fortunately, as I write (July, 2023), we are seeing more and more courageous party leaders standing up to this evil culture, but they are in for a strong fight. As we have discussed in previous chapters, these oppressive cultures have a long history of doing everything possible, no matter how cruel or evil, to find a way to retain their control of political power for generation after generation. We can expect no less here.

Chapter 22

Can the Parasitic Oppress and Persecute Cultures be Replaced with Kinder, More Loving Cultures?

You, like me, may have wondered through all the previous chapters, "Are we Christians doomed forever to be dominated and controlled by these cruel and evil oppressive cultures?"

Unfortunately, when considered in its fullness, the scope of this question is even more devastating. Although not addressed in this book, we know that these parasitic oppress and persecute cultures have also attached themselves to and dominated other major world religions such as Islam and Hinduism for centuries with similar cruelty. So, the haunting question becomes, "Is our whole world doomed to be oppressed and persecuted by these cold, dark, and cruel cultures forever with no end in sight? Can we never escape their powerful control of our religious beliefs and actions? Will the next 1,500 years be just like the past 1,500?"

These questions hung over me for weeks like one of those black clouds you see in comic strips that follow you wherever you go.

Concentrating first on our Christianity. From my study of our Christian history, it is clear, at least to me, that these cultures fully intend to remain with us forever. They will always be out there hunting for and attaching themselves, like a flea or tick, to their next willing host. But, concentrating first on our own Christianity, I could not keep from wondering, "If enough of us found the courage, could we build a different Christian culture...a culture based on justice, love, compassion, and empathy for, and service to all our fellow humans? Is that even a possibility? Could it be done? How could it be done?"

It was at this point that I wished that I could ask my wonderful wife, who passed away over two years ago. She would know. She always knew, no matter what I asked her. So, remembering Jean with tears welling in my eyes, I walked into our family room and sat in her easy chair. I sat there for a while, unable to stop the tears, apparently not really wanting to as wonderful memories of our life together traveled through my mind's eye.

Then I looked at the books on our coffee table. There it was! There was our answer as if Jean had placed it there! There was David Schwartz's best-selling book *The Magic of Thinking Big* sitting right there on our coffee table. His book is one of the best motivational books I have ever read with a simple but highly effective message: each of us can accomplish a lot more in life if we think big and set big goals as opposed to thinking small and setting small goals. I have given a copy of this book to all my children and grandchildren when they became teenagers, plus copies to lots of friends.

Then my mind went immediately to another related great book with the same theme: *Built to Last: Successful Habits of Visionary Companies*. In this fantastic business management book, Jim Collins and Jerry Porras document how successful companies and organizations establish Big Hairy Audacious Goals—not little goals but **Big Hairy Audacious Goals**, now often referred to as **BHAGS** in business management circles. Once established, all the people in these companies go to work to achieve the BHAGS with each worker doing what she or he does best. No single person accomplishes the goals. It only happens by all working together.

So, my thoughts started to come together, and I hope yours are doing the same. Given that our faith has been dominated for over 1,500 years by these cruel, parasitic oppress and persecute cultures, this is the time that we (you and I) need to think **BIG**—not small, but **BIG!** This is the time that we (yes, you and I) need to change the course of history. This is the time that we need to establish the **BIG Hairy Audacious Goal** of: *building a worldwide movement to replace the oppress and persecute cultures with a* **Love and Support Each Other (LASEO)** *culture.*

This is not a complicated culture. It is simply the culture that Jesus worked so hard to establish while He was with us in human form, and He thought so important that He gave His life for it. A culture built on doing unto others as we would have them do unto us, on loving our neighbors as ourselves, on being a good Samaritan. A culture based on feeding the hungry, giving drink to the thirsty, clothing the naked, visiting the sick and those in prison, and welcoming the strangers in our midst....a culture where we Love and Support Each Other!

David Swartz, Jim Collins, and Jerry Porras had me motivated and, in fact, convinced. We can do it! I know that it is not just a BHAG, but a Huge BHAG! Of course, I can't do it alone, and you can't do it alone. Nor can thousands of us do it alone. But all of us...millions of us... working together, with each of us doing what we, individually, do best, can do it!

You may ask, "But can we sustain the effort for 1,500 years?" and I will respond "The hosts of these oppress and persecute cultures sustained their cruel deeds for 1,500 years. Surely, we are better than them!"

So, our BHAG, for the next 1,500 years, is to be that moment in our world's history when good people come together to produce a totally different kind of Christianity...a Christianity that reaches out across all ethnic, race, gender, gender identification, and religious beliefs to form a single LASEO culture where every person is treated with love, respect, dignity, and equality. Our commitment must be to build a new culture so big and so powerful that it overwhelms the oppress and persecute cultures, causing their memberships to become smaller and smaller and smaller so that they no longer dominate our society.

To start this new movement. I invite you to join me in adopting the following:

LOVE AND SUPPORT EACH OTHER

MANIFESTO

Whereas:

- cruel and evil cultures have dominated our white Christian ancestors and their institutions for at least 1,500 years;

- these cultures have caused our Christian ancestors to oppress and persecute their victims in every one of these 1,500 years;

- the oppression and persecution of the victims have included ostracizing and keeping them in ghettos, preventing them from working in high-level jobs, holding them as slaves, preventing them from learning to read and write, taking their lands and homes, keeping them in a lower caste, segregated society and economy, preventing them from voting, lynching and burning them at the stake, shooting millions in the back of their heads, gassing millions more to death, and hundreds of other inhumane treatments.

Whereas these evil cultures have:

- used our Christian theologians, preachers, authors, and teachers to "justify" the oppression and persecution of their victims by claiming that the victims are designated by God, through the Bible, to be oppressed or are associated with Satan and are a threat to our children, our families, our Christianity and our churches;

- convinced us that our salvation is totally independent of how we treat other people;

- removed all empathy and compassion that we should have for the victims;

- rewarded those of us who actively oppress and persecute the victims as well as those of us who provide strong support for that oppression and persecution;

- punished those who object to the oppression and persecution;

- intimidated most of us to be stone silent while the oppression and persecution is taking place; and

- hidden their cruel and evil deeds behind the facades of loving Christian sermons, songs, prayers, and good deeds.

  Whereas these evil cultures are alive and well in most of our Christian institutions today and are causing us white Christians to:

- oppress and persecute women;

- oppress and persecute our LGBTQ brothers and sisters and sons and daughters;

- oppress people of color; and

- condemn Jews and commit antisemitic acts.

Whereas these cruel and evil acts, as well as others too numerous to list, often cause irreparable harm to the victims under the guise of our religion:

Therefore, I, by evidence of my signature of this document, do hereby reject all forms of oppressive Christianity and commit to building a Christianity over the next 1,500 years that is free of all oppression and persecution cultures. This different Christianity will concentrate totally on **Loving and Supporting Each Other** (hereafter referred to as **LASEO)** and will be based on the biblical commandments that we:

- love our neighbors as ourselves;

- do unto others as we would have them do unto us;

- feed the hungry, give drink to the thirsty, visit the sick and those in prison, and welcome the stranger in our midst; and

- be a "good Samaritan" to all who need our help, no matter who they are.

As a part of my **LASEO** commitment, I humbly join the millions of individuals and hundreds of cities, communities, and houses of worship of many religions in committing to the following Charter of Compassion adopted by the Council for a Parliament of the World Religions in 2009[1]:

The principle of compassion lies at the heart of all religious, ethical and spiritual traditions, calling us always to treat all others as we wish to be treated ourselves. Compassion impels us to work tirelessly to alleviate the suffering of our fellow creatures, to dethrone ourselves from the centre of our world and put another there, and to honour the inviolable sanctity of every single human being, treating everybody, without exception, with absolute justice, equity and respect.

It is also necessary in both public and private life to refrain consistently and empathically from inflicting pain. To act or speak violently out of spite, chauvinism, or self-interest, to impoverish, exploit or deny basic rights to anybody, and to incite hatred by denigrating others—even our enemies—is a denial of our common humanity.

We acknowledge that we have failed to live compassionately and that some have even increased the sum of human misery in the name of religion. We therefore call upon all men and women to restore compassion to the centre of morality and religion ~ to return to the ancient principle that any interpretation of scripture that breeds violence, hatred or disdain is illegitimate ~ to ensure that youth are given accurate and respectful information about other traditions, religions and cultures ~ to encourage a positive appreciation of cultural and religious diversity ~ to cultivate an informed empathy with the suffering of all human beings—even those regarded as enemies.

We urgently need to make compassion a clear, luminous and dynamic force in our polarized world. Rooted in a principled determination to transcend selfishness, compassion can break down political, dogmatic, ideological and religious boundaries. Born of our deep interdependence, compassion is essential to human relationships

---

[1] https://charterforcompassion.org/charter/charter

and to a fulfilled humanity. It is the path to enlightenment, and indispensable to the creation of a just economy and a peaceful global community."

_____   _____

Name   *Date*

Having made this long-term commitment and set a BHAG goal, what do we do now? I will present my suggestions, and I hope that you will join me with your own ideas and actions. Yours will, almost certainly, be far better and more successful than mine. But maybe my suggestions will get your mental thoughts flowing.

This is not going to be an easy task because these oppressive cultures have centuries of experience in holding on to their domination of our Christian beliefs and actions. And as we have seen, they have no hesitation in using every conceivable weapon in their arsenal to hold on to their power: firing people from their jobs, kicking people out of their churches, ostracizing them from society, suppressing their votes, taking their homes and lands, committing mass murders, and even going to war, to name only a few. So, it is going to take not only all our ideas, efforts, and leadership, but our commitment to a sustained movement year after year, decade after decade, and century after century. It is going to take you and me and our children and grandchildren, and their children and grandchildren for generations to come. But the sooner we start, the sooner we will reach our BHAG!

I start with Christianity because that is my own religion and the theme of this book, but this will require the help and support of all religious groups to rid the world of cruel oppressive cultures. After suggesting what we Christians can do, we will come back to what we of every religion can do because accomplishing our BHAG will require all of us from all religions working together.

So, starting with Christians:

Existing LASEO churches. First and foremost, let us begin by expressing our deepest thanks and appreciation to those small numbers of Christian churches and their leaders and members who have had the courage to reject the oppress and persecute cultures. In every age, there have been a small percentage of Christians who have stood up to the oppressive cultures of their day. Many not only stood up but risked their very lives to protect the victims of these cruel cultures. Some even gave their lives to help. These were true LASEO Christians. The shame is that they have almost always been in the minority, in fact, small minorities. Today, we are blessed with, relatively speaking, a small group of LASEO churches who have had the courage to reject the attempts of oppressive cultures to invade and mislead their membership.

We see this courage being played out today (2023) as the United Methodist church stands strong against the attempts of the oppress and persecute LGBTQs culture to take over the denomination. Rather than surrender the UMC's commitment to loving and supporting each other, its leaders are sacrificing the denomination's worldwide size and power. The invading oppress and persecute LGBTQs culture is being forced to work to capture one local UMC church at a time, and this approach, thankfully, will dramatically slow its progress. More importantly, it keeps the overall UMC intact as a LASEO denomination, now freed of the hosts of the oppress and persecute LGBTQs culture. The UMC can now rebuild itself as a more loving and compassionate world-wide church association, dedicated to treating all people with love, respect, dignity, and equality.

These LASEO churches, similar to the UMC churches, are key to our success in building a worldwide LASEO culture. They are the core, already existing organizations that we can join to build a worldwide LASEO culture. They offer us a "running start." They already know what to do, already have the organizational structures, the teaching materials, the community witnessing and service projects, the arms reaching across race, religious and ethnic aisles, and a strong history of keeping oppress and persecute cultures out of their congregations. It is almost like joining a winning team!

So, please join me in saying "thank you" to these wonderful LASEO churches who have persevered over the years while the cruel and evil oppressive cultures have dominated the majority of our other Christian organizations.

Pastors, lay leaders, and teachers in LASEO churches. We cannot say thank you enough, even if we repeat it for years, for all that the LASEO pastoral staff, lay leaders, and teachers, have done and are doing in building LASEO cultures in your churches. What you have done has been critical in preventing the oppress and persecute cultures from obtaining full domination of our Christianity. Were it not for you and your courage in prior generations, we would still be murdering innocent people as witches, yanking children from the arms of slave mothers and selling them, murdering Jews, and keeping people of color in the lowest of segregated castes. Were it not for you, women today probably could not vote, would not be holding professional jobs, and could not preach in many LASEO churches. Were it also not for you today, gay people would not be treated with respect and dignity and most likely would not be able to marry the person they love. We are a far better people because of you.

I am sure, however, that it is no surprise to you that you get no time off for the rest you so justly deserve. We need your leadership, your sermons, your lessons, and your living examples even more over the next few centuries. You are the role models that we, our children, and our grandchildren need to lead and inspire us to build a world where love and support for each other reigns supreme. If you stop, the oppressive cultures will almost certainly move aggressively to dominate more of our churches, our schools, our governments, our communities, and our world with their cruel oppression and persecution. We see their attempts to do their evil every day. But your quiet, but forceful, leadership, guidance, and words of encouragement are preventing these cultures from advancing their evil domination. Through your combined efforts, you have done it and continue to do it! We thank you and ask that you continue with no letup, maybe even redoubling your efforts!

If you are a member of an oppress and persecute culture, please leave it immediately. If we are going to defeat these cruel cultures, we must begin by denying them our support. Accordingly, if you are a member of a church or other organization that is dominated by an oppress and persecute culture, please dig deep and find the courage to leave that culture now. Please seek out and join another organization that is committed to maintaining a LASEO culture, like the LASEO churches described above.

I know from experience that it will not be easy. These oppressive cultures can give you a thousand reasons why you need to stay with them. I have personally experienced this as I've been told things like those other churches "are not true Christians; we are. They are flaming liberals; we are committed conservatives. This is where your friends are. If you leave, you will lose those friendships. You won't be any happier in another church. This is the church where your parents were longstanding members. It will take a lot of effort to find another church; why don't you put it off until next month? Etc., etc., etc. "

Why would they work so hard to hold on to even a single person? Because every day that an oppressive culture holds on to our membership is another day of victory for the culture.

But about six months ago, after my Southern Baptist Church voted to ban literature that taught that how we treated others was not part of being a servant of Christ, I, after almost fifty years of membership, finally found the courage to start looking for another church. To my surprise, after only a few months of searching, I found a Presbyterian (USA) church in Tallahassee that is committed to maintaining a LASEO culture. Also, to my surprise, the transfer was easy and rewarding. It wasn't as difficult as I had expected. I immediately found friends who shared my Christian values of respect, dignity, and equality for everybody, including women and LGBTQs. Within only weeks, they involved me in one project to help refugees relocate to our community and another to reach across racial and ethnic aisles. I was welcomed with open arms by members and staff alike. I am now using my membership, donations, and efforts to serve, not oppress and persecute, other people.

And now the oppress and persecute culture of my previous church has one fewer supporter. If one more leaves, it will have two fewer supporters, and if enough leave, it might just have no supporters at all.

If you are a "None," please consider joining our movement. We need you! "Nones," who are defined as "Americans who do not identify as having any religious affiliations," now represent 29 percent of the U.S population.[2] You are the fastest growing segment of our U.S population, projected to grow as high as 50 percent by 2070.[3] Clearly, you are having a major impact on the type of society that we have in our world.

In fact, in many ways, you have already made a major contribution to the defeat of these cruel oppressive cultures because many of you became "nones" when you could no longer tolerate the oppression and persecutions being committed in the name of Christianity. I have several friends, and have talked to others, who walked out to become "nones" following harrowing experiences in their oppress and persecute cultured churches. And when they left these churches, that reduced the power and influence of those cruel cultures.

But, if we are going to build a dominant love and support each other culture, we simply must have more from you. We must have your active support and leadership. There are about 100 million of you in our nation today (2023). You are a viable force and will be even more so in future years. Where you go, our nation is likely to go. Your values have the strong probability of becoming our values.

So, I am pleading with you. As we have already discussed, not all churches are controlled by oppressive cultures. There are LASEO churches in most of our communities with values that align with your values. If you will join us in building and supporting these churches, we can, together, build a national movement where a LASEO culture dominates our society. And when we, together, build this new culture, the old and cruel cultures will become small little groups no longer wielding the power to oppress their victims. Your participation is critical to the success of this movement. We cannot do it without you!

Within your LASEO church, join or create a small group to support each other. While participating in LASEO worship services

---

2 https://religionnews.com/2019/03/21/nones-now-as-big-as-evangelicals-catholics-in-the-us/
3https://www.msn.com/en-in/entertainment/story/projections-christians-could-fall-to-less-than-50percent-nones-could-be-more-than-50percent-in-us-by-2070/ar-AA11YeZM

is both meaningful and rewarding, it does little to change the world unless we use the inspiration and what we learn during those services. To do that, I highly recommend that you find a small group in your church that is doing things...things like serving the homeless or reaching across racial and ethnic lines to bridge relationships or doing joint projects with other religious faiths, or other projects that show love and support for others. If such a group does not exist in your house of worship, find fellow travelers and work with church officials to create one.

Smyth & Helwys Publishing Company, we need you to produce Christian study guides that teach us how to Love and Support Each Other. As committed Christians, we also need advice, information, and guidance in building our LASEO cultures. We need the thinking of LASEO theologians, ministers and authors. We need to more fully understand what our Lord requires of us, how we are to view and treat our fellow humans, and how we can best use our individual gifts to serve. We need to understand other faiths and how we can replace rejecting each other with working together to make our world a better place. In other words, we need the strong, intentional support and guidance of your company and others like it in building a Christian culture where Love and Support Each Other reigns supreme.

We need you to produce weekly lesson guides based on biblical texts that show the importance of loving and supporting each other. We need guidance on how we can use our individual gifts to serve others. We need innovative ideas for how we can provide support and help for others, both individually and collectively. We need for you to deepen our empathy and compassion for others, most especially others who are not like us.

And in doing this, you will build the writing skills of the authors, who, hopefully, will go on to write books and articles of their own. Your efforts to support their work and careers will further motivate and guide us in building and maintaining a strong and compassionate LASEO culture.

Weekend LASEO retreats. All of us need both regular encouragement and sources of new ideas as we seek to replace Christian oppress and persecute cultures with a unified Love and Support Each Other culture within the Christian church. For the last ten years or so, my wife and I attended an annual Christian weekend retreat at the Methodist Epworth by the Sea Center on St. Simons Island, Georgia. The retreats are multi-denominational and have always, unofficially, had love and support for each other as their central theme. They consist of presentations by some of the nation's leading LASEO theologians and authors who present numerous ideas about what we can do to make the world a more loving place when we return to our home churches and communities. What an uplifting experience to be among six hundred or more like-minded Christians (and sometimes those of other faiths). Originally, the retreats were named "The January Adventure." Last year, for reasons that I know not, the name was changed to "Southern Lights."

We desperately need some leading national organization, maybe one of the larger Christian seminaries with support from a national Christian foundation, to offer these kinds of annual Christian LASEO weekend retreats all over the nation—perhaps the New England Lights, the Midwest Lights, the Northwest Lights, the Southwest Lights, and the Midsouth Lights. It is my understanding that the Southern Lights retreat is financially self-supporting. I know that prior to COVID, the reservations for attendance filled up within a week of opening each year. So, after the initial founding, the suggested additional retreats should need no additional funding and will be "money makers" for the retreat centers.

If you are associated with one of the LASEO Christian seminaries or one of the national Christian foundations, would you please consider taking on this project? You might just make our world a far more loving place for generations to come!!

We need more LASEO seminary graduates. Unfortunately, the oppress and persecute cultures dominate too many of our predominately white Christian seminaries, both Protestant and Catholic. The result is that the graduates are trained to believe, teach, encourage, and model the oppression and persecution of other people, especially women, people of color, and LGBTQs. As we have discussed in previous chapters, there is little chance that these seminaries can rid their institutions of their oppressive cultures. The cultures are simply too ingrained and too strong. The sad result is that too many of our future Christian professional leaders are destined to be strong oppressive culture advocates.

The solution has to be the expansion of seminaries that have rejected the oppress and persecute cultures and teach a Love and Support Each Other Christianity. We need all of you LASEO seminaries to both increase your enrollments and to expand offerings for in-service training and short courses to provide a much larger cadre of ministers committed to and skilled at building and maintaining LASEO cultures in their communities.

National Christian publications. We need some of our national Christian magazines, like the *Sojourners, Christian Century, Christianity Today* and others, to dedicate themselves to publishing articles that promote the creation and maintenance of a Love and Support Each Other culture. Cultures have to be maintained with constant educational and inspirational materials. We need to read about the biblical history of LASEO cultures, about the importance of these cultures in serving our God and His people, to learn about innovative ideas for serving in today's modern world, and to learn about projects that we can join to build this culture. So, Christian magazine editors and authors, will you please join and help lead our LASEO movement for the next 1,500 years? What a huge difference you can make! Then after 1,500 years, you can take a well-earned week's vacation.

A LASEO Lectionary. Lectionaries which provide weekly guidance to pastors on scriptures for sermons have played a major role over the past fifty years in helping pastors to provide their congregations with both a broader and more in-depth understanding of the lessons embedded in the Christian bible. The first broadly used lectionary was the 1974 COCU (Consultation on Church Union) Lectionary which was followed by the Common Lectionary in 1983 that was then followed by the Revised Common Lectionary in 1994. These lectionaries were prepared by representatives from a large number of Catholic and Protestant church groups. My ministerial friends tell me that these lectionaries have been great aids to them as they sought to teach biblical lessons to their congregations.

In spite of the tremendous effort that went into the preparation of these lectionaries and the major improvements that they made in the sermons preached by Christian ministers, our history has shown that the lectionaries failed to rid our Christian religion of the parasitic oppress and persecute cultures that have attached themselves to us Christians and our institutions for the past 1500 plus years. A vast majority of we white Christians still, even as I write these words in 2023, allow these evil cultures to control our beliefs, policies, and behavior which result in our continued Christian oppression and persecution of women, people of color, LGBTQs and Jews. Just this week (February, 2023), The Southern Baptist Convention expelled five local churches because they have women pastors.[4]

We need our national Christian denominations that have adopted Love and Support Each Other (LASEO) cultures to come together and produce a revision to the Revised Common Lectionary that promotes the replacement of the evil oppress and persecute cultures with the LASEO culture that Jesus worked so hard to establish while He was with us in human form. Can we ask that you LASEO denominational leaders do just that? Because these lectionaries take several years to finalize, can we ask that you start soon, like within the next six months? As quickly as possible, we need hundreds of thousands of ministers preaching the Bible's Love and Support Each Other lesson every Sunday!

ALL WORLD RELIGIONS

We need all world religions to join and lead this BHAG LASEO movement.

---

[4]   https://www.al.com/news/2023/02/southern-baptists-expel-5-churches-over-women-pastors-1-over-sexual-abuse.html

While the previous sections in this chapter have concentrated on Christianity, there is no way that Christians, alone, can build this LASEO movement. It would be foolish to try. Other religions are just as important and critical. It is going to require that we of every religion come together and jointly provide the needed support and leadership as equal partners. Without our joint partnership and commitment, the movement will fail miserably, and the cruel oppress and persecute cultures will continue to dominate our world with their evil acts for another 1,500 years.

Mutual Respect. Several years ago, the company where I was employed had a contract to work with the public higher education system in Indonesia. Our project involved working with them to review and improve their processes for allocating their federal funds among their individual colleges and universities (a common issue in all public higher education funding). The contract manager in Indonesia for the project was Pak Ottomo, the chief financial officer for the nation's Department of Higher Education.

Upon my first meeting with Pak Ottomo to begin the project, he shocked me with the question: "What are your religious requirements?" I immediately wondered what that had to do with our project. I must have had a huge question mark on my face because he quickly added, "Most of the people with whom you will be working are Muslims. So, we will be stopping five times a day to pray. Whatever your religious requirements are, we want to honor those!" Those words have stuck with me ever since that conversation: "Whatever your religious requirements are, we want to honor those!"

What a wonderful man. What a wonderful attitude and respect for me and my religious beliefs. Why can we not all be Pak Ottomos with that same respect for our fellow man? My suggestion is that with a LASEO culture, we can, indeed, have that respect for each other. And if we do, maybe, just maybe, we can stop oppressing and persecuting each other!

Keep our respective religions but join together to build a common worldwide LASEO culture.

If we follow Pak Ottomo's respectful approach to our individual religious beliefs, we can both keep and build our individual beliefs *and* build a common worldwide LASEO culture. That has to be our common goal. So, I plead with the leaders of all religions, please step up to lead this worldwide movement to build this wonderful new, kind and loving culture where we love and support each other and oppress and persecute no one. I cannot do it, but you can!!

Now that I hopefully have your support, what do we do?

Let's start in our own communities by going beyond our own religions to create LASEO relationships with other religions and race/ethnic groups. We can do this in our own communities by forming small multi-religious, multi-racial, and multi-gender groups. I am a member of such a group that has been meeting monthly for over five years. We discuss how we can work together to build a better community for all our people. The group was initially formed by two of my close friends. One friend was a Baptist pastor, and the other was the CEO of a leading Florida public relations firm, who happens to be Jewish. Over these years, our group has gotten to know each other, not as people of different religions and races, but as individuals who share common concerns about our community, our world, our families, and each other. Several community-wide projects have evolved from our group. Most recently, a subgroup coordinated a meeting of over a hundred leaders of Tallahassee civic clubs and houses of worship (Jewish, Muslim, and Christians, representing all races and ethnicities) to organize our community to help the approximately three hundred war-time refugees who have recently re-located in our area.

Our group did not necessarily set out to become a LASEO group, but did so as we got to know each other and found our common bonds. My wife was a member of a similar multi-religious, multi-racial, and multi-gender group led by Rabbi Jack Romberg. He is a highly respected Jewish leader and author of *A Doorway to Heroism,*" a book about his family's experience with the Holocaust. Jean claimed on numerous occasions that her experience with this small group was, by far, the best of her life. It was through this small group that our family became involved in supporting the Holocaust Education Resource Council (HERC) that provides middle and high schoolteachers with knowledge and materials to help them teach their students about the Holocaust. This is a desperately needed program as the number of anti-Semitic acts in our nation rapidly increase.

We need millions of these smaller, intentional groups that include multi-religions, multi-races and multi-genders working to build and maintain LASEO cultures in our local communities. You can help by organizing one in your community! It is not complicated, and it costs nothing other than a little of your time. You can begin by inviting about fifteen people to join you, electing a chair, and starting by getting to know each other by asking each member to tell their life story. Then move on to discuss community issues. As the group gels, you can add other members up to about thirty in the same way that my friends invited me to join. After that, you may want to start another small group. You will be absolutely amazed at all that you learn and all that you can accomplish through your small group in creating a more loving and compassionate world. Just as importantly, you will learn that our religious beliefs have far more in common than in conflict and that each of our religions strongly support Loving and Supporting Each Other.

Interfaith America can be a huge resource for you in guiding your activities. I suggest that you research their web site at www.interfaithamerica.org. I promise you that you will be impressed and thankful.

With your help, and that of many more, we can, indeed, create millions of these small, local LASEO groups all over the world. And, by doing this, we strike a blow against the dominance of the cruel oppressive cultures in our churches, mosques, synagogues, sanghas, wards, temples, gurudwaras and communities. What a day of rejoicing that will be for both us and the victims of these evil cultures.

Companion Books from Other Religions. Following Pak Ottomo's great example of respect for the religious beliefs of others, I chose to not include other religious beliefs in this book. Yet, we all know that these oppress and persecute cultures have not limited their cruel treatments of their victims to just Christianity. They have, whenever possible, sought to attach themselves to other religions. So, I am asking that some courageous authors with other religious beliefs write books, similar to this one, that examine the cruel treatments of others caused by these evil parasitic cultures that have occurred within their religions. I am then asking that you end your book with an exploration of how we, of all religious beliefs, can both keep our individual religious beliefs and work together over the next 1500 years to permanently replace these oppress and persecute cultures with a Love and Support Each Other (LASEO) culture. **Could one of these authors be you?**

Pew Research Center and Public Religion Research Institute (PRRI), we need your objective research help. We need comprehensive research on how well our LASEO movement is achieving its goal of creating and maintaining a loving and compassionate society. We need to know if we are succeeding. We need to learn what we are doing best, what we are doing wrong, and what we can do better.

Do you already have analytical methods for measuring our individual love and compassion for our fellow man and how well we are doing in helping each other? If not, can you develop those tools? Do you have or can you develop a single societal index that measures and tracks how effectively we are loving and supporting each other...maybe, a LASEO index? Can you identify those activities that are most successful in building a LASEO culture?

Finally, will you please work with the religious publications and websites *of all religions* to widely distribute your findings so that even those of us in small community groups can use the information to guide our efforts to build loving and compassionate cultures in our own communities?

Your research is critical to our success!!

Religious and Philanthropic Foundations... Foundations like Lilly Endowment, Inc, Arthur Vining Davis Foundation, Henry Luce

Foundation, Templeton Foundation, Kern Family Foundation and others. We need both your ideas and your financial grants to create and sponsor local, regional, and national efforts to promote and support the building of LASEO projects...projects that dramatically expand a culture where we love and support each other instead of oppress and persecute each other. We need you to design and fund local and regional projects that, once successful, can be duplicated. **You are a key link in our movement.** We need your wisdom and leadership. Will each of you consider establishing an advisory "think tank" committee to explore and then design needed projects that will significantly expand the creation and expansion of local, regional, national and worldwide Love and Support Each Other cultures? We need projects that, once proven successful, can be duplicated over and over and over again, decade after decade and century after century, until our world is a world where all people are loving and supporting each other.

We need our local, regional, and national media to initiate and maintain constant messaging on building a LASEO culture. We know that the oppress and persecute cultures have their own media supporters that have been highly successful in strengthening their evil treatment of others. And we understand that market research shows that "bad news" attracts far more readers and listeners than "good news." So, this may require some financial sacrifices on your part or some creative media management at the very least. But to defeat these cruel cultures, we absolutely must have the dedicated support of the media at the local, regional, national, and worldwide levels.

So, I am pleading with our LASEO media leaders, both print and broadcasting, please give us your best leadership. It is critical. We need to hear the importance of building and maintaining a LASEO culture. We need to see and hear what others are doing to build this culture. We need to see and hear about organizations and programs that we can join. We need to especially hear about real world cases where people of all religious faiths come together to respect and honor each other and, in doing so, join hands in helping each other. We need your visionary leadership.

Social Justice Organizations such as the Southern Poverty Law Center (SPLC), the American Civil Liberties Union (ACLU), the Anti-Defamation League (ADL), the National Association of Advancement for Colored People (NAACP) and YES Magazine. You are absolutely essential to creating and maintaining a LASEO culture. We are a far better nation today because of your vision, dedication, and work to build and support justice in our nation. You have played a huge role in preventing the oppressive cultures from being even more dominant and cruel in oppressing and persecuting our fellow humans. Please continue what you are doing in fighting these cultures and their attempts to enforce their oppression and persecution through laws, ordinances and hate groups.

I know that you are already striving to replace these cruel cultures with a LASEO culture through educational programs. Can we ask that you do even more of this? And can we ask our readers to remember your organizations when they make their financial donations so that you have the resources to do more?

Educators. What a huge role you play in helping our future generations find, understand, and improve the cultures in which they will live. Next to parents, you are the most important influence on most young lives. In unfortunate cases of poor or absent parenting, you can be the most important contributor of all. Hence, it should be no surprise to you that the oppressive cultures go after you, trying to dictate what you teach and what you are never allowed to teach. Whenever possible, these cruel cultures will not let you teach the truth about their historic oppression and persecution of Native Americans, people of color, Jews, LGBTQs, and women. They will do everything they can to keep you from teaching the truth about what they are still doing today to oppress and persecute people of color, Jews, women, and LGBTQs, even to the extent of banning books that you can use, recording your lessons, and surveying your students.

I understand the pressure that you are under from these cruel cultures. But it is for this very reason that we need your courage at this time in our history. We need for you schoolteachers, college and university faculty, state school book selection committees, local school boards and administrators, college and university administrators and governing boards, and teacher and faculty unions to refuse to yield your freedom to teach the truth about these evil cultures. Instead, we need you to help us create a new LASEO culture that is committed to the truth for the next 1,500 years. It is an understatement to say that we cannot do it without you! Without you, the oppress and persecute cultures will continue to dominate our world for years to come by preventing people from learning the truth about these cultures' relentless oppression and persecution of their targeted victims.

Librarians. I understand the tremendous pressure that you, like educators, are under to perpetuate the lives of the oppressive cultures. You are under constant pressure to ban books and other publications that tell the truth about these cruel cultures. But we need you to not only be strong in the face of these evil cultures but to go further to promote the establishment of a LASEO culture. Can you arrange displays of LASEO publications? Can you list these publications in your newsletters? Can you sponsor LASEO book clubs? Can you have a special session at your regional and national association meetings on how to use your resources to build and maintain a worldwide LASEO culture?

You and your work have always been key to the building of an educated and compassionate society, and you have done it so well for centuries, sometimes in the face of evil threats. It is just as important now. In fact, your support and leadership are critical components of building and maintaining a worldwide LASEO culture. Please join us with your longtime compassion, commitment, and leadership.

Commercial Book Stores. You play a major role in the directions that our society goes...perhaps a much, much larger role than you realize in building and sustaining cultures! Can you also build displays that promote books that support LASEO cultures? Additionally, can you aggressively promote such books in your advertising with the goal of making the reading of LASEO books "the thing to do"?

Elected Governmental Officials in Oppress and Persecute Culture Districts and States. My heart also goes out to all of you

Let Justice and Mercy Flow

governmental officials who have been elected by and represent voters
controlled by oppressive cultures. You face a huge dilemma. These
cultures are unforgiving. If you start supporting LASEO polices and
laws that treat all people with respect, dignity, and equality, you will,
almost certainly not be reelected. I know that in my youth in
Mississippi, no elected official who spoke out or voted in favor of racial
equality would have ever been reelected. I am sure that it was the same
for any elected Nazi party officials in Germany in the 1930s and early
1940s who might have spoken out or voted in favor of laws that
protected the jobs, welfare, and lives of their Jewish neighbors. And
the same for any elected officials in the Southern states during
antebellum slavery. The oppressive cultures ruled who was elected and
reelected during those historical times, and they still do today.

So, I know that I am asking a lot of those of you who are governmental
officials elected by oppressive cultures when I ask that you dig deep
for the courage to speak out in favor of laws that support the building
of a Love and Support Each Other culture. In fact, I am asking so
much of you that it may cost you your job, which may affect your
ability to financially support your family. But I am asking that you
politically support laws that give every adult American citizen the same
access to registering to vote and ease of actually voting. I am asking
that you support laws that prevent any political party or body from
overruling the results of elections. I am not asking that you give any
category of people any special privileges, only that you treat all
categories with respect, dignity, and equality in all that you do and say.
If you can do these simple things, you will help provide the social and
political environment where we can all work together to build a
LASEO culture. So, I plead with our oppressive culture elected
governmental officials: join our 1,500 year initiative to build this
wonderful culture by simply vowing to treat all people in your city,
county, district, state, and nation equally.

**Elected Governmental Officials in LASEO Culture Districts and
States.** We need strong, strong leadership from you officials who have
been elected by LASEO cultures. You are building not only the legal
but, also, the political and social environment that is so crucial to the
expansion of a Love and Support Each Other culture in our nation

317

and world. We need, of course, for you to be passing the laws that ensure that every person is treated with respect, dignity, and equality, but we need more from you. We need for you to use your public platform to speak out often and loudly in support of a LASEO culture. When we read our newspapers and magazines, when we turn on our televisions, when we turn on our computers, we need to be hearing from you, not from the leaders of oppressive cultures, but from you! We need you, not them, to dominate the news with your forceful acclamations that our goal is to build and maintain a LOVE AND SUPPORT EACH OTHER culture in our communities, states, nations, and world. We need you to never let up in speaking this message.

Authors, Speakers and Leaders of all Religions. Your books, presentations, and leadership have already played major roles in encouraging people to create LASEO cultures in their communities and houses of worship. I personally know because I have read some of your books and listened to your presentations. In some ways, you are responsible for what I am writing at this moment.

We, of course, need you to continue to write and speak about the importance of replacing oppressive cultures with LASEO cultures. We need your continuing guidance and inspiration about what we can do in our local communities. But, given that we are working on a Big Hairy Audacious Goal, we need even more from you. Accordingly, I am asking that you hold your own annual retreat where you invite the leading religious authors, speakers, and organizers of all major religions to come together, think BHAG thoughts, and discuss what can be done, both individually and collectively, to more rapidly build our envisioned worldwide LASEO culture. Your BHAG vision and leadership are critical.

I am asking the renown and highly respected religious authors, speakers and leaders, Diana Butler Bass and Brian McLaren, the also highly respected Editor-in-Chief of Christianity Today, Russell Moore and the courageous visionary founder of Interfaith American, Eboo Patel, to come together to jointly plan and lead the first retreat, ensuring equitable representation from all major world religions and race/ethnic groups. I will help in whatever ways I can.

A LASEO Media Site. To those young tech/media entrepreneurs out there, we need your talent, vision, and leadership in building a LASEO media platform similar to Twitter and Facebook. We need a site where LASEO people can communicate with each other across the miles and share information about the needs of our fellow humans. We need a way to connect online to discuss and establish projects to help each other, where our LASEO authors can post their articles, and where we can encourage one another. We need this to be a BHAG LASEO site. Could this visionary tech/media entrepreneur be you? Would one of you foundations consider funding such a project?

An Escape Route for Religious Leaders Captured by Oppressive Cultures. My heart goes out to those professional religious leaders (priests, sisters, ministers, imams, swamis, et. al.) who are currently employed by religious organizations controlled by oppress and persecute cultures. From history, we know that these cultures will "eat you alive" if you object to their oppression and persecution or even if you try to leave.

Imagine with me for a moment that you are a Catholic priest or sister or a Southern Baptist minister and you have decided that you can no longer support their cruel ideologies, and you want to get a job with a LASEO organization. In most cases, given the current job market for religious leaders, you will have to start a "word of mouth" search which means that there is a real chance that your current oppressive culture employer will learn about your search. As soon as that happens, you will almost certainly lose your job.

But that's not all—the culture will often try to destroy your reputation, making it difficult for you to find employment elsewhere. We saw this earlier in Chapter 12 when we discussed what happened to the careers of twenty-eight Mississippi Methodist ministers who signed a manifesto in the 1960s supporting racial integration. Eighteen lost their jobs, and the remaining ten had their lifetime careers limited to small churches paying low salaries.

So, we need an escape route for these professional religious leaders trapped in oppressive culture jobs, a bit like the Underground Railroad that slaves used to escape. One way that this route can be built is through the establishment of a worldwide website where all LASEO religious organizations can post their job openings (along with specific requirements unique to each religious group) and applicants can *confidentially* investigate and apply. We need some large LASEO organization to step forward to build and manage this site for the next 1,500 years.

A Worldwide Love and Support Each Other Session. Remember, as David Swartz says so convincingly in his book, "There is magic in thinking big." And as Jim Collins and Jerry Porras establish so well in their book, "Success comes from setting Big Hairy Audacious Goals." So, I ask the Parliament of World Religions and Interfaith America, both of which already have a tremendously successful history of thinking and acting big, to think bigger than you have ever thought before. Think big hairy audacious thoughts...ones so big that maybe even God will rejoice and say "Finally, at last!"

I am asking that the Parliament and Interfaith America join together to assemble representatives from worldwide religious institutions, foundations, religious research organizations, social justice organizations, religious publishing organizations and secular media for a weekend retreat with a single agenda item for each representative to address: What can my institution/organization do to advance the building of a worldwide LASEO culture?

I suggest that all the individuals, institutions, and organizations mentioned in this chapter be invited but know that many more need to be included. I do not know all of them, but you do.

If my intuition is right, this meeting can build on your past accomplishments to launch a world-wide, 1,500-year crusade of love, empathy, and compassion that replaces the cruel and evil oppressive cultures that have dominated our religions and our society for the past 1,500 years.

Movement Leaders. We know from history that every movement needs dynamic leaders...leaders who see the vision of what can be; leaders who know how to lead; leaders who are so committed that they will never give up, leaders who all of us respect and want to follow; leaders who are willing to sacrifice their own welfare to serve others; leaders who will never rest until the movement is well established. We need millions of these leaders. We need them in every community, every state, and every nation. Could one of these leaders be **YOU**?

For sure, it is going to take all of us. It is going to take YOU. It is going to take ME. Cultures, whether good or bad, are built around people and supported by them. So, it is going to take all of us to build and maintain a LASEO couture. That means the officers of the national organizations. That means the religious authors and speakers. That means our friends and our family. **Most especially, it means you and me.** So, please, do not close this book and move on to, maybe, a more entertaining one. Instead, please think **BIG.** Make a list of what you are going to start doing this week: maybe leave the oppressive culture that you have been supporting to join a loving culture or call a couple of friends about starting a small group or explore what your organization can do to build a beautiful love and support each other culture.

I Leave You Now with This Challenge. A young boy approached his grandfather with his hands behind his back. In his hands, he held a caterpillar.

The boy said to his grandfather, "I have a caterpillar in my hands. Is it alive or dead?"

The grandfather quickly realized that if he said "alive," the young boy would squeeze the caterpillar to death and hold out a dead caterpillar. If he said "dead," the boy would hold out a live caterpillar.

So, after a few moments of thought, with a smile the wise old grandfather responded, "As you will, my son, as you will."

To my fellow women and men, you hold our future in your hands. Will our future generations hold out a dead society smashed to death

Ken Boutwell

by cruel oppress and persecute cultures or a beautifully molted culture dedicated to loving and supporting each other?

It will be "As you will, my sisters and brothers, as you will."

Appendix A

Letter to Methodist Minister

August 26, 2019

3431 Cedar Lane Drive
Tallahassee, Florida 32312

Dear Dr. _____,

Just as Jesus, as documented in the fifth chapter of Mark, stopped on his way to an urgent destination to hear the story of a woman who, because of her desperation, reached out to just touch His cloak, I am reaching out to "touch your cloak", hoping that you will take the time to hear my story. I apologize in advance for its length, but hope that, like Jesus, you will take the time to "hear" it.

Recently, I was having dinner with my sister-in-law, Nanci Youngblood, and her sister, Marilyn Casey. I mentioned a really good *Born of Conviction* book that I had recently read about the careers of 28 young white Mississippi Methodist ministers who had the compassion and courage to sign a manifesto in about 1963 (I forget the exact year) that, in essence, called on white Christians to support the equal treatment of black people. I came away from that book with a tremendous admiration for those 28 ministers who, in spite of knowing the costs that they most likely would have to pay, still had the courage to sign that petition. As the book so vividly portrays, most of them did, indeed, pay those costs with losses of friends, family and jobs and setbacks in their careers. If my memory is correct, you were one of the leaders in both writing the manifesto and getting others to sign it.

To my shame today, while you were risking everything to do what was right in those days, I was on the other side—even to the extent of writing a letter to a state Baptist magazine editor defending white Christians' racial integration resistance.

I was born and raised on a farm outside of Newton, Mississippi. We had black sharecroppers on our farm, who were, "obviously", inferior to our white family. I still remember my mother crying when she heard that the U.S. Supreme Court had ruled that schools had to be integrated. My father was more vocal, and I remember when we drove by a black church with lots of parked cars on a week night, he speculated that they were secretly plotting to take over our country. We had a black lady who, using outside wash pots and tubs and scrub boards, along with outside clothes lines, did the hard hand labor of our weekly laundry and ironing. She also helped clean the house but was never allowed to share our table for meals. She knew that her place was to eat alone in another room. No black man was ever allowed into our home except on those rare occasions when help was needed to make some repairs or move furniture. When black men needed something, they could knock on the door, but my father or mother always went outside to talk to them—even on the coldest winter days. They knew their place. When our family and friends did talk about blacks (or "niggers" as many whites privately called them in those days), it often was about how lazy or dishonest or uneducated or unclean or immoral or alcoholic they were as both individuals and a race. As the Civil Rights movement gained momentum, my Baptist church stationed deacons with shotguns at the church entrances to keep blacks out. Rev. Germany, the pastor father of a girl that I was dating, was beaten unconscious because he was building a seminary for black students and had meals with black people in his home. (His beating is briefly described in the *Born of Conviction* book.) At about the same time, I was threatened by a man I had never before met at a country store near my home. After asking if I was dating Reverend Germany's daughter and my responding "yes", he popped out a switch blade knife and said, "Anyone who will date one of them is no better than they are". Fortunately, at the age of 17, I was very fast on my feet!

The beating of Rev. Germany, the murder of Emmett Till and the murder and burial of three young Civil Rights workers under a pond dam in our neighboring Neshoba County were all viewed as justified homicides by some of my friends and fellow church members.

While I was not aware of your manifesto at the time, we were aware of other white people, like you, who were trying to force unwanted racial integration on innocent white people. According to our pastor, as well as lots of other pastors (including the very vocal Bob Jones) and lay leaders at that time, such integration was in direct conflict with what the Bible says. As proven in white church after white church in those days, the support of racial integration was a sin so deplorable that it could get a pastor fired or a lay leader relieved of his or her position. Or, as in Rev. Germany's case, beaten unconscious. Segregationist leaders like George Wallace, Orval Faubus, Lester Maddox, and Ross Barnett were greatly admired because they had the courage to stand up to those, including our morally corrupt federal government, who were forcing racial integration on our innocent white communities. It was in this dangerous environment that you and the other 27 Methodist ministers had both the courage and audacity to "speak out".

To my shame now, over 55 years later, it was in this same environment that I was a staunch segregationist. I may have known, deep down, that my position and actions were wrong, but I could not let my father and mother, my grandmother, my uncles, aunts and cousins, my church and my high school and college friends down. They would have "disowned" me if I had done what you did. Besides, the Bible was perfectly clear, without any doubt, that God prohibited the intermingling of races. To support such intermingling was a sin against both God and the children of intermingled marriages. While I and my family ignored lots of biblical "laws" (we, of course, never admitted that we were ignoring them), we never even considered not obeying the laws demanding the separation of the races. Besides, there would be huge costs to pay, if we did, and I was unwilling to pay those costs. YET, YOU WERE!

But God and life moves in strange ways. Even people like I was in those days can change—even within the threatening environment that existed at that time. I still remember the chair that he was sitting in and where I was sitting in his office. It was my first year in graduate school at N.C. State University and Dr. Seagraves, one of my professors, had invited me to his office to "just talk". I felt honored by his invitation and figured that he was going to talk about my future as an economist—what type of career I wanted and what courses I needed to be successful in that career. But that is not what he talked about, at all. He initially talked about his life values and asked about mine, including what type of person I wanted to be. He then built on that discussion to talk about the cruel oppression of black people and how racial segregation kept them in poverty generation after generation. He argued that black people could be treated equally and lifted out of poverty without harming white people in any way. In fact, if they were lifted out of poverty, we would all benefit economically and socially. It was a win/win for all of us, he passionately argued.

My conversation with Dr. Seagraves did not cause me to have an immediate conversion but did cause me to start thinking—which is probably all that this very caring professor was seeking. I remember going home and talking to my newly wed wife and was somewhat surprised that, although also from near Newton, Mississippi, she shared Dr. Seagraves' values. Those two conversations were pivotable points in my and my wife's lives. We did not start participating in the Civil Rights protests nor did we start speaking out as you did. But I stopped telling racist jokes and wrote no more letters to editors trying to justify racial segregation. Fortunately, since we were now living in North Carolina, Jean and I did not have to worry about offending our parents and extended family, nor our church or even our college friends as we quietly made our transition from staunch segregationists to supporters of equal rights for blacks.

Upon completion of graduate school, my career took us to Washington, D.C. where racial equality was beginning to emerge. We found ourselves working and socializing with more black people on an equal basis and they were wonderful people—nothing like my church had told me they were. Dr. Seagraves was right, Jean and I had lost nothing by the more equal treatment of black people. Our salaries were not reduced. Our restaurant meals were no less enjoyable when black families sat at a nearby table. Our second child was delivered by a wonderful black physician and our son was no less healthy.

We had changed and the world around us was changing, but my Mississippi church pastor remained as firm as ever in his oppression of black people. The Bible said that the races should be kept separated and he was committed to obeying the Bible. He visited us in D.C., and we took him downtown to see the capital. There, he confronted a mixed-race couple who happened to be walking close to us from the parking lot to the capital and were holding hands. He jumped in front of the couple with his hands on his hips and, in a condescending voice, said, "You ought to be ashamed of yourselves!" Even in this case, unlike you and the other 27 ministers, Jean and I remained quiet and said nothing to him, although we did try to act like we were not with him.

In spite of our own transition, we just did not have the courage to speak out against our Pastor's, our family's, our friends' and our Mississippi home church's oppression and, really, persecution of blacks. When we returned to Mississippi to visit with family, we kept quiet when our family, friends and former church members damned the "outsiders" who were forcing racial integration on them. We kept quiet when their churches founded private schools so that their children would not have to go to school with blacks. We kept quiet when some of our family and friends continued to denigrate blacks, tell racist jokes and use the word "nigger" in private conversations. It was not that our family, friends and fellow church members were bad people. They weren't. They were good people. But we were a people who had become victims of a Bible-based Christian culture where oppressing and persecuting blacks was expected and failure to do so could have dire consequences. Hence, few of us had the courage to be the first to openly break with that culture. You did and we didn't.

Today, however, we have finally had the courage to proudly count ourselves among those who fully support equal treatment of all people regardless of race, gender, economic status or place of birth. I even founded a management consulting firm (MGT of America, Inc.) that became the national leader in conducting race and gender disparity studies that are required to establish special governmental programs to help women and minority owned businesses overcome the effects of historic discrimination. But none of this ever required the courage and personal costs that you and your family paid. In fact, we got paid for our studies.

Now, I hope that you understand the devastation that I felt when Nanci and Marilyn told me of the strong position that you have taken against the equal treatment of our LGBT sons and daughters and brothers and sisters. I kept asking "Are you sure that this is the same person?" But they assured me that that is, indeed, the position that you have taken in a most forceful way and that your leadership is having a huge impact on the treatment of LGBTs by those who respect your leadership.

While my balloon has been deflated, I am sure that your life's journey since those difficult Civil Rights years has led you to your current position. For some reason, my journey led me in a different direction.

Just as I strongly supported the oppression of blacks back in my early years, I also strongly supported the oppression of LGBTs—maybe even more so. To my shame again, I laughed at and told lots of gay jokes that ridiculed LGBTs, especially when I was in the army. I viewed LGBTs as people who had intentionally chosen a sinful life style and were actively recruiting others to join them. They were predatory people to be feared, avoided and kept out of all positions where they would have contact with "the rest of us", especially children. No matter how kind, serving and loving they were, they were still lost sinners who could easily become straight and be saved if they would only repent and give their life to Christ. I knew because my church, my Christian friends, my Bible and my Sunday school literature told me so. Oppressing and persecuting them was, in my mind, totally justified and could actually help them see and repent of their sin. I proudly participated. Of course, I never viewed it as oppression and persecution. Oppressors and persecutors never do, whether it be killing witches, marching native Americans on the Trail of Tears, enslaving blacks, prohibiting women from preaching in our churches, making and enforcing Jim Crow laws or oppressing LGBT people. Instead, we, (particularly, we Christians) justify our actions by demonizing the victims as villains who have earned their own punishment and we have been really good, over the years, at using the Bible to justify that persecution. I am ashamed to admit today, I have an early history of doing just that.

My "Dr. Seagraves" moment came about 20 years ago when I took a weekend boat trip with the CEO of a company whose board of directors, I chair. On that trip were several other men, including a Methodist minister, who had a gay brother. It was one of those trips where we had a lot of time to talk and where, as the weekend progressed, we became more and more comfortable in discussing confidential, personal issues. On the evening of the second day, the minister opened up about his gay brother and the horrible way that his parents, other family members and his church had treated his brother—totally and openly condemning, ridiculing and rejecting him. As he described the relationships, tears welled in his eyes. Words were not necessary for my new minister friend to communicate both the love and compassion that he felt for his brother and the dilemma that he faced as whether to speak out in support of his brother and almost certainly lose his pastoral job. His face and the tears dwelling in his eyes said all that needed to be said. But he did say something that I will forever remember. He said his brother once said to him "Jerry, do you think that I would have chosen this life style if I had had any other choice. Do you think that I enjoy having my family, my church, my Christian friends—everybody—condemn me as a sinner and treat me like scum?" (After 20 years, those may not be the exact words, but they are the exact message.)

That was, indeed, my "Dr. Seagraves" turning point. When I returned home, I couldn't get the minister's brother's comments out of my mind. What if I had I been wrong all of those years? Was I guilty of making another person's life (the only life he or she would ever have) miserable for something that he or she was born with? Was I guilty of not treating another person the way I, myself, wanted to be treated? How did I know that simply being gay was a sin? How did I know, for sure, that that sin could easily be "cured" and go away forever by the simple act of accepting Jesus as one's lord and savior? Would I suffer in any way if I treated my fellow LGBT brothers and sisters with respect, dignity and equality? Simply put, was I being the same sinful person I was being back when I strongly supported the oppression of my black brothers and sisters? These questions would not leave me alone and forced me to start doing what research I could about whether being gay was a choice or a born-with trait. I found an extensive number of Bible-based articles by religious authors condemning the LGBT life style; all saying, with authority, that being gay was a chosen sin that could easily be altered by counseling and religious conversion. In many ways, those articles were very similar to the large number of articles produced by white Christian authors in the 1950s and '60s using the Bible to condemn racial integration and equality. I did find some persuasive personal testimonies of changed individuals. But I also found follow-up confessions that, in essence, stated "I claimed that I had changed because of tremendous pressure from my family, friends and fellow Christians. I can no longer live that lie." The number of objective scientific studies was limited, but all that I found concluded that being gay was an inherited trait, not a chosen life style or mental illness. Further, it was a trait that could not be "cured" by counseling or religious conversion. The general scientific conclusion was that the self-reported changes were made, not by counseling or spiritual conversion, but by suppressing natural preferences, often under pressure from family, friends and fellow church members. The natural preferences never went away, too often leading to a disastrous life for both the gay person and his or her family members.

It was difficult, but I came to admit, privately at first, that I had been wrong all of those years about LGBT people, just as I had been wrong about racial segregation. Their gender preference was not the sin, my anti-gayness along with my oppression and persecution was really the sin. Over the following years after that conversation with my new Methodist friend and my study of scientific research, I had the opportunity to work with and become friends with several gay and lesbian people. I quickly came to realize that my family, friends and church (especially my church through the sermons and Sunday school literature) had lied to me and I, to my shame, had, in turn, lied to others. Other than their born-with gender identification, my gay and lesbian friends and fellow workers were no different than me or my family members and friends. They had none of the characteristics that I had been told. They were good people. They wanted to be successful in life. They hurt when others hurt. They felt personally hurt, just like me, when others condemned them. They wanted to be loved by their parents and other family members. They wanted to be a member of a church and to be loved by their fellow church members. They wanted to marry the one who they loved. They wanted to help others. They wanted the same career opportunities as others have. They just simply wanted to be who God made them to be. They were just like me in all ways except their sexual orientation. And their sexual orientation was not hurting me or anyone else in any way, just as the equal treatment of blacks never hurt me.

But I still had the biblical prohibitions to deal with. The Bible is perfectly clear as to gay relationships: such a relationship is so sinful that the punishment is "death to both parties". You can't get much clearer than that. What was I going to do with that very explicit "commandment"? For starters, I knew for sure that I was not going to be faithful to that biblical mandate. I was not going to kill my LGBT friends, just because the Bible said that was what was supposed to be done. So, already, I was not being faithful to the Bible. Then it occurred to me that there might be other biblical "mandates" that I was also not obeying and began a biblical search. To my surprise, it took only a few hours to find that I had been, basically, ignoring lots of biblical "mandates" or "guides" my whole life—-mandates and guides like killing witches (Exodus 22:18), putting all who work on the sabbath to death (*Exodus 35:2*), owning slaves and passing them on to my children (*Leviticus 25: 44-45 and Ephesians 6.5*} and prohibiting women from speaking in church (*1 Cor. 14: 33-35)*—to name just a few. Now, what was I going to do? Why was I holding on to the biblical LGBT prohibitions while ignoring other biblical mandates or guides? If I was ignoring other biblical passages, I had lost my claim that I was opposed to LGBT relationships because all biblical passages had to be obeyed. I still believed that the Bible was "God's word", but why was I being faithful to one passage and not to others? Why were my Christian friends doing the same? What criterion was I using to choose one and ignore others? What criteria were my friends using? Was it fear of condemnation from family, friends or church? Was it an unproven opinion that gayness is a sinful choice, not a natural born trait? Was it a desire to force my LGBT friends and family members to behave like I thought they should? Was it the same fears that had prevented me from speaking out on racial equality all those years? I still don't know. What I do know is that it was not because I am faithful to all biblical passages. I have never been and neither have any of my Christian friends, no matter what we claim.

We all have to choose which Bible "mandates" or "guides" we will follow. For some of us the criteria may be subconscious. For others, it may be loyal adherence to church doctrine. For still others, the choices may be made after much prayer and study. And, for almost all of us, family and peer pressures play a big role.

I wrestled with my own criteria for over a year—maybe 2 years. After a lot of prayer, study and soul searching, I have concluded that the criterion that I will use in choosing which biblical passages to be faithful to is: "Does it hurt or help another person?"—or in other words does the passage comply with Jesus' mandates that I "love my neighbors as I love myself" and "do unto others as I would have them do to me." With that chosen criterion, I now ask of each biblical passage if it will harm or help another person? If it harms, I will not be faithful to it. Accordingly, I will not kill witches nor homosexuals nor those who work on the sabbath, no matter what the Bible says. I will not be faithful to the passages that prohibit women from speaking in churches. I will treat women, homosexuals and people of other races with dignity, love, respect and equality. I will "love them as I love myself" and "treat them as I want to be treated".

All of this is interesting, but you are probably wondering at this point, why I care enough to write this letter. There must be more—and there is. A few years ago, I took some extra vegetables from my garden to a couple friend of ours. When they came to the door, I could immediately tell that they were hurting. They insisted that I come in. I already knew that their Christian faith meant everything to them, as well as to their son and his family. I knew that they were heavily involved in their church's manna program. I knew they had contributed to the construction of a new church building and their son had recently spent many days volunteering to clean up the trash and landscape the grounds around the new building. I knew that their entire family, including their teenage grandchildren, were at church almost every Sunday. I knew that he sometimes taught Sunday school lessons. I knew that their grandson was a very active youth leader and a member of the church's praise band that played at every Sunday morning service. They were dedicated Christians who were proud of their church and their fellow Christians. As we sat down, they began. Their previous pastor had retired, and a new interim pastor had been appointed. Soon thereafter, one of the deacons, just prior to the beginning of a Sunday morning service, called one of their friends off to the side and told her that she, her lesbian partner and their two children were no longer welcome at their church—they needed to find another church. But it was not the "humiliated blow to their friend's self-worth" that was hurting them at that moment; it was the "arrow that had been thrust into their own hearts". The new pastor had just called their grandson in and told him that, because he (the pastor) had heard that their grandson was gay, the church was immediately removing him from the praise band and all of his volunteer youth leadership positions. He could still come to church, but that was all. At this point in their story, tears welled in their eyes and mine as well. "How could any Christian be so cruel and do so in God's name?", I couldn't help but wonder.

My friends said that they had to leave their church. So, since they were Baptists, we talked about their joining our Baptist church. They did and we enjoyed worshiping together until about a year later when the U.S. Supreme Court ruled in favor of same sex marriages. According to our friends (we were out of town that Sunday), that ruling caused our Sunday School teacher (a wonderful person, by the way, who, had he known, would have been much more sensitive) to use part of his time to first condemn the court and its decision and then to condemn gay people who want to marry their partners and those who support gay marriages. Some class members joined in to add more condemnations of this violation of God's biblical laws. Our friends went home and spent the afternoon Googling what national church leaders were saying about the new court ruling and about how churches should treat LGBT people. I don't have to tell you what they found, just that an arsenal of arrows was launched into their already punctured hearts. The following week, they asked our church to remove their names from its membership roster. They still worship God but say that it will never again be through a church.

Not long after this event, Jean and I participated in a religious retreat at Epworth by the Sea. At this annual retreat, the moderator always asks for a show of hands for different church denominations. This year, she included the "nones" and I was startled at the large number of hands that went up, including a couple sitting near us. At the next break, I asked the couple about their "none" association. The wife told their story of how they and their lesbian daughter were repeatedly ridiculed and condemned by their fellow church members after their daughter married her lesbian partner. The condemnations caused them to leave their church and, ultimately, all churches. They both vowed that they were still Christians dedicated to serving God and His people, but never again through a church. The conference speakers went on to briefly discuss the ten-year annual declines in evangelical Christian church memberships in the U.S. and I didn't have to wonder why. The large number of raised "none" hands combined with my new friends' story and my old Tallahassee friends' experiences, including their Google searches, told me why.

As the weekend progressed, I had a hard time concentrating on what the speakers were saying. My mind kept wondering to the question of how we had reached the point where, just like back in the Civil Rights era, we had all become victims of a Christian culture where the oppression and persecution of our LGBT brothers and sisters was not only expected but mandated. How did we get to this place where speaking out against this oppression will get a pastor fired, a lay leader relieved of his or her responsibilities and a member ridiculed? Did we never really leave that culture where the same happened when a Christian spoke out against the expected oppression and persecution of blacks? Did we just add the oppression and persecution of our LGBT brothers and sisters and expand "expected" to "mandated"? Are we doomed to be the prisoners of this culture forever?

Now, as I come to the end of my story, just as the woman who reached out to touch Jesus's cloak then pleaded for his help, I now plead for your help. I plead with the humble request that you use the tremendous respect with which you are held by Christians all over this nation to openly support the treatment of all homosexuals with respect, dignity, love and equality. I do not have the platform that you have so successfully built that will cause people to listen to me, but you do. You have had a highly successful career as a pastor, writer, editor and head of a prestigious seminary. Few people ever achieve what you have achieved. Because of that success, people from all walks of life look to you for leadership. What you say and do matters—in fact, matters a lot!

Somewhere today, there is a child wrestling with when and how to tell his or her parents that he is gay or she, a lesbian. Your leadership will help determine whether that child is embraced with love and affection or ridiculed and rejected by his or her parents. Somewhere today, there is a homosexual who is wrestling with the decision to commit suicide because of the way he or she has been treated by his or her family, friends and fellow Christians. Your leadership may determine the decision that that hurting person makes. Somewhere today, there is a gay church member who is living in fear that their pastor or church board will expel them from their church choir or praise band or Sunday school teacher position. Your leadership may help determine whether they get to stay or are removed. Somewhere today, there is a gay or lesbian couple who, along with their children, is fearful that they will be asked by a deacon to leave the church that they love so much. Your leadership may play a major role in what that deacon does. Somewhere today, there is a highly qualified Christian homosexual who has been called by God to serve as a professional in his or her church. Your leadership may determine how that church's governing body responds to the person's application. In lots of places all over the world, thousands and thousands and thousands of homosexuals and their families are hurting today far more than you and I have or ever will hurt because of the oppression and persecution by fellow Christians. Your leadership will either help perpetuate that persecution and hurt or replace both with love, respect, dignity and equality.

I know that this is a lot to ask of you, especially in light of the public position that you have already taken. But Felix Frankfurter, a Supreme Court Justice, once, when asked how he explained a reversal of a previous decision he had rendered on an almost identical court case, responded, 'Wisdom too often never comes, and so one ought not to reject it merely because it comes later." As you might expect, this quote has helped me on more than one occasion.

I understand, however, that if you honor my request, you will, almost certainly, experience, all over again, those horrible condemnations that you received from many of your fellow Christians back when you helped write and signed the racial equality manifesto. But you had the compassion, love, courage and audacity to show that leadership back then and I plead that you do so one more time by showing the same compassion, love, courage and audacity for our homosexual sons and daughter and brothers and sisters that you showed back in the 1960s for our black brothers and sisters. If you do, I promise to drive to Memphis and treat you to the best dinner I can afford so that you will have at least one remaining friend. I will start saving now and when we get together, I will tell you the rest of my story.

Most sincerely,
Ken Boutwell

Ken Boutwell

www.ingramcontent.com/pod-product-compliance
Lightning Source LLC
Chambersburg PA
CBHW051003140626
46546CB00016B/142